Finding Your Perfect Match

Pepper Schwartz, Ph.D.

A PERIGEE BOOK

THE BERKLEY PUBLISHING GROUP
Published by the Penguin Group
Penguin Group (USA) Inc.
375 Hudson Street, New York, New York 10014, USA
Penguin Group (Canada), 90 Eglinton Avenue East, Suite 700, Toronto, Ontario M4P 2Y3, Canada
(a division of Pearson Penguin Canada Inc.)
Penguin Books Ltd., 80 Strand, London WC2R 0RL, England
Penguin Group Ireland, 25 St. Stephen's Green, Dublin 2, Ireland (a division of Penguin Books Ltd.)
Penguin Group (Australia), 250 Camberwell Road, Camberwell, Victoria 3124, Australia
(a division of Pearson Australia Group Pty. Ltd.)
Penguin Books India Pvt. Ltd., 11 Community Centre, Panchsheel Park, New Delhi—110 017, India
Penguin Group (NZ), cnr. Airborne and Rosedale Roads, Albany, Auckland 1310, New Zealand
(a division of Pearson New Zealand Ltd.)
Penguin Books (South Africa) (Pty.) Ltd., 24 Sturdee Avenue, Rosebank, Johannesburg 2196,
South Africa
Penguin Books Ltd., Registered Offices: 80 Strand, London WC2R 0RL, England

PRINTING HISTORY
Perigee trade paperback edition / January 2006

ISBN: 0-399-53244-7
Special Markets ISBN: 0-399-53293-5

To my children, Ryder and Cooper, whom I adore and whose love and support makes all things possible. And to everyone at Rosebud River Ranch, who back me up again and again, so that I have the time, peace of mind, and encouragement to write. Right now, in this special place we all love . . . I thank you for all the things you do for me.

Contents

Part One

Why You Need This Book

Are you tired of dating and feeling exhausted from failed relationships? Are you ready to commit to discovering what it takes to find the love of your life? If you are really ready to do the emotional and psychological work to determine the person you should be with, then this book will give you the insights you need to accomplish your goal. I'm going to give you the benefit of what I've learned in more than thirty years as an academic in the field of sociology and as a relationship expert. *Finding Your Perfect Match* is based on real social science. It is going to take you, step by step, on a rewarding journey that will help you understand more about yourself and make the wisest choices in your search for your life partner. The essence of this book is simple but powerful: My approach can help anyone understand his or her personality and will identify and underline the characteristics that are essential for creating the match of a lifetime. The series of questions as presented here, and the resulting analysis of your personality will be inspirational. Why? Because you will find out things about yourself you might not have known, and discover what similarities—and differences to look for in a potential partner.

I developed the Duet® Total Compatibility System, which forms the basis of this book, in conjunction with PerfectMatch.com, a pioneer in the online dating arena, because chances are, you don't quite understand why you pick the people you do, or why the people you pick don't pick you or stay with you. If you're like most people, you've made some mistakes and wasted a lot of precious time. Those detours have probably shaken your faith in your ability to find the right person.

This book will help you feel more confident about your ability to choose the right person for you in the future. *Finding Your Perfect Match* starts with a series of simple yet extremely important questions—about your personality, most specifically the parts of your personality that will matter most in a romantic relationship. Duet® is not about being good or bad, or right or wrong, just simply about understanding who you are, what you want, and therefore, who you should be with. It has been my experience that most people who are having trouble finding their soul mate don't need therapy, but do need insight; and this book will help you have that inner vision of who you are, and what kind of person will be compatible with you.

This book explores eight of your most important personality characteristics—and shows how they work when viewed from two different perspectives: those personality characteristics that tend to produce compatibility when similarly matched with another person, and those characteristics that might often work well with someone whose profile is different from yours. When you understand these two sets of perspectives, you will have an ideal guide for finding your perfect match.

However, understanding yourself and how to find a truly compatible partner for life is only the first, albeit important, step. Equally important, you need to understand what lifestyle patterns and habits of behavior and belief also need to be in sync because even the most compatible of couples can be defeated if they don't have some of the same values, goals, and lifestyle choices in common. I will explain what those essential areas of compatibility are and why you need someone who is on the same wavelength as you are when it comes to certain choices and habits. From all this you will be able to identify your own "negotiables" and "deal breakers"— there really is no self-test that can help you do that. Like the millions of people who have used Duet® to find the love of their lives, the self-knowledge that you gain from Duet® and this book will help you to make the most informed decisions about what matters most to you—and what you can set aside in the spirit of compromise and generosity.

I do, as all social scientists must, realize that no system is ever perfect, no finding ever written in stone, and that research on intimate relationships is in constant change, new findings modifying old ones, old ones being validated, or central information being replaced by new theories and data. This book does not offer a flawless theory of compatibility; people are too complex to be able to completely cover every aspect of the personality that is important in mate selection, nor can I adequately factor in how chemistry will affect any given emotional connection. Still, I have absolute confidence that there are powerful, credible tools for you to use in this book, insights that will help you find a perfect match if you use them in your life. My sincere hope is that this book will be a turning point in your life and it will help you be a more aware person, able to employ new ways of picking a long-term partner, and able to avoid old illusions and emotional dead ends. I am excited about offering you this system of self-analysis and compatibility characteristics.

—Pepper Schwartz, Ph.D.

1

The Love Diagnostic for a Perfect Match

The most important part of this book is taking the quizzes and getting the information about your personality and your lifestyle priorities. So we won't spend much time reviewing the science behind these tests, but I will give you just enough information to motivate you to take these quizzes and to have confidence in what they tell you.

The Duet® Total Compatibility System shares it's roots with the well-known Myers-Briggs Type Indicator.® Myers-Briggs, based on Jungian philosophy, was developed by Katherine Cook Briggs and Isabelle Briggs Myers, and refined over the last sixty years. It is based on the idea that in order to put together good teams for organizational productivity, managers need to know which personality types are important for essential components of jobs and which personality types might work best together to create a superbly functioning team. For example, one type of personality characteristic that is revealed is the tendency to want to come to closure on a task. While one type of person on this personality axis is generally in a hurry to get answers, get results, and move ahead, another at the opposite end of the continuum may be more reluctant to move ahead quickly and instead is happiest "brainstorming" and allowing as much time and participation in the creative process so that the best path is revealed. The beauty of understanding these two different approaches is that one is not "better" than the other: both are useful in getting the job done. But it might be best to have both kinds of people represented on the team so that ideas have enough time to float, but eventually someone pushes the group to end the discussion and actually get on with a plan. Both kinds of people are capable and necessary, but you could see how they might frustrate each other if each did not know that their respective approaches were valuable and needed. Understanding the personality characteristics of the other team member, as well as knowing their own personal approach, helps an individual understand what is happening, why it is happening, and why it might be annoying. It also helps each person accept those differences and value and cope with someone quite unlike themselves. Instead of being angry with each other, they can not only accept opposing styles, they can appreciate them!

Of course, you are not trying to put together an organizational team. But, there are some things you can take from this system and apply successfully to romance. You have to know what are the ways you approach and practice love. You need to know which characteristics fundamentally annoy you and which characteristics fit together nicely.

Sometimes you want someone just like yourself—or the other person will make you nuts! But in some areas of personality, it's the differences between us that create attraction, admiration, and good teamwork. The trick is discovering what the important characteristics for romantic compatibility are, and finding out when you want someone with the same approach as you have, and when you want someone who is not exactly like you but complements your needs and desires.

It is also important to think about how these characteristics come together to result in a personality profile. That is one of the inspired parts of the Myers-Briggs test. It describes four important characteristics but then shows how each characteristic has an impact on the others.

The first category in Myers-Briggs is Introverts (I) versus Extroverts (E). The way Myers-Briggs defines these terms is particular to the interpretation developed by the psychoanalyst Carl Jung. Introverts are private people who need solitude to recharge their batteries. On the other hand, Extroverts, when tired, need to be around people in order to be energized. An Introvert will be exhausted by being in a group for two hours; an Extrovert will be continually recharged.

The second category is Sensing (S) versus Intuitive (N). The designers of the Myers-Briggs felt this trait shapes personality more than any of the others. Sensing people are realists. They believe what is here and now is more important. The future is hazy, and therefore should be somewhat discounted in current decision making. Intuitives are people who prefer the future to the present. They value possibility more than reality. While Sensing people value a bird in the hand, Intuitives value the possibility of getting the two birds in the bush. Sensing people are linear thinkers: B follows A, C comes before D, etc. They value rules over logic and consider themselves to be realistic and down to earth. They think that Intuitives tend to be dreamers. On the other hand, Intuitives will think, even speak, in branching patterns, and parallel ideas. Only later do they put all the ideas together. Intuitives value logic over rules. They would consider Sensing people to be potentially close-minded, narrow thinking, and pessimistic.

The third category is Thinking (T) versus Feeling (F). Stereotypically, people would think of men as Thinking and women as Feeling. This is the only attribute of the Myers-Briggs that seems to be gender based. The Thinker values logic while the Feeler values a person's feelings first. The Thinker sees a problem and tries to solve it. The Feeler is more likely to listen to the emotions underneath the problem. Tending to the *feelings* rather than trying to solve the problem itself. The Thinker tends to be pragmatic and the Feeler tends to be sensitive.

The fourth category is Judging (J) versus Perceiving (P). This area deals with the degree of order a person needs to have in their life. A Judging person keeps an orderly desk and an orderly room. A Perceiving personality tolerates and perhaps even likes messiness. When there is a difficult decision to be made, Judging people like closure and Perceivers prefer to keep the options open. Once a difficult decision is made a Judging person feels relieved while a Perceiver feels uncomfortable having the door closed. Judging people like to do one task at a time and then move on to another. Perceivers, who prefer to do a little bit of a lot of things and keep moving back and forth between tasks, tend to be more scattered, yet also more creative. Artists are more likely to be Perceivers while an accountant is more likely to be a Judging personality.

In Myers-Briggs it is not just the characteristics themselves that are important but the way they are put together. Taken down to four basic areas, the characteristics are grouped as: Sensing/Judging (SJ), Sensing/Perceiving (SP), Intuitive/Feeling (NF), and Intuitive/Thinking (NT). The Intuitives and the Sensing personalities are believed to be so different from each other that they are often incompatible. The system does qualify these types, however, by whether or not a Sensing person is also a Perceiver or a Judging person. If you are an Intuitive, it is whether you are also a Feeling or Thinking person. In this system, the Intuitive/Feeling is attracted to the Intuitive/Thinking, and the Sensing/Judging is attracted to the Sensing/Perceiving. Similarity and difference are part of the chemistry. There are also sixteen major possibilities of how these characteristics sort together.

The same general theory that drives Myers-Briggs also underlies Duet®. First, because Duet® is focused on emotional characteristics, there are many differences, however. In fact, Duet® overlaps only with one characteristic in the Myers-Briggs—that is, the Introvert/Extrovert. But Duet® uses it in a way that is calibrated for romantic relationships. Second, Myers-Briggs is based on the Jungian psychoanalytic theory of Archetypes, what Jung believed to be the elemental parts of all personality types. Duet®, however, uses characteristics based on research from the sociology and psychology of love and compatibility. Third, while the Myers-Briggs test indicates who should be attracted to—or put off by—one another on teams and in general interaction, Duet® also indicates which kinds of people will be compatible in emotionally serious relationships. Behavioral science research has not been very enlightening about which personalities are necessarily attracted to each other. While some of the same characteristics that make people love and commit to each other may be involved initially in attraction, revelatory tests in Duet® are not meant to measure simple attraction.

Finally, Duet® has *eight* characteristics rather than four, two personality profiles instead of one, and creates one set of characteristics that work most harmoniously with a similar person and another profile of characteristics that might work equally well with someone similar to you *or* different from you. Each of the eight characteristics is an important aspect of how you love and live with someone but, like the Myers-Briggs psychological assessment, you will also need to think about the way these characteristics work together to further define the way each personality functions in a romantic relationship.

One important caveat: The eight characteristics that form the basis of the Duet® Total Compatibility System are not the only personal qualities that matter in relationships. This book does not cover *every* personality trait you own that might affect compatibility. But Duet® doesn't have to be encyclopedic to be extremely useful. Moreover, if you had to review every single aspect of your personality in order to use a compatibility system to find a partner, you might get so exhausted at the prospect of all this introspection that you would give up before you might ever see the benefit. Recognizing that too much complexity is overwhelming, I've tried to highlight just those aspects of relationship compatibility that I believe research in social psychology finds most compelling. In addition, at the end of this book, as an important auxiliary aide, I review some practical aspects of love and life that might get in the way of making good choices—even though you will certainly have a greater understanding of yourself and others! Other issues, such as being overwhelmed by physical chemistry when there are plenty of signals that you have different goals and values, or having different viewpoints and traditions about money or sex, will be discussed as core considerations that can make or break a relationship. In fact, throughout this book, I'll be offering you the occasional pep talk as your relationship coach about what I think works best for your personality type. The result, I hope, is that you will have the best tools to find a great love and discover ways to avoid any habits that have undermined your attempts to achieve a satisfying love life. Finding love is much more than chance or chemistry. It is a combination of self-knowledge, understanding the object of your affections, and exercising the emotional maturity to act on what you now know is in your best long-term interest. You have to make the choice to move away from superficial, impulsive, or destructive choices and move toward true compatibility. In essence, it means picking a compatible rather than incompatible, but still alluring, person. It means respecting who you are, and finding someone who will do the same and want the same.

In the end, however, it is your own choice, and your ability to listen to your own good sense, that will make the difference between getting into a relationship that will be a duet—or a disaster.

2

The Eight Essential Compatibility Characteristics

Romantic Impulsivity · **Personal Energy** · **Outlook** · **Predictability** · **Flexibility** · **Decision-Making Style** · **Emotionality** · **Self-Nurturing**

The first four of the eight key personality characteristics are linked together because they usually produce compatibility when they are shared by each person in a couple. However, when a couple does not share the second four characteristics, the relationship can still thrive; in fact, these differences between them might add to chemistry or attractiveness of the relationship.

Similarity Factors

1. Romantic Impulsivity

> *"'Tis better to have loved and lost*
> *Than never to have loved at all."*
> —In Memoriam, A.H.H., *Alfred Lord Tennyson*

The quote may be Tennyson's, but the sentiment is pure Bridget Jones, the hapless English heroine, frantically and enthusiastically looking for love, centering her whole life around the pursuit and throwing herself into the search with the most open and vulnerable of hearts. In *Bridget Jones's Diary*, Bridget falls in love with Mark Darcy, her direct emotional opposite. A careful man, Darcy is capable of great loyalty and feeling, but is not one to jump into a pool without checking the water level. Much of popular culture celebrates the impulsive lover who creates sexual tension when he or she madly pursues a more emotionally conservative target. In real life, as in the movies or romantic novels, this mismatch can be more than a bit dicey.

Romantic Impulsivity is an important characteristic because it describes the way one falls in love, and if two people are different in this aspect of their personalities, one may frighten the other off before a match can even be tested.

If you are impulsive and you don't control it, you are probably quite the risk taker. When you are excited about something or someone, you get an overall body response: perhaps a quickening of your heartbeat, shortness of breath, an overwhelming need to enter into the conquest and conquer the object of your heart's desire!

When in the throes of early infatuation, a romantically impulsive person is emotionally and physically proactive. It is not uncommon to call a lot, say romantic things early on in the relationship, rely on your instincts—and follow them seemingly regardless of the consequence. However, if you are a person who lets caution rule instinct you believe that time and a clearer understanding of the other person should prevail over immediate feelings or that illusive feeling of instant connection. You may consider impulsive people to be insincere, superficial, or off-putting. On the one hand, we have a person who could meet someone and instantly be thinking "this is the one" and on the other end of the spectrum, a person who feels that the only way to trust their own feelings is to let them develop over time, cautiously playing their cards close to the chest until they believe their feelings about the other person are solidly based on in-depth information and experience.

The gossip programs and newspapers are full of examples of both kinds of people. Of course, the gossip columnists love the impulsive celebs who make better stories than the more private and cautious ones. Impulsivity is the stuff that great romantic stories—and scandals—are made of.

Why Romantic Impulsivity Is Important for Compatibility

A significant difference in a couple's levels of Romantic Impulsivity can end a relationship as quickly as it might ignite it. One person instinctively pushes, the other instinctively backs away. But even if the two people get through the courtship phase—when even the most risk-averse individual may abandon their usual caution under an intoxicating adrenaline rush—this difference can create issues over the life of a relationship. Chances are that a person's most innate responses in a romantic situation will be mirrored in other aspects of their lives, and two people who find themselves basking in the glow of love-conquers-all may all too quickly find each other to be annoying and frustrating.

Alternately, there are always those whose natural inclinations—either being too impulsive or impossibly reticent—have cost them a potentially great relationship in the past. They may look beyond the moment and seek out a partner who can provide a balance for them. But, for the most part, those who share similar temperaments in romantic impulsiveness (or lack thereof!) may have an easier passage to a long-term relationship because they share a sense of kinship with and trust in one another.

2. Personal Energy

"If a man insisted always on being serious, and never allowed himself a bit of fun and relaxation, he would go mad or become unstable without knowing it."
—*Herodotus*

"Bite off more than you can chew, then chew it. Plan more than you can do, then do it."

—*Anonymous*

Think of the Energizer Bunny married to a sloth . . . Or consider the classic duos of stage, screen, and television that have used different levels of intensity to create comic repartee: the Smothers Brothers, Dean Martin and Jerry Lewis, or George Burns and Gracie Allen. As much fun as these partners had with one another, it is more likely that in "real life" couples with similar levels of energy are more likely to be compatible. For example, consider Hillary and Bill Clinton, or Elizabeth and Bob Dole—the quintessential "power couples." However well or mismatched they might be on other personality characteristics, it is clear even to the casual observer, that each member of these couples lives life at a fast pace with similar levels of energy and ambition. Neither of them is pushing the other to be more intense nor is either one pulling back, insisting on a less hectic life.

These partners have a pace and intensity that is natural for them. No one pace is objectively better than any other, but sharing the same approach can make a difference. People naturally have different amounts of energy. But in a relationship, if one is happiest speeding around, doing things, being places, happy to take on the world—while the other wants to stop and smell the roses and take life slowly and easy, the chances are that one partner will feel either held back or pressured to keep up.

Why Personal Energy Is Important
We often think about different energy levels with the common labels of Type A or Type B behaviors. There is a plethora of research on their differences and why they may have trouble with one another. Whenever a

couple spends time together their energy levels come into play—from how fast they wake up in the morning to their tolerance for downtime to the much loftier issues such as the investments in their careers, their parenting styles, and so on. While lovers may be willing to accommodate a leisurely stroll along the beach or a speed walk up the nearest mountain, at the end of the day, constant accommodation can be taxing and frustrating.

It's not inconceivable that one member of a couple could change their ways—being introduced to a new activity that really energizes them or being seduced by the benefits of meditation. However, the pace at which you live, and the personal energy you can bring to bear, is one of your most defining personal traits. It shapes your activities, your goals and intentions, your conversation, and ultimately, your personality. As well, it is one of the core elements that determine your compatibility with another person. But like all personality traits, the natural level of your personal energy is neither good nor bad—it simply is. It can bring a couple together, or alienate them. One couple I know well seemed ideally suited for each other in many ways—similar in values, intelligence, education, and a mutual love of travel, art, and animals. The problem with Gene and Patti, however, was that he liked a day exploring just one of their mutual interests, and she tried to pack them all in! "She made me tired," he said. "I felt like she could never just enjoy life. I wanted to just hang out on weekends; she couldn't enjoy just sitting around reading the paper and vegging out. When we went to New York, she had to see all the galleries, rather than just pick a few. I felt rushed and pressed. I was awed by her energy and I admired her: I just didn't want to live like that."

3. Outlook

"After all, tomorrow is another day."
—*Scarlett O'Hara in* Gone with the Wind

Peoples' attitudes and mood ranges from cheerful and upbeat to serious and earnest and many nuances in between. At the extremes you'll find the Pollyannas of the world for whom every glass is half-full, every cloud has a silver lining, and every story has a happy ending. At the other, are the Eeyores, that sad-faced donkey from Winnie the Pooh for whom everything is gloomy. Most of us fall somewhere in between, avoiding the extreme pathologies of being manic or depressive. But how one views the world—whether through rose-colored glasses or in the harsh glare of daylight—will have an impact over the long term in any relationship.

There is nothing wrong with either of these two emotional approaches to the world, but if one person always feels the other is "raining on her parade," always seeing the downside, never totally going with the optimism and high spirits of the moment, it can be frustrating, perhaps even provocative. Meanwhile, the partner's take on this may be to see that kind of optimism as simplistic or even scary. They see the downsides that require caution (if only to avoid disappointment and disillusionment) and they stop trusting their partner's instinctive impulse to see the brightest side of everything. Keenan, a lawyer I interviewed, prided himself on his cynical, world-weary approach to life. He fell in love with a model named Lila who looked like his sexual ideal, but she had a quite different temperament than he did. She was a much younger woman who had not developed any of his cynicism. Whenever he would talk doom-and-gloom politics, and rail against governmental policies, she would try and come up with reasons why it wasn't so bad or offer solutions for positive changes. She felt he always saw the dark of things and that he never gave anything a chance to work. He would treat her somewhat contemptuously in front of others whenever the debate turned to political problems. The last straw was when he quite publicly referred to her as Ms. "Why Can't We All be Friends?" They saw the world very differently and over time it became obnoxiously obvious to both of them.

Why Outlook Is Important

Temperament defines the feelings you have daily about every important event and every decision. If you are a sunny person, you generally like to be around other optimists—you like feeling buoyant. You don't like being brought down because, for better or for worse, people like to have their moods validated and reinforced. "Why are you so happy when there is nothing to be especially happy about?" seems an unnecessarily cruel question to one with an optimistic outlook. But not everyone can tolerate the Pollyannas of the world. Whether it is in their nature—or the water—New Yorkers are famously suspicious of strangers who smile at them on the street. It's all a matter of perception. On the flip side, think of the old cliché, misery loves company. Natural-born pessimists may find comfort in their darker view of the world and prefer not to have someone try to cheer them up. Sharing mood is another form of validation of one's worldview, and in general, people like to know that the way they see the world is shared by their partner.

4. Predictability

"To explore strange, new worlds; to seek out new life and new civilizations; to go where no one has gone before."
—Star Trek

How you adapt to the unknown is the foundation of lifestyle. If you draw comfort from surrounding yourself with familiar patterns and places, you are not going to be happy with someone for whom the very thought of predictable days, weeks, and places fills them with an urge to run. Remember the movie *The Runaway Bride* or Jennifer Wilbanks, the real-life runaway bride? Neither the movie's heroine, nor Ms. Wilbanks, had a unique reaction to making a lifetime commitment. Of course some people bolt from an imminent marriage because they think they are marrying the wrong person. But not infrequently, it is just the act of signing up for a certain way of life, certain expectations, and a kind of stability that freaks out some prospective brides and grooms and makes them bolt. Other people with the same issues might marry, but they never can commit to buying a house or really settling down. They become anxious at the very idea of living happily ever after in "Pleasantville." Some people prefer a military life or working for an international corporation that assigns them to a different part of the world every few years; other people get depressed thinking about even the possibility of moving across town.

For some people, the essence of happiness is found in having control and predictability in their everyday lives. Many people prefer to follow in the footsteps of their parents: They will stay in the same neighborhood, attend the same church, synagogue or mosque, shop at the same stores, and take the same vacations they did as a child. They prefer going to the schools their parents went to, and they may have a cottage to go to in the summer that has been in the family for years. They have a few close friends (or perhaps many) but they are the ones they have had since childhood. They may try a few new things—but that isn't generally what they feel most comfortable doing. They find comfort in knowing where they are headed, and pretty sure that they'll like it when they get there. Next year is pretty predictable from the last year. They don't do really well with change. Here's a true story: Alan, for example, fell in love with Misty, who was also deeply in love with him. But Alan had a set routine that gave him pleasure and Misty thought it was too narrow and tried to broaden his horizons. He liked to stay home on weekends; she got him involved in a gourmet club. He liked having a few friends they would see every so often and did not enjoy all the new people she introduced from her large circle of friends. She wanted to travel the world, while he just wanted his annual fishing trip and a weekend place where they could "hide out" during most of their vacation. He started withdrawing from the relationship because he found that he was always doing things he didn't want to do and never getting enough time with the activities that made him happy.

The opposite of this need for predictability is the passion for variety. When life becomes predictable, people who like variety feel trapped. They may like the friends they have, but they enjoy meeting new ones just as much. They don't like to backtrack, may like to move a lot, but certainly enjoy many places and experiences and may even have wanderlust. A person who likes variety may have had trouble "settling down," but once they do commit, they want to be with someone who keeps their lives moving, creating novel experiences, and always up for a new adventure, hobby, location, or game. They are worried about boredom, and may even sink into depression if life seems to be the "same old, same old." Variety is not only the "spice of life," it is what makes life enjoyable. They don't need the thrill of burning a mortgage or the sense of security that staying in the same job forever might give someone else. At one extreme they could be Foreign Service professionals who expect to move to new countries every couple of years, and learn to love it. Or, they may stay put while changing jobs, hobbies, or activities regularly.

Why Predictability Is Important

One of the key elements of relationship success is a feeling of security. For some variety seekers it is the security of never worrying about being bored. They want to know that the person with whom they ski, jog, or mountain climb won't stop and settle into a sedentary, predictable life. If they have ever taken off spontaneously for a three-month trip around Europe, they want to feel that something like that could happen again. For others, it is the absolute surety that your partner will always be there, your favorite chair will be in the right place, and the season's tickets will be yours every year. Security in getting what you want, what you've been led to expect, is a core value to both perspectives, but obviously the details are extraordinarily different.

Again, both of these are completely acceptable patterns, but if the person who craves variety and the person who craves predictability find themselves together, they are going to feel betrayed and angry and worst of all, trapped. This is not just a lifestyle difference; it is a deep psychic need that seeks expression in lifestyle choices. Different approaches in this category will almost always lead to great unhappiness and feelings of life being out of balance. The only way to avoid those feelings would be to live parallel lives—where one person stays in a known universe while the other one lives their passion for change and challenge. This can work sometimes, but most often it leads to a lack of intimacy and finally, a drifting away—or linking up with another person.

Complementary Factors

While having similarity in the first four characteristics often leads to better relationships, a lot depends on how these characteristics mix and match. We will come back to the personality profiles on these characteristics in

Chapters 7 and 12 but for now, let's look at the next four personality factors that reveal why *being different*, rather than similar, might work in a long-term relationship. These characteristics possess what social science calls complementary factors.

5. Flexibility

"The thing that is really hard, and really amazing, is giving up on being perfect and beginning the work of becoming yourself."
—Anna Quindlen

"He who every morning plans the transaction of the day and follows out that plan, carries a thread that will guide him through the maze of the most busy life. But where no plan is laid, where the disposal of time is surrendered merely to the chance of incidence, chaos will soon reign."
—Victor Hugo

People have different levels of perfectionism, of wanting and needing things to be a certain way. In fact, some people feel so strongly about certain ways of thinking or doing things that any other way is simply unacceptable. There are people who live in small towns and would not, could not, live anywhere else. There are people who have a certain routine in the morning and no other routine feels comfortable or desirable. Depending on how compulsive they are, people who need things to be a certain way might become angry or have an anxiety attack if things don't go the way they want. For example, take a little thing like how the grass is cut or the flower beds tended.

Dillon was a master gardener and had very strong feelings about what his garden should look like. He felt that his landscaping should always be in perfect shape. As he traveled quite a bit for his work, he wanted his wife Carol, to keep up the place while he was gone. But Carol didn't even notice if the gardens needed weeding or whether the grass was cut to a certain height. She didn't walk around the house with the same eye for gardening he did, so she accepted a certain disarray. When Dillon returned, he rather testily reminded her that he needed her cooperation about keeping the gardens and lawns just so. Carol thought he was exaggerating his concern for effect. But out of the blue, at least it seemed so to her, he had a major fit about what a slob she was and how much it bothered him. She couldn't understand why all of this was so important to him.

Other people don't have inflexible demands. They are happy in the country or the city. They are willing to wake up at 5 A.M. or at 7 A.M. or go to sleep early or late. They really have very few must-do's or must-haves on their wish list. They are often very accommodating to other people's needs, and take pleasure in their ability to do so. In general, they are highly adaptable and happy under a number of conditions. This carefree attitude can make a highly structured person upset if the highly flexible person is always suggesting alternatives ("Well, yes, we could do it this way, but what about if we did it this way, or this way, or perhaps that way . . .") or if they refuse to make a decision, feeling that any way the other person decides is okay with them. This might seem like it would delight the partner who needs everything a certain way, but sometimes it also means that the flexible person is never really taking responsibility for a decision, which can be especially annoying to the person who is doing the planning. And this situation becomes particularly problematic when things don't work out as planned and the planner is having to accept all the blame.

Why Flexibility Is Important

There may be no problem if two people who are very flexible create a relationship. There will be give and take and easy negotiation, because neither person has a lot of stake in most daily decisions. But, like the comparable types from Myers-Briggs, if neither partner pushes for closure, they may never be able to make a decision on anything, including getting and staying together. However, a truly flexible person is a lot less common than one with a strong sense of what their life should look like. And this may become more evident as people age and they have formed an emotional and perhaps financial investment in a way of life.

People who have had strong and inflexible demands about the shape of their lives from their very earliest years are highly unlikely to change. If they meet someone just like themselves, someone with the same goals, values, and behavior in every important category, the two of them can be an amazingly happy and well-adjusted couple. However, the chances of meeting someone *exactly* like themselves is a whole lot less likely than meeting someone who will adapt to their patterns and wishes. This pattern may work, if the inflexible person isn't so narcissistic that they refuse to give the other person some role in the design of their life together! If on the other hand, the structured personality falls in love because of uncontrollable erotic attraction or some other factor, a mismatch on this personality characteristic means at the least a lifetime of challenges, and at worst, a disaster. If a highly inflexible person is attracted to someone who is also very opinionated and leads a life that is very different, there is no doubt this will be a tempestuous and maybe short-lived match. A much, much better situation for them is a connection with someone who is willing to cater to a person with very different preferences. This is a situation where the difference between two people may make love possible. Later we will talk about what group of characteristics in a potential partner will be most likely to suit someone who is more rigidly attached to a specific lifestyle, attitudes and beliefs.

6. Decision-Making Style

"Many women feel it is natural to consult with their partners at every turn, while many men automatically make more decisions without consulting their partners. This may reflect a broad difference in conceptions of decision-making. Women expect decisions to be discussed first and made by consensus."

—Debra Tannen, You Just Don't Understand

Every couple must figure out how to make decisions, how to negotiate differences, and how to deal with competitiveness or other parts of a relationship where each individual would (consciously or subconsciously) like an advantage over the other. While the idea picture of a long-term relationship assumes that all decision making will be collaborative with each loving partner demonstrating flexibility and understanding, the reality is somewhat different. Over the years, people stop being as sacrificial, generous, or unselfish as they were when they were dating. This is very human; most of us are not going to be nominated for sainthood, and sometimes we are going to love ourselves more than we love our partner. Even if we are as selfless as Mother Teresa, we may feel that it's necessary to win an argument when we feel that our partner's welfare, our children's welfare, or the relationship's welfare, would be better served by following our advice rather than our partner's.

How we go about dealing with conflict, getting our way, or accommodating someone else's desires, is critical. This factor is really all about how we gather, or share, power—and how important power is to us.

There is certainly a range of behavior and preference regarding decision making. At one end is the person who likes to be the primary decision maker in the relationship and is willing to take on the responsibility of guiding the relationship and the couple's future. On the other end of the continuum is the individual who is much more willing to let their partner take on the responsibility of the direction of the couple's life, and who is grateful for their leadership. One person likes to be in control, and the other is willing to give up control and live with the consequences. The two people may be collaborative on decisions, talk them through, and decide together, or let one person have "the final say."

In some successful relationships, one person is clearly dominant and the other person enjoys that division of emotional and practical labor. In a situation where people are badly matched, the dominant person is seen as willful and oppressive and the other partner is either seen as weak or argumentative. If both partners have no big desire to lead, both partners are likely to have a consultative style and negotiate plans and positions more often, taking turns on who compromises, who decides, and who carries out decisions. In this case, they may evolve into a "peer" relationship, two people who operate on the basis of romantic friendship rather than a hierarchy. Dominance may change according to the topic or skill involved, or both people may take turns sharing responsibilities and solving problems or creating plans. Sometimes, over the life cycle, people may change from one power style to another. Consider this example: Bill met Samantha when she was an undergraduate student and he was a teaching assistant in the department. She thought he was brilliant and deferred to him in all things. She bragged to her friends about how much he knew about genetics and she was fascinated by his thesis project. Over time, however, Samantha's own talents were recognized by the department and she got an internship with a senior professor. She won a prize for the best undergraduate project and she was accepted into the graduate program for the following year. As graduate students together, while Samantha still respected Bill, she felt more like a peer than the adoring young student she was when she met him.

Samantha felt that there was a lot of conflict over intellectual questions that were, in reality, conflict over her changing role in the relationship. Eventually Bill left the relationship and got involved with someone else who was not in school and who did not challenge him. Samantha became involved with another fellow graduate student who liked her ambition and her forthrightness.

Why Decision Making Is Important

You've heard the term *power struggle*. You can see it when it's happening. Two dominant types won't budge from their positions and they will use everything they can think of (within their moral and ethical boundaries) to get their way. Dominant personalities can enjoy struggle, to a point. But if everything is competitive, if each is truly unhappy unless they are in control, there is going to be a constant undercurrent of dissatisfaction and anger. Anger is an archenemy of compatibility and anything that continually creates it and never resolves the provacation is, within reason, to be avoided. That is why it may be critical for someone with a dominant personality to be with someone who is willing to compromise, who likes to follow rather than to lead, and who, while not a doormat (which could lead to contempt) knows when to step back. Of course it also works to have two people together, neither of whom needs to be dominant, both of whom like to negotiate and compromise. Even here, however, there may be problems with similarity if one person really does want to follow and is looking for someone else to lead. In this case, difference between partners is actually a good thing since someone who wants to be led may feel contempt for a partner who is unwilling to lead or unsuited to leadership.

7. Emotionality

"The first time I didn't feel it, but this time I feel it and I can't deny the fact that you like me, right now, you like me."
    —*Sally Fields accepting an Oscar at the Academy Awards*

While one's everyday outlook is a critical aspect of how someone experiences the world and how you experience the world with them and through them, day-to-day mood isn't the only aspect of temperament that is a core element of compatibility, The other major issue is how someone acts under extreme conditions: when they are challenged, worried, frightened, confused—or even madly in love. Some people are passionate in their emotions: they react with volumes of language, high emotion, quick anger (often quickly dissolved as well), and quickly formulated strong opinions. A stereotype of this kind of person would be a tempestuous "Latin Lover", full of heat, intensity, and passion.

The other end of the stereotype scale would be the cooler "Nordic" personality or the reserved Asian demeanor. This kind of person does not like emotional displays and tends to remain calm and thoughtful. They are often slower to anger or react. They have a much longer fuse before they blow up, and blowing up is rare. They tend to think first when confronted with challenges, rather than react, keeping their emotions to themselves until they are sure about how they feel.

Non-emotional types are often picked as leaders in business because they can keep their heads clear and logical while others are giving into their emotions. They may not have any better answers ultimately, but for the moment when other people are venting, they may have a more objective vision of the situation. A good example can be found in the story of Marco and Hilda, who were an interesting mix of these personality types. They practiced architecture together and their different natures complemented each other. Marco was the designer, the effusive creative free thinker of the two, talking a mile a minute, changing direction of design at unpredictable times, and getting upset or frustrated daily. Hilda was the person who negotiated the contracts, talked price, and soothed Marco when he became exasperated with the client—which he almost always did. She was cool, orderly, and determined. He was disorganized, passionate, and impulsive. They felt like they made a good design team because they counteracted each other!

Why Emotionality Is Important

The way people react during periods of intense feeling or crisis makes a difference in how they solve conflict, and also how safe they feel with their partner when things get rough. Two passionate people may do well together because they understand this style of emotional expression and they both respect the process of venting and feeling anger, outrage, or emotional distress. Research shows that people who communicate their feelings tend to do well as a couple, even if they do it at the top of their lungs. Nonetheless, having equally hot tempers and quickly aroused emotions may sometimes result in destructive conflict. Similarity here can be problematic with calmer personalities as well. When both partners have cooler temperaments, for example, it might be comfortable for each of them, but it is also possible that both parties would always prefer to shelve issues rather than disrupt the peace—or put them away until they can be handled sensibly—which might mean that sometimes the issues don't get handled at all. Many "cooler" couples create a relationship that becomes distant because they avoid discussing tougher issues. Things start to go sideways because the couple is slowly disconnecting. Two passionate people can break up in a fury, or two temperate people can just drift away because the relationship diminishes in importance and intimacy.

In both cases, the result is undesirable: problems that might have been handled better are not, and the relationship suffers. The best style of communication may work well when both partners are neither *too* hotheaded nor *too* reserved. But if the difference in temperaments is significant, it could possibly be good for the couple. Therefore, it might be better to find someone who balances the hotter personality with some natural restraint. Similarity here can work, of course, but there is a lot to be said for difference on this characteristic. Calmer people can help modify the passionate person's reactions and avoid overdramatizing and ramping up of an argument. Likewise, cooler and more emotionally collected people can learn to understand and express their own feelings and get in touch with their partner's. Difference in this category may cause some initial serious conflicts, but may also increase personal and couple growth and interdependence.

8. Self-Nurturing

"It's the friends you can call up at four A.M. that matter."
            —Marlene Dietrich

"I owe my success to having listened respectfully to the very best advice, and then going away and doing the exact opposite."
            —G. K. Chesterton

How you confront and deal with deeply personal psychological challenges could be the most important romantic characteristic of all—or at least it appears to be for most women. It might also be the most highly "gendered" characteristic of the group; that is to say, the one characteristic that is more likely to divide along male and female lines. This factor refers to how your internal psychology works: it measures how you comfort yourself, and how you want someone else to relate to you when you are confused or distressed. For many people, and certainly most women, the resolution of distress is the essence of intimacy: Do you share when something important and perhaps troubling is happening to you, or, do you become silent, contemplative and need only your own counsel until you figure out how you feel and what you want to do about it?

How you self-nurture aligns with a more general personality characteristic—whether you are an introvert or an extrovert. Introversion

can be defined in a number of ways, but the essence of the concept in social psychology is that an introvert seeks internal ratification rather than ex-
ternal validation. In everyday language, this means an introvert talks to him
or herself to examine a difficult problem or feeling while an extrovert
needs other people's feedback to decide what is right or wrong, good or
bad, for them. Introverts stay inside their own heads to feel, think, and
puzzle things out. In general, they need only a few people in their lives.
They get their energy from a small number of deep relationships rather
than many friends, and they need more private time than social time.

Extroverts, on the other hand, gain their emotional satisfaction and
equilibrium from other people. They may not like to be alone very much
because being alone deprives them of the strength and support they draw
from interacting with other people. They get energy from sources and, often from many different people. When they are sad or excited or tense,
they need to talk at least to a close friend, but often to *many* close friends.
They need to check in, share, vent, and confer. Without the ability to do
this, they can feel lonely, even desperate.

Why Self-Nurturing Is Important

In general, women, even women with strong introvert tendencies, define
intimacy by the level of emotional sharing in the relationship. Sharing confidences, experiences, and feelings is the coin of love and friendship for the
majority of women.

Most men on the other hand have more often been taught to keep what
they perceive to be their weaknesses or insecurities to themselves. It requires a lot more angst for a man to share his innermost fears or failures
than it does for a woman. Women will likely make a confidante of another
woman whom they have just met because there is rapport between the
two. Men find this female facility for easy intimacy disconcerting. They often feel it leaves one's flank exposed unnecessarily. Because women tend to
reveal their deepest and most troubling feelings and most men don't, difference over "opening up" can be a primary area of incompatibility in romantic relationships.

One partner's reluctance to be open is lessened, however, if the introvert feels comfortable enough to at least be vulnerable with the most sig-

nificant person in their life. So while it might really be best if two introverts were together and two extroverts were together, given how most
men and women have been conditioned, this would leave many more
women looking for an extroverted male than are to be found. Of course,
there are many males who are "people persons." But that is the surface
characteristic, not the deeper core characteristic of sharing one's deepest
intimate feelings or not, which is what we are talking about here. So, the
best that many women can do is to find a man who is aware of his reluctance to expose and share and who seeks a woman who will help him do
this. It's a real challenge to find a man who can be vulnerable and open in
the same way a woman is. True sharing has to come from a solid position
of strength and self-confidence, rather than from someone who is simply
lost in the world. Women are not looking for someone who is emotionally
unstable, just someone who knows how to express deeply held feelings and
open up to her. That said, I do not want to overemphasize gender univer-
sals. There are certainly men who want to open up and exchange intima-
cies as part of what they want in a long-term relationship. And there are
women who are very private and do not like someone asking them how
they feel, checking their emotional temperature, or intuiting their mood
and wanting to find out more. I have interviewed lesbian couples where
one partner complained about the other's ability to readily "open up and let
me help her sort out her feelings." While there is a probability of more
men on one side of this characteristic and more women on the other, it is
not a completely predictable division by gender.

What is important is that most relationships do need a certain amount
of sharing to create and maintain intimacy; so for a long-term relationship
to be emotionally intense, there is usually the need for at least one extrovert in the relationship. Whether or not the extrovert will be happy with
their match depends on how much the introverted partner is able to break
the mold and confide and communicate. As we analyze this characteristic
and others in Part Two of this book, a great part of our discussion will be
about the fit between people who are similar on these characteristics and
people who are different—and how to use this knowledge in order to create the most compatible relationship possible.

Part Two

Understanding and Using the Duet® Total Compatibility System

In order to understand your romantic personality, the next eight chapters present a series of short tests designed to analyze the way you love. Each chapter will have a short self-scored quiz to help you know yourself better. You will receive an overall score that will tell you whether or not you are a romantic risk taker or are risk avoidant, whether you are an extrovert or an introvert, and so on. Then, under the heading of "explanations," I will explain what each question measured and what that tells you—not only about you but also about people who may have answered that question differently. At the end of each of the two groups of four personality characteristics, I will show you how each characteristic fits with the other three in the group and how they modify each other. Furthermore, you will find suggestions about which personality profiles would be simpatico with yours, which *might* be, and which are usually not compatible.

The first four set of "similarity" characteristics usually work well with someone who is similar to you—so most of the suggestions of compatible profiles will be close to your own. The second set of "complementary" characteristics can either work with similar or different profiles and so suggestions of matches will be both similar and complementary. Finally, since relationships do not begin or stay together based on personality alone, the final part of the book will discuss what lifestyle and personal is-sues you need to consider and whether or not you need to be similar or dif-ferent on some of the challenges these present. The last two chapters concentrate on using your new knowledge to find a perfect match, and once found, keeping it!

Being Similar

Romantic Impulsivity · Personal Energy · Outlook · Predictability

In general, when people describe their "soul mate" they are referring to someone who fits them as if they were made for each other. This feeling usually comes from a shared way of experiencing life, and a jointly held set of values and goals. Less conscious and distinguishable, but extremely important, is the way their personalities mesh. Most studies show that similarity produces this seamless integration of two people's psychological comfort with one another This may mean culturally familiar background characteristics such as shared class, ethnic, religious, or racial backgrounds, but it may also include the ways people think about and react to life's situations. Of course we know that not every characteristic has to be similar and in future chapters we will talk about when differences between partners might be the mortar that cements a feeling of belonging together. However, the following personality patterns may do best between partners when the two partners are similarly matched.

3

Romantic Impulsivity

The following quiz measures your romanticism, your impulsivity, and some associated factors. People who are romantically impulsive tend to trust their intuitions and act on the rush of strong attraction and intense connection. There might be many barriers, but they are not likely to be discouraged by impracticality or other blockades that might stop the faint of heart. Risk takers love being swept away and don't want too many hesitations to spoil the ride. Their opposite is people who are extremely risk avoidant, and to whom risk is a turn-off rather than a turn-on. Risk avoiders try to slow down the romance so they can see who this other person really is.

Please mark True or False

T   F   **1.** Almost every time I have been in love I had an overall physical response when we met: my heart beat faster, I got sweaty palms, I felt a bit hyper, I was overly talkative, or became uncharacteristically shy.

T   F   **2.** If I am deeply attracted to someone immediately, I will trust my emotions and I am willing to start a serious relationship right away.

T F **3.** I trust my romantic instincts. If I am seriously drawn to someone, I don't care about traditional matching characteristics (like a certain age or financial status). I go for it!

T F **4.** When it comes to romance, I believe that it is better to go for it and risk getting burned than to hesitate and never know what might have happened.

T F **5.** If there was a contest I had almost no chance of winning, I'd still enter, even if there was a fee. I'd think at least I'd have a chance to win!

T F **6.** I've never regretted putting all my feelings on the line and making myself vulnerable—even if I didn't get the person I originally wanted.

T F **7.** If I felt deeply in love after a couple of months of being with someone I would be willing to get engaged or move in together.

Scoring

Give yourself one point for every True answer.

Give yourself the letter R (Risk Taker) if you have more True answers than False answers.

Give yourself the letter X (Risk Avoider) if you have more False answers than True.

The bigger the gap between True and False answers, the more intense you are in this characteristic.

What Your Answers Say About You

---

1. Almost every time I have been in love I had an overall physical response when we met: my heart beat faster, I got sweaty palms, I felt a bit hyper, I was overly talkative, or became uncharacteristically shy.

R (Risk Taker) While it's not always the case, really impulsive people often have an overall body response that excites them and makes them more likely to act in the moment. You feel excited, nervous, and you want to act dramatically. This could mean you are more likely to have sex when another person might wait. Or you tell deep personal truths about yourself, or you just talk a lot as if you had to say everything all at one sitting. You are pumped! And it increases the intimacy or at least feelings of connection right away. This can be pretty heady, especially if you are getting the same kind of response from the person you are with. However, if you are with a Risk Avoider rather than another Risk Taker you may feel them withdrawing, being silent, or, after sex, feel a loss of connection rather than an increase.

X (Risk Avoider) If you are a Risk Avoider, a Risk Taker may scare you away for various reasons, but most of all because you don't believe that true emotions can be understood without some time spent experiencing the other person. You enjoy but will not rely on your immediate attractions. You are unlikely to have the same overall intense physiological arousal when you meet someone you are interested in; attraction yes, but not an intense overwhelming bodily response. If you are very attracted to someone, you tend not to trust your feelings enough to depend on your emotional or physical response. You may distrust someone who does and while you are less likely than a Risk Taker to jump into bed with someone right away, if you do, it is less as an act of love than an act of lust.

---

2. If I am deeply attracted to someone immediately, I will trust my emotions and I am willing to start a serious relationship right away.

R (Risk Taker) Because you are impulsive, you don't want to wait for a lot of information. You tend to make snap decisions and are ready to act on them. A romantic personality feeds off emotional highs and feelings of heartfelt connection. Your emotions are your revealed wisdom to yourself. Because you are impulsive, you don't wait for concurrence. When you believe in the relationship, you are often the one who presses for more commitment early on—because you don't want to waste time when your emotions are giving you such clear signals. If you are with another Risk Taker, they are right there with you, helping to develop and deepen the relationship right from the beginning. If you are with a Risk Avoider, they might be asking for more space, more time, even if they started out quite interested. If you don't give them that space and time and lower the pressure, they might back off entirely.

X (Risk Avoider) You are less likely to trust your emotions no matter how promising the start of the relationship may be. You like a person who is, like you, more cautious about giving away their heart (or for that matter, body). You feel more comfortable starting out slowly and exploring your interest in the other person than declaring the relationship to be serious right away. If you feel pressured to define the relationship as serious right away, you may back away altogether. At the very least, it may make you feel that your partner is less picky or careful than you are—and perhaps that makes this relationship less special since they jumped in so easily. You can be friendly, romantic and interested—but you have an internal reserve that you want respected until such time when you feel like going to the next level. If you are with a Risk Taker they may feel insulted or underappreciated while you are taking the time you need to find out whether or not this is a relationship that should go to the next level.

---

3. I trust my romantic instincts. If I am seriously drawn to someone, I don't care about traditional matching characteristics (like a certain age or financial status). I go for it!

R (Risk Taker) You listen to your body a lot; sometimes too much. Because you are impulsive, you are likely to respond to your first instincts and act on them. If you are physically drawn to someone, it is easy for you to overlook the details—and sometimes those details are important (like the person has three young children and you really aren't excited about the prospect of raising small children). Your type of love style has been described by John Lee in the book *The Colors of Love* as Eros—passionate attraction is the main thing that leads you into a relationship and you are likely to have very specific and nonflexible erotic tastes that if triggered, set your courtship in motion. You may have regretted some of your past choices, but this impulse is too strong a part of your emotional makeup to deny.

X (Risk Avoider) One way or another, you have learned that your romantic instincts are not always on target. Perhaps you have acted impulsively once—or against your better judgment—and gotten burned. Whatever the source of your cautiousness, you look carefully before you leap—not matter how drawn to a person you are. Over time you have probably come to believe that certain characteristics are very important (such as whether a person is doing well at their job, or whether they like children, etc.) and you listen very carefully to what a person says concerning the areas that matter to you. It is not that you won't give your heart—you just don't give it easily.

---

4. When it comes to romance, I believe that it is better to go for it and risk getting burned than to hesitate and never know what might have happened.

R (Risk Taker) As true romantics, Risk Takers are willing to accept the consequences for acts that might be rash or could be wonderful. That's what it means to be a risk taker. It's not that you don't recognize that you could be wrong and there could be a downside. You are willing to take your lumps in order to get a chance at something marvelous. You are the entrepreneurial spirit of romance! The most fun for you is to be with someone who, just like you, is willing to go full throttle into a romantic relationship. On the other hand, if both of you are Risk Takers, you may well stand a better chance of being burned, because neither one of you wants to slow down the falling-in-love process until you determine what the practical issues of your relationship are. Neither of you want to diminish or complicate those wonderful sensations that come with falling in love.

X (Risk Avoider) You can't quite understand why someone would answer true to this question. You have experience that tells you that impulsive action is much more likely to have negative than positive consequences, and the sting of those negative consequences continue, even in memory. At some point you think it is just dumb to place yourself in a possibly painful position. Not only are you not going to do it; but you are a little wary of anyone who would. While it might allow you to fall in love more easily if you gave in to your romantic impulses, you generally are a bit put off by someone who falls head over heels in love with you too quickly.

---

5. If there was a contest I had almost no chance of winning, I'd still enter, even if there was a fee. I'd think at least I'd have a chance to win!

R (Risk Taker) This question measures not only the willingness to lose but to be optimistic about romance. Most people look at the odds and unless they are strongly favorable, they don't take a risk, unless the cost is minimal. For example, even someone risk avoidant might buy a one-dollar lottery ticket, but they certainly aren't going to buy an expensive one. On the other hand, someone who is a risk taker generally believes that *someone* has to win against all odds, so it might as well be them. You might be willing to fall in love with someone who lives 5,000 miles away because you believe love can conquer anything; but if the person who is the object of your desire is not a risk taker, your romantic commitment to having a relationship no matter what it takes to do it may be rejected as unrealistic, even foolish.

X (Risk Avoider) It's not that you are pessimistic; you just look at hard facts and come to sensible conclusions. You believe statistics, and unless a risk is low-cost (let's say a coffee at a nearby place to meet a blind date) you demur and won't spend the time and effort it takes to play a long shot. You generally have a conscious calculus of odds in your head, and you don't believe you can conquer fundamental differences or overcome difficult practical considerations that end up being very important in maintaining a good relationship. Someone else may be too sure that every issue can be surmounted, but you will be skeptical, thinking they are not being logical or realistic. On the other hand, if you meet someone exciting but there is some block to the progress of the relationship (say one of you is finishing school, or you are in a long-distance relationship) you might need to be with someone who believes in the possibility of long shots. If the person, like you, feels overwhelmed by difficulties rather than inspired by possibilities, the whole relationship may never get started.

---

6. I've never regretted putting all my feelings on the line and making myself vulnerable—even if I didn't get the person I originally wanted.

R (Risk Taker) Risk Takers are usually emotionally open. In fact, you often get a kind of hormonal high letting the other person know who you are, how you feel, and what you have experienced—even if it is a painful story to tell such as talking about a failed relationship in which you admit that you were mostly at fault. You are willing to be vulnerable and face disapproval in the search of intimacy. You probably have found however, that this is a high-risk maneuver: letting people know the not-so-pretty parts of your history may put some people off immediately—and for good. But you just can't help it. It's who you are. Most Risk Takers are pretty resilient however, which allows them to take emotional risks that other people would never even consider.

X (Risk Avoider) You don't reveal your "backstage" self early or often. You're not necessarily dishonest—you just don't think you owe an early relationship the deeper and more vulnerable aspects of your personality and history. You may appreciate openness in others, as it helps you to understand the other person's character. But you may also find that that kind of self-exposure asks too much of you and you don't want things to proceed so quickly. Early intimacy might, in fact, be a deal breaker for you. If it is, you may want to warn the person that you are on a "need-to-know" schedule when it comes to confessionals and deeper secrets. This might turn off some potential partners, but if that's the way you feel, it might save a relationship from burning itself out before it begins.

7. If I felt deeply in love after a couple of months of being with someone I would be willing to get engaged or move in together.

R (Risk Taker) This is the quintessential measure of how much of a romantic you are and how much you believe in your first emotions and impulses.
Many people have fallen in love quickly, but it is something else again if
you are willing to make an important commitment, such as living together
or getting married. Then you are really willing to take big risks based on
your new but intense emotions. Many of us feel like we know that this person is *the one*, but acting on that feeling very quickly is the mark of a true
Risk Taker. Chances are that you can't possibly know *everything* you need to
know about this person. But you are willing to find out those things as you
go along, rather than being sidetracked with too much information before
you get involved. This can turn out very badly—or not. There are the hor-
ror stories of post–Las Vegas binges and the "Oh my God" response when
one person wakes up beside the consequences of what they have done in
the heat of the moment. But there are also stories about couples who sur-
vived whirlwind romances to go on to celebrate their fiftieth anniversaries.
The odds are against quick commitments—but they are not 100 percent
against them. If you are a true Risk Taker, of course, you don't care much
about odds.

X (Risk Avoider) The last thing you would ever do is move in with someone,
or make a public statement like an engagement, before you knew them for
quite a while. No matter how much you were attracted to someone, no
matter how close you had become, you would want time together before
you would consider moving out of your place, or having someone move in.
You think that this haste to co-habitate is a decision based on a temporary
state of mind and ultimately to be regretted. In a more charitable mood,
you might believe that they just have more guts than you do—or better
instincts—and you wish them well. But you think it is unlikely that things
will end up okay. You think of that old Cole Porter lyric, that the love affair
was "too hot, not to cool down." You want, no matter what, to get to

know someone before you change your life—or their's—for the better or worse. If you are dating someone who relies on their instincts and is ready to get serious right away, it may be flattering, but it is also unnerving and you may discount that person more than you should. It's just a different style, but you may think it connotes a more superficial approach to love.

Romantic Assessment

Being a Risk Taker (R) in romance means that you are more likely to be impulsive and intense about the way you relate to someone. You get everything on the table early, and you go with your instincts. However, your impulsivity can either be flattering and appealing to someone, or really off-putting. If you are infatuated, and sure of your emotions, you'd like to receive the same enthusiasm back. You want to leap ahead and not wait as the other person cautiously moves forward—or pulls back. Maybe a Risk-Avoider would be attractive to you because you would find them to be something of a challenge. But true Risk Avoiders are not being coy; they really don't like to be pressured, and they don't respect someone who is so *much* less cautious than they are. People who are risk averse do not avoid love. Rather, they see themselves as people who love deeply and therefore are more careful about proceeding—both for their own feelings and to avoid hurting the feelings of someone who is in love with them but of whom they are not yet sure. Each approach has its advantages—but each tends not to respect the other. Occasionally, the risk-taking romantic is so appealing that a risk-averse people throws usual caution away and lets themself get closer, faster than they would ever before. It could work out. But there is also the possibility of "risk-averse regret"—a delayed pullback, a sometimes dramatic reaction with unfortunate consequences.

Bottom line: Similarity in Romantic Impulsivity often makes for the best match. Proceed cautiously if you are seeing someone dramatically different from you in this category.

4

Personal Energy

This quiz measures the intensity of your everyday life. It helps you take a look at some of the dimensions of how much energy you have and how you use it. You will find out if you are a High Energy (A) or Relaxed (B) type. But you probably already have a good idea if you are the classic hyperkinetic personality who can't do enough things in a day, or alternatively, the kind of person who wants a more laidback kind of life. This quiz will certainly tell you if you are an A type or a B type, but it will also explain a lot more about what other characteristics line up with each personality trait, and how those traits affect a relationship.

Please Mark True or False

T   F   **1.** Work is at the core of my identity. I give it a lot of energy. When I fail, I am inclined to feel bad about myself. When I succeed, I feel like I am terrific.

T   F   **2.** When I want to be successful at something, I am totally committed to that effort. I can be like that whether it is a job, a sport I play, or a hobby.

T   F   **3.** Even if I am in love, a great deal of my energy goes elsewhere. I invest heavily in my job, my friends, my other interests. I have a lot of energy and I use it in multiple ways.

T   F   **4.** Wherever I am, I am often the center of attention. Most of the time, people can feel my charisma and intensity.

T   F   **5.** Anyone who knows me would describe me as a classic Type A personality: driven, busy, and ambitious about what I'm doing whether it is a volunteer or paid position.

T   F   **6.** When I travel, I am happiest when I have a packed schedule and see new things each day. It's not that I'm against a beach resort but if I were on a beach, you would see me doing water sports or sight-seeing. There is only so much lying around I can do!

T   F   **7.** I can't help it: I finish people's sentences for them more than occasionally. I have trouble waiting for the rest of what someone is going to say when I know what it's going to be!

Scoring

Give yourself one point for every True answer.

Give yourself the letter A (High Energy) if you have more True answers than False answers.

Give yourself the letter B (Relaxed) if you have more False answers than True answers.

The bigger the gap between True and False answers, the more intense you are in this characteristic

What Your Answers Say About You

1. Work is at the core of my identity. I give it a lot of energy. When I fail, I am inclined to feel bad about myself. When I succeed, I feel great about who I am.

A (High Energy While High Energy (A) types are not always workaholics, it is a commonly associated trait. High Energy types are more likely to attack work as if their self-worth depended on it, and frequently, although not always, it does. If you are a true A type you usually cannot help but work hard—even if it is just a job rather than a career. In fact, even if it is a job you don't like, it just isn't in you to do it lackadaisically. You want to throw yourself into your work and if you become alienated from what you are doing, it is really hard on you. A bad day at the job is likely to make you very upset. It can be hard for you to shake off that feeling. When things are going well, you throw yourself into your work all the more, and in general, you need someone who understands that this is your nature, your pleasure, and a more or less integral part of your personality. While you enjoy having a partner who cares enough about you to counsel you not to overdue it, usually you really don't want someone who wants you to be less attached to your work or the degree of performance you expect from yourself. If you are with a Relaxed (B) type who tells you not to take things *too* seriously, or doesn't support you in your intense commitment to what you do, you can feel isolated, unappreciated, or held back. If you commit to another A type who is extremely engaged with their work you may admire and understand each other better, however the downside here is that no one may be taking the time to attend to the needs of the relationship.

B (Relaxed) You are less likely than an A type to think of your job as central to your identity but even if you do, you have more boundaries between your work and your state of mind. You are likely to keep your work in balance to other parts of your life, less likely to sacrifice personal or family time to work, and in general more likely to take issues at work in stride. Because you see work as a part of life rather than at the core of it, it may be very hard on you to have a partner who often puts you in second place (or further down the list) when work demands or opportunities arise. While you may admire an A type, and enjoy the success and perhaps money that comes with their work commitments, you are not so happy about the time it takes away from the relationship and from family. If you are a B type yourself but attracted to hardworking or career-obsessed A types, you may often find yourself in the same fix: this is the kind of person you want, but they won't give you the emotional and physical time that you need. This is a common dilemma when a B type commits to an A type workaholic: you want an ambitious, skillful, and successful partner, but over time their absence from you and the home starts to undercut the emotional connection you once had. (A types often stop obsessing about work long enough to fall in love and start a relationship. But once that is accomplished they go back to their intense connection to their work.) B types who fall in love with A types had better understand that a workaholic is not going to have them uppermost in their mind.

---

2. When I want to be successful at something, I am totally committed to that effort. I can be like that whether it is a job, a sport I play, or a hobby.

A (High Energy) A types are not just A types at work. They are A types at most places and at most times. Most A types feel driven and competitive; so whether it's on the tennis court, making model trains, or doing crossword puzzles, they attack each activity with intensity and the will to win, or at least the will to do as well as they possibly can against either an opponent or their own past performance. They can be a real pain in the neck to the B type, who wants a friendly game of tennis or an easy stroll around the golf course. An A type may not be aware of how much tension their intensity brings to a game or conversation, because it is perfectly natural for them to be on high alert all the time—and this state of mind doesn't cause them stress. Laid-back B types, however, can feel their blood temperature go up in response to a frustrated A type who visibly expresses anger or disappointment if they don't meet their own high expectations. B types may worry that an A type is not enjoying what they are doing because they are so bothered by how it's going. But the typical A type may only be mildly stressed, if that. A types are generally intense, and being intense about getting a job done or getting the garden just right seems natural to them. If you are an A type, you don't really understand why everyone feels that *you* should lighten up!

B (Relaxed) You are more interested in the activity than the outcome. You might like to win—but that's not the point. If you are a B type, you more than likely are looking for more time to enjoy life, slow it down, and make more space for the things you like to do, rather than maximizing the intensity of what you do at work or play. The idea of playing a sport for blood is unattractive at best. It annoys you if the person you are playing with can't enjoy it as a game. Even if you played or play competitive team sports, you want to support the team more than you want to be a star. You may work hard and play with gusto—but A types are exponentially more ambitious than you are. That's just not what you want for yourself. If you are teamed up with an A type for doubles tennis or hiking or just about anything, it may take the joy out of it for you because they are driving themselves hard, while you want to do the sport in your own way and with your own goals.

---

3. Even if I am in love, a great deal of my energy still goes elsewhere. I invest heavily in my job, my friends, my other interests. I have a lot of energy and I use it in multiple ways.

A (High Energy) High Energy A types typically—though not always—are juggling many responsibilities and activities. As an A type, it is unlikely that you are simply going to drop everything when you are in love. You have responsibilities that don't go away when you fall in love, and since you are an intense person, your activities and business relationships are used to your in-depth attention. You may be very focused when you are in love, and perhaps you put everything you have into winning someone over and spending those first heady months of infatuation wrapped up in your romance. But inevitably, sooner rather than later, you have to manage *all* the interests and duties you have in your life, and that means your love interest will have to fit into an already busy life. You may be able to handle all of this better than most anyone, but some things will fall through the cracks. It is possible that if the person who loves you is a Relaxed B rather than a High Energy A, they may feel a sense of deprivation as you start to allot your time according to your previously packed schedule. A lover who is not as busy as you may get upset if they think they are no longer such an obvious priority for you.

B (Relaxed) Your vision of love and romance is synonymous with spending time together. And private time counts the most. Love is more likely to be a major priority of yours than someone who is an A type. While they may love you deeply, their more complex and other-directed lives may seem antithetical to your romantic needs. You are able to focus on one person, and when you are in love you much prefer that person to be at the center of your life. If you are with someone who loves you but does not see you as their number one priority, setting aside as much time for you as *you* want, you are likely to feel neglected and even unloved. You really want someone who puts the relationship first and whose other commitments, however complex, are clearly second. Similarity on this characteristic is important—or, if you do fall in love with a High Intensity A type, you had better be very clear from the beginning about your expectations.

---

4. Wherever I am, I am often the center of attention. Most of the time, people can feel my charisma and intensity.

A (High Energy) You can't help it—parties and people often revolve around you. It may be because you fill in the spaces, keep the conversation going, or have other attributes that often make you the center of attention. It may just be that your energy and style is infectious. Or maybe it's because the things you say and the stories you start shape subsequent conversation. Sometimes it's a big responsibility to keep everything going and you may choose to retreat in some social contexts, but if you use your usual fund of energy, you are much more likely to be the one who people encourage to speak more, the person people want to listen to, and the person most likely to inject energy into the room. A types who are also introverts try to avoid the spotlight, which naturally searches for them. In general, their strategy is not to go to places where they are thrust into being the star of the show. True enough, unless you conscientiously avoid this social role, you will find that you will be the center of attention often—and B types may come to feel that your behavior is, at least, tiresome, or at worst, all about your big ego. While this is not always necessarily the case, many people who avoid the limelight themselves do not generally understand what drives another person to seek it. They may not understand that it is perfectly natural, and even generous for you to keep everyone entertained and interested. On the other hand, B types may be as entertained as anyone else by your A type behavior—and happy that it's you doing all the work and not them!

B (Relaxed) You like being the audience rather than the performer. You are more likely to find yourself engaged in one-on-one conversations rather than having a crowd gather around you. And while you are glad to talk about things that mean something to you, you don't feel pressured to create a social success for everyone present by keeping them amused, interested, or engaged. You may have as much ego as a High Energy A type but you don't feel as much responsibility or need to be the life of the party or the storyteller for the group. In fact, you feel quite the opposite about social interaction: You don't like to "perform" and you are more likely to hang back than push yourself forward. You may admire a partner who likes to be at the center of things because it means you don't have to, especially if you are one of the hosts. But you might also think that all this expended energy is a waste, and you could wish you had a partner more like you, who was more conservative in social settings.

5. Anyone who knows me would describe me as a classic Type A personality: driven, busy, and ambitious about what I'm doing whether it is a volunteer or paid position.

A (High Energy) If you are a classic Type A personality, chances are someone—maybe many people—have labeled you as such. You might have heard comments such as, "Do you ever sleep?" or "Do you ever slow down?" or "You have more energy than anyone I know." There might be an implied criticism in their comments, but you take pride in being character-ized this way. After all, you are remarkably consistent: You are the same compulsively busy person in every aspect of you life—at work, at home, or at play. It is not exterior to your character. You don't force yourself to be this active; it is just who you are.

B (Relaxed) No one tells you you are moving too fast—in fact, quite to the contrary. Some people may mistake your laidback nature for laziness. You get comments such as, "You take everything in stride," "You are quiet but extremely competent," or "How do you stay so balanced?" Your energy tends to calm things down rather than speed things up. Other Relaxed B types like to work with you or be around you. You mix easily with more different kinds of people than an A type does. You may like an A type who will encourage you to get out more, try new things, and do more than you would not otherwise have attempted. On the other hand, you may find A types frenetic and out of control, and be afraid that they would stir up anx-iety or tension in your life.

---

6. When I travel, I am happiest when I have a packed schedule and see new things each day. It's not that I'm against a beach resort but if I were on a beach, you would see me doing water sports or sight-seeing. There is only so much lying around that I can do!

A (High Energy) It is hard for you to lie on a beach. You would rather be snorkeling, collecting shells, or doing water sports. If you go to a place with tourist attractions it would be next to impossible for you not to want to see them—all of them. If you were with someone who wanted to just pick a place and stay there rather than explore, you would have to wrestle with the gnawing desire to see what was out there. You would fit best with someone who also has the urge to do, see, and go . . . or would at least feel comfortable with you going on jaunts by yourself or with friends. However, if you occasionally find that you tire yourself out and never really have a "vacation" you might appreciate a partner who takes life at a slower pace and makes you feel comfortable with not pushing yourself and seeing every single thing that could be seen. If you tried slowing down, you might enjoy someone who helped you truly relax—or at least could bring that element to some of the trips or vacations you took together. Because you are an A type, you may never have experienced the joys to which a B type can introduce you: casual strolls through the park; long, lazy mornings reading the paper; slow-paced dinners that go late into the evening.

B (Relaxed) Your idea of a vacation is relaxation, relaxation, relaxation. While you might want to tour on a given day, you wouldn't want to cram so much into it that you ended up feeling like you needed a vacation to recover. You would rather miss something and not bring tension into the day then try too hard to do it all. If you were with a High Energy A type who is anxious because they didn't get to all three museums, or every beach on the north shore, or connect with three different people who they promised to look up, you would likely being to feel stressed, which is exactly what you want to avoid on a vacation. Vacations with an A type could be very difficult for you and cause more problems for the relationship rather than help repair it. On the other hand, if you are with an A type, you could negotiate taking some vacations at a leisurely pace and others more intensely. Certainly agreement on what a vacation is supposed to accomplish and what each person needed in order to have a good time would be a necessary part of vacation planning if you were with someone whose approach was radically different from your own.

> **7.** I can't help it: I finish people's sentences for them more than occasionally. I have trouble waiting for the rest of what someone is going to say when I know what it's going to be!

A (High Energy) Of course you finish other people's sentences—and exhibit a lot of other seemingly impulsive behaviors! You might be demonstrating a certain level of Attention Deficit Disorder. You know what the speaker is going to say next—or at least you think you do—and you want to get that answer out right away. You have trouble waiting for people to finish their thoughts. After all, you've already integrated what they've said and now you've got the answer! The brighter you are and the more you can intuit the gist of the issue, the more you find yourself thinking ahead and ready to remedy the situation before someone else is finished articulating the problem.

If you are not too rude, you will find yourself appreciated for your agile mind and quick answers. On the other hand, not letting people finish their sentences exhibits a certain amount of aggressiveness and desire for control that a partner could come to resent. You might, for example, have a B-type partner who allows you to interrupt, but is secretly stewing about it.

You could be seen as arrogant, which generally fosters resentment. Just as problematic, by jumping into the conversation midstream, you may miss nuances—or the whole intention of what your partner was trying to say. If your partner is the same type as you, they may be willing to go back and forth, until they get their point made. But others who don't share your propensities, will eventually, be cowed into silence, or driven to angry retorts.

B (Relaxed) In general, you think interrupting is bad form and you don't do it. Even if you know where a conversation is going, even if you are bored, you wait your turn and you don't like it when someone doesn't wait their turn as well. You may put up with someone who interrupts you but it is more likely you're offended by that type of behavior. If you are with a High Energy A type who consistently does this to you, you may need to bring it to their attention since they are probably unaware of how much they do it, or the impact that it is having. Otherwise, the A type may assume that you understand how the conversation game is played and that they expect that you can join in. You know that this is not your style and you do not want to get in the habit of fighting for verbal turf. If you are with an A type and want to mitigate this problem, you will probably have to make a big deal about it since it is unlikely that someone who interrupts will stop on their own will. The interruptions may be part of a larger set of issues that differences in the levels of energy present for a couple. Fixing it, or at least toning it down, might buy you some satisfaction. The easier course may be to be with another B type like yourself who is not in such a hurry about anything—including getting the last word.

Romantic Assessment

Differences in energy and intensity are not minor problems in a relationship. After all, a lot of relationship time is spent *doing* things, not discussing important social or family issues. That means being in sync about whether or not you want to do the same amount of socializing, how you want to spend weekday time together, what plans will happen on weekend nights, and what Sunday mornings will look like. This characteristic also affects one of the bigger issues that occurs in relationships: how will time be divided amongst responsibilities at work, friendship, children, family members, each other—and time alone. The A type person might think, "Okay, I can give my partner the early morning, divide up the afternoon between a tennis game with my buddy and time with the kids at the park, and then get back for dinner before I sit down at the computer to get those reports done." And they will feel good about hitting all their bases. However this isn't really going to do it for the B type, who wanted the whole day to spend with their partner, and for whom nothing less than the whole day is going to feel right.

Of course it doesn't always have to be that way. Under the best of circumstances, the B type in a couple will enjoy watching the A type partner do their thing, and will like being the stabilizing influence that keeps their spouse from spinning out of orbit. Likewise, the super-active partner could appreciate having someone who tethers them to earth and, over time, teaches them to ramp down a bit. Each person can get better at seeing when to modify each other, when to operate independently, and when to enable each other's preferential pace.

Under tougher circumstances however, the A type could feel like the proverbial "fast horse hitched to a slow cart" while the B type feels lonely or pressured—never getting enough of their partner's time or attention. Even when they do, they feel that life is going at a pace that causes them anxiety rather than enjoyment. If some kind of compromise isn't reached, the B person might see their partner as someone who is acting out inner insecurities that they don't respect, while the A person could feel lonely or frustrated, longing for a partner who wants to share life with the same gusto that they embrace.

Bottom Line: If two people are more closely aligned when it comes to personal energy levels, it allows them to create a mutually satisfying lifestyle more easily.

5

Outlook

This quiz maps your daily disposition. How you view the world in everyday circumstances is an important part of personality and a critical element in what makes people feel comfortable and potentially intimate with one another. This quiz will help you decide whether you are an optimist about life or whether you are more cautious about what will happen in any given period of time. Other aspects of how you apply optimism or caution in romance will also be analyzed here so that you can be better informed about how your perspective and expectations affect an intimate relationship.

Please mark True or False

T F **1.** I am usually happy when I wake up in the morning.

T F **2.** If I am in a relationship, unless there is obvious information to the contrary, I feel secure and loved.

T F **3.** I expect the person I love to be honest and true to me. I don't feel the need to be checking up on them, as suspicious thoughts almost never cross my mind.

T F **4.** When I start something new, I expect it to work out. I tend to get going right away and trust that I can correct problems along the way rather than having to do long periods of research before I begin.

T   F   **5.** Just because something has failed before, doesn't mean it will fail again. I don't let past disappointments weigh too heavily in my expectations of future likelihood of success.

T   F   **6.** When I meet someone and there are big complications (a long commuting distance, entanglements from a previous relationship, etc.) it doesn't deter me. I figure if this relationship is worth having we can work just about anything out.

T   F   **7.** I believe you can "teach an old dog new tricks," that "tomorrow will be a brighter day," and that you can "forgive and forget." All the clichés aside, I believe people can change and you can repair a badly hurt relationship.

Scoring

Give yourself one point for every True answer.

Give yourself the letter O (Optimistic) if you have more True answers than False answers.

Give yourself the letter C (Cautious) if you have more False answers than True answers.

The bigger the gap between True and False answers, the more intense you are in this characteristic.

What Your Answers Say About You

---

1. I am usually happy when I wake up in the morning.

O (Optimistic) You are sunny most of the time, and the proof of your happy disposition is that you are sunny even in the morning. Only the most incurable of optimists manages to pull that off! There are optimists that are not morning people—so this isn't an essential characteristic of optimism. But it is true that someone who starts each day with a positive attitude is a pleasure to be around—at least to another optimist. That said, it can be at best, irrelevant, or at worst, annoying, to someone whose biorhythms may not be in sync with yours.

Likewise, you may feel that someone who doesn't want to engage at the start of the day is a "downer" for you. While this difference of temperament may seem trivial, over a long period of time, a partner's *general* mood becomes quite important. Imagine years of mornings during which you are walking on eggshells from the moment the alarm goes off. Well, it might be a simple matter to cope with a crabby partner for the hour or so it takes for you to get out the door. If, however, this same circumstance was pervasive—twenty-four hours a day—the effect on your attitude could be dramatic. Everyone has times when they are down or quiet or just want some privacy. But a true optimist keeps seeing the positives no matter what time of day—or night. In general, an Optimistic person wants someone who will help them sustain that happy feeling. A partner whose mood veers from cautious to skeptical to pessimistic or gloomy may eventually rub all the sharp points off their partner's star and drive them away in search of some who can appreciate and reciprocate their optimism.

C (Cautious) What might strike others as being moody or crabby in your morning disposition may simply be that you are preoccupied—waking up concerned about the day ahead. You are not necessarily "down" in the morning but probably this isn't the high point of your day emotionally. You may start the day slowly or be all brusque and businesslike, but you don't understand how anyone would wake up happy unless there was something remarkably wonderful to be happy about. You might enjoy someone who is a happy camper in the morning because it would bring a little sunshine into your morning, or it might just bug you because you really just want to get on with it—and the Pollyanna whistling in the shower is distracting and annoying. But how you interact with your partner in the early hours of the day will not necessarily make or break your relationship. If you find that your moods are rarely in sync the problem is more serious. While a naturally optimistic person can perk you up and make your day lighter and happier, if that same optimism is not tempered, you might want someone with a disposition more like your own. It's not that misery loves company, although that may be true from time to time. It's just that we tend to appreciate someone whose emotions are similar to ours. It justifies the way we are feeling and makes us believe that we inhabit the same world and are dealing with the same problems.

---

2. If I am in a relationship, unless there is obvious information to the contrary, I feel secure and loved.

O (Optimist) Everyone wants to feel secure that the person they love returns their affections. But some people are constantly worried that the person they love could fall out of love with them. This is not the way you go through life. Because you are optimistic in general, it is also easy to be optimistic about the future you will have with someone. You are not blind, but you tend to think that everything can be worked out, so even if there are problems, you not only assume that they can be fixed, you assume that your partner believes the same thing. This is not always the case.

An Optimist who is paired with a Cautious or potentially pessimistic person might not realize that their partner fails to share their vision and firm belief in a future together. An Optimist might let issues slide without addressing their partner's abiding concerns, assuming that everything will come together eventually. A partner who is more cautious and self-protective might want to cut and run at an earlier point. Two optimists are likely to have the same level of faith in the resilience of the relationship; an Optimist with a Cautious type might not be really experiencing the same relationship in the same way as their partner does.

C (Cautious) What has made you cautious about love? Usually it is some romantic experience that worked out badly and has made you more anxious about relationships in general. Once someone has been left, betrayed, or disappointed, it is hard for Cautious types not to be affected in other relationships down the line. Some people are irrepressibly optimistic. No matter what negative things might have happened in the past, they believe that these things will not happen again in the future—or that they could see them coming and ward them off. They take each episode as an independent learning experience. As a Cautious type, however, you feel vulnerable. You need someone who is very reassuring about the relationship. There is still the issue of whether or not you are reassurable. Assuming you might be, you may need an Optimist to convince you that a relationship is possible, that a partner could and would be faithful and committed. If you are with another person who is cautious about whether or not love is real or whether it can last, the two of you may convince yourselves that love is too tenuous to invest in. On the other hand, someone as cautious as you are may reassure you that each of you is serious and that someone like you will try to avoid playing with your emotions—or their own—frivolously.

---

3. I expect the person I love to be honest and true to me. I don't feel the need to be checking up on them as suspicious thoughts almost never cross my mind.

O (Optimistic) You are not a suspicious person. You don't want to be a suspicious person. You feel good about people in general, and feel particularly trusting of someone you love and who you believe loves you. You don't torture yourself with doubts; you *need* to believe in the person you are with. Even if you have had an experience to the contrary, you haven't let the experience of betrayal change your belief that once you give your trust you it will be honored.

You do not generalize from one person who betrayed you to all others. Trust is natural to you and it is a key ingredient in the way you love someone. It will, of course, make you vulnerable if you are with someone who doesn't deserve your trust. And you do run the risk of being shocked and feeling stupid if your partner does two-time you. Also, you might feel hurt if you are with someone who worries about fidelity more than you do. You would feel insulted if you find them checking up on you. In fact, being with a deeply suspicious partner would be so unflattering and worrisome to you that it would be cause enough to end the relationship.

C (Cautious) Your experience, or your assessment of human nature, makes you naturally cautious when it comes to putting your trust in another person. You may be tempted to keep close tabs on someone with whom you are involved if there is anything about them that makes you feel insecure. You will need someone who doesn't arouse any fears in you; otherwise you might start backing away from the relationship, or making your partner defensive and upset. On the other hand, you may not expect your partner to be true to you because you don't think that total fidelity is possible in the world. You may consider this just being realistic—about yourself, or a partner—and if you do feel this way, you will need to be with someone who shares your attitudes and values. This philosophy, whether it is an "open marriage" (where partners agree to be non-monogamous) or a "don't ask, don't tell" policy will feel dishonest and unloving unless you have a partner who feels *exactly* the same way you do.

---

4. When I start something new, I expect it to work out. I tend to get going right away and trust that I can correct problems along the way rather than having to do long periods of research before I begin.

O (Optimistic) You approach love like you do other projects: confident of success and a happy ending. You are willing to get in deep pretty early on because you trust your intuition. You don't do love with a "shopping list" that has to be checked off. Once you connect, you are willing to give it your all and then see what happens. You don't do background checks online—except for fun; and you are unlikely to hedge your bets by keeping a lot of other people in the picture until you are dead certain that "this is the one" for you. Part of the fun of falling in love is just letting yourself get swept away. You can do this because you feel strong enough emotionally to withstand disappointment should it occur. Your natural optimism leads you to believe that *this* relationship will be just terrific. Even though you may have been mistaken in the past, you still approach new relationships with the same enthusiasm and positive expectations. It's the way you like to love—and you don't want too much caution to ruin the romantic beginning and progress of the relationship. If you are with someone like you, it's a heady experience for both of you. If you are with someone overly cautious, it can dampen the experience for you and may undermine your joy in—and commitment to—the relationship.

C (Cautious) In general, it makes you anxious to get deeply emotionally involved quickly. You may have doubts about your potential mate, even if you are very interested and sexually attracted. The more information you have, the more comfortable you feel. Also, you may rely on experiencing pivotal events in a relationship that reassure you—or alternatively, make you feel that you are with the wrong person. You may feel really uncomfortable with someone who wants to invest in the relationship with what you consider inadequate information about each other's personality, goals, values, or habits. In general you will feel more secure with someone who will proceed as cautiously, and with increasing personal disclosure, as you do. On the other hand, sometimes it is exciting and oddly reassuring to you to be involved with someone who feels so sure that you are a good team that they have no hesitations about commitment. Under the right circumstances, this dynamic might move a relationship along more swiftly than it would if you were with a person who likes to be as careful as you do.

---

5. Just because romance has failed before doesn't mean it will fail again. I don't let past relationships weigh too heavily in my expectations of future likelihood of success.

O (Optimist) Maybe the defining characteristic of a romantic optimist is that no matter how many lumps and bumps they get looking for love, they never feel that love is impossible—or even unlikely! Like everyone else, you've had your share of romantic disappointments but they don't squash your enthusiasm or expectation that you will eventually find your soul mate.

When you meet someone who seems jaded, someone who has let their past disappointments shape their future expectations, you find it an unattractive characteristic. You haven't lost your enthusiasm, and you don't want to be with someone who has lost their hope and interest. You are emotionally resilient. In fact you are so emotionally resilient that you may not recognize how truly cautious someone can be about love. If you meet someone who has reservations about you, or relationships in general, you might not know how hard these attitudes are to change, because you are so confident that problems will be resolved and love will triumph in the end. You need to be careful that you don't invest a lot of emotional energy and time into someone who intimated to you at the beginning that they had been in failed relationships before and think it will be too hard to make this one work. An optimist might not heed this warning signal, but a more cautious person would—and has a good chance of being correct.

C (Cautious) You believe that the best prediction of the future is the past. You feel that you are shaped greatly by your past relationships and you take your cues from the lessons that these experiences have taught you. You feel that people who don't take past relationships into account are in denial, have no ability to grow, or are doomed to make the same mistakes because they are not educable. You find it more interesting—and comforting—to talk with someone as cautious as yourself about the likelihood of similar situations having similar outcomes than to try to engage with people who seem to feel the past has nothing to teach them. Generally their optimism will not influence your attitudes or reservations about the success of a relationship in which issues exist that derailed things in the past.

---

6. When I meet someone and there are big complications (a long commuting distance, entanglements from a previous relationship, etc.) it doesn't deter me. I figure if this relationship is worth having, we can work just about anything out.

O (Optimist) You are not intimidated by romantic challenges because you think that love will conquer all. You are not only optimistic; you may also underestimate the difficulties to be overcome because you don't want to give up on love—even if it means commuting between countries or states. In the past, you may have twisted yourself into a pretzel when love called—and you are still prepared to do it again and again. It's not that you are necessarily attracted to the long shot, but you are willing to put effort in when it's in the interests of romance. When there are serious difficulties, however, it will really help if the other person is an optimist like yourself. As much as you are willing to do, you need someone who will take encouragement from your attitude, and be willing to meet you halfway. At the very least, you will need to know that you have your partner's support to let you do what needs to be done to keep the relationship alive.

C (Cautious) When you learn that a potential mate must take a job halfway around the world, or that they have two children under the age of three while you have none of your own, you can't help but focus on the problems ahead of you. You try to be realistic about what you can accomplish and what chance you really have to construct a long-term relationship or marriage with someone who now lives far away or who comes with a lot of baggage that you would have to help carry. You look at the facts: What would it cost to commute? What effort would it take to help parent another person's young children? What economic sacrifice would you have to make to be committed to someone with financial problems? In all likelihood, you will bail out. It's not that you couldn't see loving this person—it's just that you feel that your efforts are unlikely to pay off or you will be saddled with some serious challenges that you don't feel you can take on. You prefer the better bet of someone who lives nearby, someone whose life fits easily with yours. You might be flattered that someone more optimistic than you would be willing to commute a long way, or take on your children as their own. However, you know that a lot of people start things they can't finish. You shy away from long shots.

7. I believe you can "teach an old dog new tricks" that "tomorrow will be a brighter day," and that you can "forgive and forget." All the clichés aside, I believe people can change and that a badly hurt relationship can be repaired.

O (Optimist) It takes a lot for you to say a relationship is over. If you were committed to someone at one time, you tend to feel that the relationship can be saved, even though some pretty ugly things have occurred. You are willing to go to therapy or give someone a second chance because you believe people can and do change for the better. If you are with another optimist, they are as likely as you would be to do whatever psychological work and practical adjustments are necessary. Someone more cautious than you, however, is less likely to be convinced that change is possible. If you are with another optimist it is more likely that your partner will believe that things can be different next time. Both of you could be kidding yourselves, of course, but on the other hand, this attitude often opens the door for another chance. And many relationships have been saved by reuniting one more time to talk, negotiate, and effect change.

C (Cautious) There is the old saying, "Fool me once, shame on you. Fool me twice, shame on me." You are not in the forgiveness business. You are not an optimist—and you are particularly not optimistic about people changing the way they act in an intimate relationship. Unlike an optimist, who is highly motivated to want to give the relationship another chance, you are reluctant to believe that a positive resolution is likely enough to warrant opening yourself up to pain and disappointment again. If you don't believe in putting in the work to save a troubled relationship, chances are it's because you experienced or observed unsuccessful attempts at relationship rehabilitation and lost your belief in the restoration of love, trust, or commitments once any or all of these have been shattered. You will need a very convincing optimist to make you believe you should try again. If you are with another cautious or even pessimistic person, chances are that even one bad incident between you will drive you both away from each other.

Romantic Assessment

The way you feel about chances for love, marital happiness, fidelity, and the personal growth and change of two partners will be an important variable to consider in a long-term relationship. If you are optimistic, you expect the best, try to tolerate or get over the worst, and are very likely to be willing to stick with the relationship for better or for worse. That's because you really do believe that things work out most of the time, that you could make an estranged husband love you again, or tame a playboy who hasn't ever settled down. Optimists are great relationship savers and maintainers—but the downside is that your outlook may keep you in a relationship that isn't healthy for you. Given your usual desire to believe in the resilience of your relationships, it would help if you had someone who felt the same way you do and would put in similar effort. If you are a cautious person, you may feel that some people are unduly optimistic and are not being realistic. You could feel trapped if you are with a person who cannot see the problems of the relationship the way you do. It may seem to you that your concerns are not taken seriously and that their optimism is really an attachment to the relationship per se rather than a realistic reaction to what is going on between the two of you.

There is also the chance that an Optimist will see your more critical approach to life as judgmental, which it may be. Optimists favor giving approval over disapproval, faith over cynicism, and assume value where you might reserve judgment. These differences could seem highly discordant to both of you.

On the other hand, there are times when a relationship might profit from at least one Optimist in the couple. It is not that a Cautious person is always negative, but sometimes it is hard for them to take a leap of faith and believe that a new or troubled relationship is worth the effort. A Cautious person is always evaluating their chances of being hurt or throwing good years after bad. An Optimist may not be cautious enough for his or her own good, but they do give a relationship every chance because they believe almost any chance at all is worth taking. When an Optimist runs out of positive feelings about chances for relationship survival, it is usually after an ugly truth has been revealed and acknowledged or after much time and energy has been expended to no avail. In general, two Optimists give a relationship its best chance, and one optimist can help pull a relationship through some tough times. Two Cautious partners may be less likely to believe in the relationship right away, but they also may be good at uncovering relationship weaknesses, which means that they can be discussed and fixed. The balance between blind belief in the relationship and attention to its problems and challenges is a delicate one—but that is why one positive sensibility and one given to criticism might be a good mixture if the two people are not at polar opposites of the spectrum.

Importantly, someone may be too cautious—an extremely cautious person may have a darker vision of human nature that makes them too suspicious and even paranoid about their partner's commitment or fidelity. Someone too sunny and optimistic may not want to see the signs of their partner's discontent or coverups. However, extremes of almost any personality characteristic may create incompatibility.

Bottom Line: Two people who are *realistically* optimistic or *realistically* cautious probably constitute the best foundation for a good relationship—enough caution to proceed slowly until issues are faced and solved, and enough resilience to be willing to do whatever is needed to amend a relationship that has become unstable because violations of love or trust occurred.

6

Predictability

This quiz measures how much your happiness in a relationship is affected by the level of predictability versus the level of change and variety that you prefer in your life with your partner. Some people find comfort in knowing that once they find something they like, they will be able to repeat that wonderful experience. For example, many couples intend to put down roots in a community, raise their children there, and be in that same neighborhood when the grandchildren come along. Other people find the idea of repeating or sustaining a pattern over and over again suffocating. People who need variety in their lives could become bored or depressed at the thought of the kind of life that brings great pleasure to people who like predictability.

Please mark True or False

T   F   **1.** If I find a great restaurant or getaway, I prefer to return with my partner again and again. I'd rather do that than risk trying someplace new, even though someplace new could turn out to be wonderful. I like to stick with the wonderful place I know.

T   F   **2.** I have a small number of friends that I treasure and take care of. I don't have time for a lot of new friends in my life.

T   F   **3.** I'm a person who attaches emotionally to one person at a time. If I'm content in my relationship, I couldn't be drawn out of it, or into a new relationship or into an intimate adventure, even if the person was extremely attractive.

T   F   **4.** I would love to have a place to go to every weekend and/or most vacations.

T   F   **5.** I like my partner to dress and look a certain way. I don't like them to change simply according to fad or fashion.

T   F   **6.** I have certain ways that I enjoy being intimate. Once my partner and I learn how to please each other, I'm content not to experiment further.

T   F   **7.** When I am committed to someone, I am rock solid. I never wonder about what I am missing or whether or not I should be with someone else in a different kind of life.

Scoring

Give yourself one point for every True answer.

Give yourself the letter P (Predictable) if you have more True answers than False answers.

Give yourself the letter V (Variety) if you have more False answers than True answers.

The bigger the gap between True and False answers, the more intense you are in this characteristic.

What Your Answers Say About You

1. If I find a great restaurant or getaway, I prefer to return with my partner again and again. I'd rather do that than risk trying someplace new, even though someplace new could turn out to be wonderful. I like to stick with the wonderful place I know.

P (Predictable) For you, familiarity makes the heart grow fonder. The more you like something, the more you want of it. You are more secure and emotionally stronger when you are in familiar circumstances. You like waiters who know your name or hotel staff that know which room you prefer when you go on vacation. You don't really like surprises, because in your experience, a lot of them turn out to create problems or disappointments. You see yourself as someone who digs in deeper rather than spreading yourself too thin. It's not that you aren't occasionally curious or that you never do new things, but your greatest comfort and pleasure exists within the things you've grown to know and love. It would disturb you if you had a partner who wanted to take you away from those things too often. On the other hand, if you find someone exactly like yourself, you had better like the same habitats and outings. After all, two people who both like a predictable environment, but can't agree on what that environment should be, could find it difficult to be together!

V (Variety) You are endlessly curious and you want to experience a lot of different activities, destinations, vacations, and perhaps even jobs. You think of life as an adventure and want to get as much out of it as you can. You feel trapped at the idea of going to the same vacation spot every year or eating at the same restaurant almost every night. It's not that you don't have favorite places, but rather that you will often sacrifice one of those favorites in the service of a beguiling new destination. If you have a partner who really doesn't like to try new things or activities or go to new places, you may feel confined, and eventually become frustrated and angry.

If you don't want to feel you are missing anything, you might think a good compromise is to start traveling and doing things on your own, which is fine up to a point. However, it can cause emotional distance in a relationship if your independent life starts taking up too much of what could be "together." You would do best with someone like yourself, or at least someone who doesn't inhabit such a small world that you feel stifled.

---

2. I have a small number of friends that I treasure and take care of. I don't have time for a lot of new friends in my life.

P (Predictable) You have a small circle of family and friends in your life and you are happy with that. You don't need a great number of friends and acquaintances around you. In fact, you don't feel that you could have really meaningful relationships with such a large group. And besides, you don't feel the necessity to put out the energy it would take to add new ones to your intimate group. You like the comfort of people who know your history, and you know them equally well. If you are with someone who is a "people person," you have trouble getting enthusiastic about meeting their friends. In general, you are not a party animal: even a large dinner party at home may make you feel uncomfortable when the horde invades your privacy. You prefer couple to couple outings, when you can really get to know other people on a more than superficial basis.

V (Variety) You are the "people person" that a Predictable personality is afraid of! You probably have a wide circle of friends and acquaintances, but even if you don't have many really close friends, you are always open to meeting new people and you enjoy getting to know them. You don't mind if you have dinner parties where nothing extraordinary or really intimate gets said—you like to hear people's stories and you like watching people interact with one another. You may be a "party animal" or simply enjoy big gatherings. You like to see what's going on and at least participate, if not instigate. It would make you feel unhappy or constrained if you were with someone who never wanted to meet your friends or take advantage of the interesting people you came across. You have trouble understanding why a partner wouldn't want to at least meet most of the people you really like.

3. I'm a person who attaches emotionally to one person at a time. If I'm content in my relationship, I couldn't be drawn out of it, or into a new relationship or into an intimate adventure, even if the person was extremely attractive.

P (Predictable) You probably have never been much of a "dater." At least since after your teenage years, you have always wanted a relationship more than just "hooking up." You are not the kind of person who wants to juggle a number of people. Instead, you prefer a sequential kind of dating rather than having a different person on different days of the week. You think of yourself as a person who, once committed, is extremely focused in a romantic relationship. You want to be with someone who is as serious as you are about dating "with a purpose." You want someone who appreciates the fact that you know what you want and, once committed, will be steadfast. If you break up with someone, you are happiest when you find that you are getting back into a groove with a new serious relationship. You are wary of people who are known to play the field. While they may look good at first blush, you find it hard to accept that they will ever give themselves completely and forever.

V (Variety) Your dating/relationship patterns reflect your outgoing people-pleasing personality. You've gotten a lot out of the experiences you've had and there is a part of you that finds it hard to give up the chance to meet some new, intriguing person. You notice interesting, attractive people in your environment, and you are tempted. You worry about boredom. If you do concentrate on one person, or think about making a commitment to one person, they have to be engaging enough to keep you committed. You need a partner that will help keep life interesting—socially, sexually, and emotionally—or you just might find yourself back in the dating marketplace. You might do well with someone else more like yourself who would keep you on your toes and make you work harder on the relationship—or perhaps someone who can commit strongly to the relationship and who can inspire you to do the same. But ultimately if you are the kind of person who likes to keep your options open, you may have to decide if that's what you really want forever. If it isn't, then you'll have to find the kind of person who will help you fulfill your needs for variety in your life—inside one relationship.

---

4. I would love to have a place to go to every weekend and/or most vacations.

P (Predictable) You tend to be "nester." You like to build yourself a warm, comfortable place and then take the time to enjoy it. The idea of moving homes every couple of years—or even at all—probably stresses you out. You take that same approach to vacations or weekends. Once you've found a place that will satisfy your needs, you can't imagine why you would exchange it just to try something new. In general, you would prefer to be a member of a community where you feel at home, rather than be constantly interacting with strangers in different places. This doesn't mean that you never want to go someplace new; but comfort and familiarity are a bonus to you. Having your own place with your own things makes you happy. You would prefer a partner who had the same impulse to nest because it would give you a sense of comfort and connection.

V (Variety) You enjoy going to that cabin in the woods or a favorite B and B, but the idea of doing one or even both of those time after time, week after week, probably makes you feel trapped. You want to explore, see new things, and check off as many adventures as you can on your long "places to see before I die" list. If you were with someone who was a weekend nester, or always wanted to go to the same place for vacations, you would feel constrained and maybe even deprived. You might be able to do it for a while, but you'd probably come to resent it over the years.

Yet if there was some sort of compromise—a mixture of a favorite place with an occasional adventure, this situation could work out nicely. In fact, someone less adventurous than you could end up introducing you to the simpler pleasures of one place and community relationships. Likewise, you could spice up someone else's life that was a little too predictable. You could add the new experiences and new places that could add interest to your relationship. It all depends on how intense your desire for new experience is and how determined your partner is to have predictability.

---

5. I like my partner to dress and look a certain way. I don't like them to change simply according to fad or fashion.

P (Predictable) You have certain ways that you like your partner to look and it can really upset you if they change. You are sensitive to fluctuations in weight, radical changes of hair, anything that really changes the look of the person. Although these things are minor to some people, they are important to you. Your partner needs to know this ahead of time or they won't understand how crucial this can be in terms of how attractive you find them. If you are with someone who feels the same way, you will both agree that it's important to maintain your look and dress up to each other's standards as much possible. People who don't share your attitude in this regard may feel that you are superficial because they don't understand your need for physical predictability. Over time, you may be disconcerted to find them changing in ways that you don't like.

V (Variety) Once you find someone you are attracted to, you still find them attractive even if they try on a number of variations of dress and hairstyles. You may even prefer someone who is fashionable—someone who likes to take on a new look or tries the newer styles each season. In fact, you may be much more drawn to someone who has an adventurous style rather than someone who has found one niche and sticks to it. How people dress or wear their hair may not, in fact, be that important to you, but it's probably a plus when you are with someone who's not afraid to try something new.

---

6. I have certain ways that I enjoy being intimate. Once my partner and I learn how to please each other, I'm content not to experiment further.

P (Predictable) You are not the kind of person who gets easily bored with a sexual routine. Once you have figured out what pleases you and what pleases your partner, you are not too interested in sitting down with a copy of the *Kama Sutra* to learn ancient sexual tricks. Sex to you is about more than sexual variety, and if you have a partner that wants to shake things up too much, you may feel that it makes sex less authentic, more artificial or superficial. You are not necessarily against change—but you don't think your sex life should be graded on how many new things you try. You develop a sexual style and unless either of you complains, you are happy with the status quo. You do best with someone who feels the same way. You really wouldn't want to feel like a lab rat in a series of sex experiments. And, equally important, you don't want to be pressured out of your comfort zone

V (Variety) You like variety in general but you really like variety in bed. You like to mix up what you do, what order you do it in, and whether or not it's playful or serious. You really want someone who feels the same way you do. Otherwise you start to get bored and wonder how you are going to do the same thing with the same person for the next forty years. Someone with the same perspective as you have will keep sexual energy alive by trying new things and being adventurous and remaining open to your suggestions. In fact, it is the variety of your sexual behaviors and the trust between you that actually allows you to try innovative things. In turn, your shared adventures make you feel more intimate and more emotionally connected with your partner. If a partner refused to try new things in bed, or found some of the things you wanted to do gross and unloving, any limits they'd place on your sex life would bother you. In fact, if your partner wanted to repeat the same pattern most times the two of you made love, it might be a source of serious discontent that would make you less happy with the whole relationship. Depending on how important sex is to you, you might end up looking elsewhere. You would definitely be happiest with someone who thinks of sex both as a physical as well as an emotional need and who is ready to explore some adventurous and playful sexual ideas with you.

---

7. When I am committed to someone, I am rock solid. I never wonder about what I am missing or whether or not I should be with someone else in a different kind of life.

P (Predictable) You were made to be married. The only thing that breaks up a relationship for you is being left—or falling out of love, which you wouldn't do lightly. If you do break up, it is much more likely to happen because something is wrong with the relationship itself, *not* because you are interested in someone else. You are not the kind of person who flirts seriously with anyone else or keeps an eye on the horizon for someone better. When you are in, you are in 100 percent, and it takes an enormous unsolvable problem or horrible revelation to shake your commitment to the one you love. You need to be with someone who feels the same way. In fact, you naturally assume that the person you are with feels the same way. After all, you chose them, which makes it all that much more vital that you do not pair up with someone who's "in love with being in love." That may seem to be the kind of person you want, but in fact it's exactly the opposite. You'd be well advised to know your partner's track record because if it's littered with many short-lived relationships, you might be headed for trouble.

V (Variety) It's not that you cannot commit—or stay committed—but this doesn't come easily for you. If you meet someone who never doubts, never waivers, and never looks—no, *never even thinks about someone else*—you need to be very conscious about the differences between you. You are not like that. However, you might do well with someone who has the capacity for unflagging loyalty. Sometimes you need to be inspired by your partner to accept that one person can be your "whole world." On the other hand, you have to be honest with yourself and fair to others who are not as open to variety as you might be. If you are still cruising the room with your eyes, engaging in playful flirtation, or exchanging intimate e-mails with new people online, you have to ask yourself if you are really ready to forego the romantic variety you have enjoyed most of your life. It's a hard corner to turn for a playful lover. If you aren't ready to give up the hunt or the thrill of discovering that next, new, and wonderful person, then make sure you are hanging out with people who share your feelings, and who don't assume that romance automatically means commitment or a stable relationship.

Romantic Assessment

It is unlikely that someone who takes this quiz gets seven out of seven answers that are entirely on the Predictable or Variety side of the equation. What you might want to pay attention to is how intensely you seek a steady, predictable course or how upsetting the very idea of predictability is. Small differences about this approach to life are not a big deal. As you've seen in some of the explanations of the questions, there are even circumstances under which being with someone different from yourself might support the relationship.

For example, if you have a tendency to have trouble committing and settling in with one person, it might be really good for you to have someone who expects full commitment, who gives it, and helps you understand how important commitment would be to your future happiness in this—or any—partnership. If you have grown up enjoying the company of a large number of dates and spent a big part of your adulthood enjoying numerous relationships, you may find it hard to settle for a life with only one person. But in all likelihood you may be looking to change that pattern to find a satisfying lifelong relationship. Rest assured, it's possible for you to "settle down" without settling for less or denying your fundamental nature by creating variety within a relationship. If you can't come to terms with making one choice over all others you will not only scuttle your own dreams of lifelong connection with a soul mate—you will also be detrimental to those people who are looking for a lasting love.

The challenge for you if you strongly crave predictability in a relationship is to make sure that a prospective mate shares your expectations for the future. In other words, ask yourself are you dating a person who is capable of having a strong desire for continuity and commitment? Are you sure that their commitment to a shared future is as strong as the commitment you are ready to make for them? There are people who crave variety within a relationship and if they get it they are quite content. But there are others who are in love with being in love, and variety for them means changing partners or having other partners on the side. Wanting variety in a relationship is not a danger signal for those who are looking for a lifetime monogamous commitment, but you do have to make sure that a person who is a strong V (Variety) personality is able to find that variety within the relationship with *you* and you only.

Bottom Line: It is usually better to pick someone similar on the predictability scale. People who want variety will not want to be bored and people who want predictability will not want to be pushed into a series of experiences they really don't enjoy. When opposites do attract it is important to understand that some major compromises and accommodations may be in order.

7

Perfect Matches Based on Similarity

The next step in understanding yourself—and your perfect match—is to discover how Romantic Impulsivity, Personal Energy, Outlook, and Predictability affect each other. Now that you've completed the quizzes in the preceding section, you will be able to determine your four-letter profile, such as RAOV or RBCP, for the first half of the Duet® Total Compatibility System. This chapter will show how each characteristic affects the others, moderating or intensifying certain aspects of your personality. Once you have reviewed your own profile, you might want to look at the others to see which appeal to you and which might make a good match based on the analyses provided. Be aware, however, that these four characteristics are just a part of a romantic personality. These first four characteristics most predictably create a positive match when two people's profiles are similar to one another. (I will also review additional critical parts of your romantic personality, characteristics that could be either similar or complementary to someone else, in future chapters.)

Combinations of Personality Traits

RAOV:
Risk Taker, High Energy, Optimistic, Seeks Variety

An RAOV is an unleashed personality. There is nothing in this personality type that holds back. These people are willing to put it all on the line, act quickly, expect success, and if they fail, they still expect success the next time. They also like change, because a changing environment means new opportunity, another chance, or a better mate. A person with this personality profile isn't going to be happy with a partner who holds them back, who tells them they "can't," or who too often sees the downsides or predicts disaster. RAOVs match well with someone like themselves. They especially like someone who will be excited, confident, and positive about love—and each other.

Matches to Consider
If you are looking for a true soul mate, chances are you'll be drawn to someone similar to rather than different from yourself. Another RAOV could well be your perfect match.

RACV (Risk Taker, High Energy, Cautious, Seeks Variety): This person is a risk-taking, high-energy person like yourself but is a little more cautious about making decisions or taking action. You might benefit by the cautious nature of someone who can help you avoid some of the negative consequences of your more impulsive decisions.

RBOPs (Risk Taker, Relaxed, Optimistic, Predictable) are great lovers and are willing to be romantic and share your optimistic approach to the relationship yet take life a little easier than you do. The appealing contrast is that they are less likely to search out greener pastures, which could help solidify your relationship and help the two of you stay together.

XAOVs (Risk Avoider, High Energy, Optimistic, Seeks Variety) are your counterpart in every way except for the fact that they are less impulsive than you might be about getting into a relationship or opening up quickly. Otherwise they share your high energy, optimism, and enjoyment of new experiences. An XAOV might be perfect for you if you have gone out on too shaky a romantic ledge a few times and prefer someone who would help the relationship build more slowly into a more solid structure.

RACV:
Risk Taker, High Energy, Cautious, Seeks Variety

An RACV is inventive and aggressive, yet takes time to assess risk. This person explores options and is willing to invest a lot to make their dreams and ambitions come true. They are likely to have wide-ranging interests and they try hard to avoid boredom. Yet they are realists and don't presume that all their endeavors will work out. If an RACV has a little bit of "attitude" they might be seen as "awesome" yet perhaps a challenge to keep engaged over the long haul.

Matches to Consider
Your matched profile, an RACV, offers the likeliest chance for a soul mate, if you are drawn to similarity.

RAOV (Risk Taker, High Energy, Optimistic, Seeks Variety) is very similar to you, except that you are more cautious about the possible downsides of the relationship. If you think that you would be better off with someone with a sunnier approach to issues than you have (and who would have a more positive approach to solving relationship conflicts), this might be a good match. An RAOV also has a good chance of being a soul mate, helping you trust your instincts and reinforcing your feelings about each other.

XAOV (Risk Avoider, High Energy, Optimistic, Seeks Variety): If you feel you need someone who will help pace the progress of the relationship, allowing you both the time to work through issues, an XAOV might be an ideal choice. They will recognize the challenges, but with an optimistic outlook. Your RACV and the XAOV profiles are very much alike yet the difference in the way you begin a relationship may help the relationship eventually get a firm footing.

XACV (Risk Avoider, High Energy, Cautious, Seeks Variety) is also a very similar profile. Less willing than you are to be open and vulnerable right away, perhaps because they are less trusting of their intuitions, an XACV is otherwise a high-energy person who does put the same thought into the relationship as you do. If you can reassure an XACV that *this* is the right relationship, you two could have a lot of fun together.

RBOV:
Risk Taker, Relaxed, Optimistic, Seeks Variety

This personality type usually exudes romantic confidence, which allows them to fall in love rather quickly. RBOVs are likely to throw themselves into a relationship wholeheartedly if they believe that this is "the one" and they are likely to want someone who will do the same. Their ability to focus on the relationship and take the time to develop it means that RBOVs generally combine intense romanticism with the practical caretaking that nurtures love. Attachment, however, does not mean predictability. RBOVs don't want to be bored. They like to mix things up, which means they need someone who will spend the time with them to enjoy life on their terms. RBOVs are optimistic enough to try new things and may be attracted to a more energetic personality than their own—but they want to see the other person's energy directed at them and the relationship.

Matches to Consider
Another RBOV is your potential soul mate, if you are attracted to similarity and, therefore, could be your perfect match.

RAOV (Risk Taker, High Energy, Optimistic, Seeks Variety): If you admire high energy and drive, then this person might complement you. Like you in every other way, they can be entertaining and exciting, which could enhance this part of your character. You might want to be careful, however, if they are an extreme version of a High Energy A type since you might not get as much attention as you would ideally like.

RBCV (Risk Taker, Relaxed, Cautious, Seeks Variety) is a similar profile to your own. You both are likely to be romantic and impulsive about love, except that RBCVs are more cautious about making a commitment and may not have the trust and belief in the relationship that you do. On the good side, you are both people who are likely to put the relationship first and use it to explore new experiences together.

XBOV (Risk Avoider, Relaxed, Optimistic, Seeks Variety): If you appreciate a person who puts on the brakes and is "the voice of reason" more often than yourself, then an XBOV might be a good choice for you. You, on the other hand, will be the leader when it comes to acting on impulses and intuition.

RBCV:
Risk Taker, Relaxed, Cautious, Seeks Variety

RBCVs are willing to consider romantic and other kinds of opportunities that could have a significant chance of failure. Still, they are not impulsive and they might say that they will take calculated risks, not silly ones. Their adventurousness and ability to act from the heart is tempered by a slower and more cautious approach to romance than an RAOV. But do not make the mistake of thinking that their Relaxed B–type approach implies a lack of interest or drive. They have a conservative side but this type of person wants a full and varied life and is willing to try new things and take on challenges. Nonetheless, they probably feel more respect for someone who is Relaxed (B) and Cautious (C) rather than a Risk Taking (R), High Energy (A) person who moves too fast, too soon, and risks making unconsidered choices.

Matches to Consider

A person with the same personality profile is soul mate potential, if you are attracted to similarity.

RACVs (Risk Taker, High Energy, Cautious, Seeks Variety) share your romanticism, your realism about issues and challenges in life, and your lifestyle choices. The major difference is RAVCs are more active, more aggressive, and perhaps more ambitious. This difference energizes a lot of relationships, so if it is attractive to you, an RACV would be a good choice.

RBOV (Risk Taker, Relaxed, Optimistic, Seeks Variety): If you find yourself a bit (or a lot) more pessimistic about life and love than you might prefer, then you might want someone like an RBOV who will not only counteract your more negative impulses but help you drive the relationship forward. An RBOV also shares your romanticism and will help keep things interesting because they, too, seek variety.

XBCV (Risk Avoider, Relaxed, Cautious, Seeks Variety): If you want someone who has a similar temperament to yours but who is less romantic and impulsive about love, an XBCV would be a good choice. Sometimes we are drawn to people who keep their distance longer than we do, and allow us to have the emotional freedom to pursue our feelings without worrying that the relationship will get too serious too quickly. If you respect someone who goes into a relationship more slowly than you do, this would be a good choice.

RAOP:
Risk Taker, High Energy, Optimistic, Predictable

An RAOP is a dynamic combination of will and drive when it comes to courting. They charge into the dating world to find the one they love and they can usually handle the ups and downs of the dating game very well. Their take-charge, go-after-what-they-want-and-expect-to-get-it profile is tempered by the fact that they prize predictability. They may be at ease in the dating market—but they are not "players." This is the kind of person who knows his or her strong points and would probably like to see those same strengths in another person. Once an RAOP knows they are on firm, familiar, and worthy ground, they will take on a tough project or go after a romantic relationship with a lot of enthusiasm and a hardy self-confidence that they can make things work out. However, they will have this kind of confidence if they feel they are on familiar footing, that is, if the person they are interested in is the kind of person they have loved in the past. In general, an RAOP likes dating a similar kind of person (same class, a certain look, similar goals and values) rather than dating someone exotic. They are looking for a life partner, or at the very least, a steady dating partner. They take their risks elsewhere.

Matches to Consider
Another RAOP, being the same as your personality profile, would be your perfect match if you are drawn to similarity.

RACP (Risk Taker, High Energy, Cautious, Predictable) is a good match. RACPs are also romantic, high energy, and looking for the same kind of attachment to a predictable and solid lifestyle that you are. They will not have the same optimistic approach to life you have, but if you want someone who will help you think through things more critically than you might otherwise do, an RACP would fit the bill.

RBOP (Risk Taker, Relaxed, Optimistic, Predictable): In general, matching on the level of energy is important. However, sometimes people are looking for someone who will slow them down, put ambition in a more controlled or modest place in their lives, and center on the relationship. If cranking down the intensity of your life (or having a partner who is not as busy and job-absorbed as you are) appeals to you, you might want to try an RBOP.

XAOP (Risk Avoider, High Energy, Optimistic, Predictable): If you have enough romanticism for two, you might appreciate an XAOP. They share your lifestyle values, your optimistic outlook, and high energy but they are less impulsive. If you think your relationships may have suffered by being too hot, too soon, finding someone who is a bit more Risk Avoidant might be a better long-term bet.

RACP:
Risk Taker, High Energy, Cautious, Predictable

RACPs will take a chance on love but not too much of one. They have a cautious vein that moderates their romantic enthusiasm. An RACP is intense in love and will go after a desirable partner with singular focus. But they also believe in managed risk and they want to minimize the possibility of hurt or loss. They are analytical, even in love, applying logic to every situation. Even as they are pursuing someone, or encouraging advances, they will hold back, considering all aspects of a potential relationship. They know the kind of life they want to live and they are looking for someone who will fit into it. This attitude prevents them from being overly impulsive. Because they want predictability, they tend to go for a specific type of person rather than dating widely diverse kinds of people. They definitely need someone who is similar to them: a devoted partner with whom they can share a high-octane life with a rather tight circle of good friends and predictable activities.

Matches to Consider
RACP is exactly the same profile as you and, if you are drawn to similarity, this could be your perfect match.

RAOP (Risk Taker, High Energy, Optimistic, Predictable): If you have a tendency to see too many problems and pitfalls in love and are not confident in your own resilience, you might want to pick an RAOP. They share your energy and romanticism, but are more likely to be problem solvers and help show you a way to believe in the relationship.

RBCPs (Risk Taker, Relaxed, Cautious, Predictable) might be good for you because they are more likely than you are to put serious time and intensity into the relationship to get it going and keep it going. A match on energy is important, but if you are an extreme High Energy A type, having someone who is satisfied with less of your undivided energy and focus is a good thing.

XACP (Risk Avoider, High Energy, Cautious, Predictable): You might want someone who is exactly like you, but not so impulsive about love. Over time, impulsive people have a high chance of being burned, and finding someone who makes this less likely to happen can be very attractive. You want a long-term relationship, so being with someone who sets up the beginning of the relationship more cautiously, nurturing it for the long run, might be really valuable.

RBOP:
Risk Taker, Relaxed, Optimistic, Predictable

An RBOP is a very attractive kind of person to many different kinds of people because their pursuit of someone is steadfast rather than aggressive—a full, open-hearted jump into love. They are not however, the kind of person who is "in love with being in love" and their enthusiasms are straightforward: what you see is what you get. They make time to develop a relationship since this is their style in other parts of their lives as well. Like other types who are dating "with a purpose," they are in no hurry; they are optimistic about love, but they like to savor the moment and don't want to plunge ahead and bypass the good parts. They may be the one to initiate a relationship, but they will let it develop at its own pace. They are homebodies, family builders, deep lovers rather than sequential daters.

Matches to Consider
Another RBOP, being the same personality profile, is an ideal match if you are attracted to someone similar.

RAOV (Risk Taker, High Energy, Optimistic, Seeks Variety): If you want to change your life, you probably couldn't do better than to choose a Risk

Taking, High Energy A type who is going to rev up the pace and bring new experiences into the relationship.

RBOV (Risk Taker, Relaxed, Optimistic, Seeks Variety): If the High Energy A type of the RAOV puts you off but you don't want to fall into predictable patterns, then the RBOV might suit your needs.

RAOP (Risk Taker, High Energy, Optimistic, Predictable): If you are attracted to more energy in a person, or want someone to take the lead economic role in your relationship, an RAOP would be a good choice, since they are positive sorts of people who like the same kind of day-to-day life you do. You do have to be careful, however, to make sure that a High Energy A type will still be able to make time enough for you in their busy lives.

XBOP (Risk Avoider, Relaxed, Optimistic, Predictable): This profile is exactly the same as yours except for having much less tolerance for emotional risk. If you are emotionally open and forward, you might help them to get involved in the relationship more quickly than they naturally would. If they like your romantic panache, they will easily be drawn to your temperament, which is very similar to their own.

RBCP:
Risk Taker, Relaxed, Cautious, Predictable

RBCPs have a nice romantic style. They are imaginative, open to love, but rarely superficially romantic. Analytical people by nature who make a careful entry into the world of love, they are looking for something long lasting that completes a life they already enjoy. They date purposefully and are willing to be aggressive in their pursuit of someone who excites them. But once they've found that certain someone, they don't keep playing the field. In fact, once they are sure of their choice, an RBCP is willing to put everything on the line.

They don't really gamble, even if the relationship seems to be off to a strong start. They will hold off on a serious commitment until they feel they have the information—and the confidence—they need. They might like a High Energy partner if there are other important similarities in what they want out of life. But they would be cautious about an A type because in general they are looking for balance and stability in their relationships. RBCPs like routine and they don't want someone who will be bored by it.

Matches to Consider
RBCP, being your exact profile, will probably be a perfect match if you are attracted to someone similar to you in most respects.

RACP (Risk Taker, High Energy, Cautious, Predictable): You might want to try someone like yourself, but with higher energy. As long as your energy levels aren't way out of sync, energy exchange between A and B types can help bring balance into a relationship.

RBOP (Risk Taker, Relaxed, Optimistic, Predictable): As long as an RBOP isn't unrealistic, having some difference in outlook can be productive for a relationship. They see the bright side, you see some of the clouds, and together you can find a balanced approach to a project, problem, or process.

XBOPs (Risk Avoider, Relaxed, Optimistic, Predictable) are not as romantic as you are. This could be a turn-off—or a challenge. They balance you in a couple of ways. They would slow down the relationship and give it a chance to mature into something important. And once they were convinced it was good, they would be more able to believe in it, and prop it up in hard times. The differences in this case might help support the relationship.

XAOP:
Risk Avoider, High Energy, Optimistic, Predictable

The X in this profile is a very important fact and should be considered an important characteristic in dating. An XAOP takes love slower, either because they are shy, because they come to decisions slowly and carefully, or because their trust has been abused in the past. Their self-protective instincts did not operate well enough to save them from uncomfortable or dangerous mistakes. The high energy and optimism mean the previous dicey experiences did not cause bitterness and that they remain a positive force in their own lives and the lives of others, even though they may be cautious about love for some good reason. Since they are not comfortable with romantic impulsivity, they give considerable thought to whether or not they should let the relationship proceed.

They don't want a lot of dramatic dead-end love affairs, and are uncomfortable about falling head over heels in love. Rather they prefer to let serious relationships develop and may be looking for a companion more than a passionate lover. If they continue in a relationship, chances are they are hoping this will be a love connection with an infinite future. They are optimistic that it could happen, but they will be looking for someone who is a known quantity to them, serious about commitment, and similar in values and lifestyle.

Matches to Consider

An XAOP has the same personality profile as you do. If you are attracted to similarity and looking for a soul mate, this could be your perfect match.

RAOP (Risk Taker, High Energy, Optimistic, Predictable): You find that you are too cautious about falling in love, and are not confident enough at the beginning of a relationship to give it a chance to be what it could be, you might want to choose someone who will help you take that romantic leap of faith. Maybe you should let yourself be drawn to people who impulsively pursue you, relying on their intuitive knowledge about how good the two of you might be together. If you give up a little control at the beginning, you might encourage deeper and more passionate feelings. You can take this chance since you will feel comfortable with their other personality characteristics.

XBOP (Risk Avoider, Relaxed, Optimistic, Predictable): Sometimes High Energy A types like you need someone who calms them down rather than matches their energy, volt to volt. It sometimes works better when there are not two ambitious, super-busy people in the relationship. The real question is, how relaxed might this person really be? If they are enthusiastic and active in the most important areas of your life together, this match could work very well.

RACPs (Risk Taker, High Energy, Cautious, Predictable): RACPS are more romantic and adventurous, but since they are moderated by a cautious approach to problems and issues in the relationship, they might feel familiar enough for you to be confident about their emotional attachment to you. Other than their romanticism, theirs is a pretty stable profile and would probably be a very good match for you. And you might enjoy a little romantic push!

XBCP:
Risk Avoider, Relaxed, Cautious, Predictable

An XBCP is generally conservative about love. They don't like high drama and romantic excess. They are not risk takers generally and so don't proceed impulsively even if they feel they are "in love." An XBCP has a very coherent, comfortable personality. They want a steady, calm, uncomplicated emotional life. They look for balance: a stable home, a relationship with a trustworthy, commited partner who accommodates their lifestyle, and work that does not overwhelm family life. XBCPs may not be the most ambitious people, but they prefer a life that enables a relationship. There is only so much sacrifice they will make at the cost of this relationship. They truly want a companion and they will guard against those things in life that would undermine that central desire. This type of person is usually monogamous and wants to find a partner who also is loyal and content with a lifelong vow. They are emotionally conservative and would do best with someone who shares their outlook and temperament.

Matches to Consider
XBCP is your perfect match if you are looking for a soul mate and are drawn to someone whose profile is identical to yours.

XACPs (Risk Avoider, High Energy, Cautious, Predictable) are conservative like yourself, except that they are more high energy and more likely to put work, money, or achievement at the center of their identity. If this kind of person is exciting to you, this could be a great match since every other aspect of temperament is similar, and lifestyle preferences are in sync with your own.

XBOPs (Risk Avoider, Relaxed, Optimistic, Predictable) share your general approach to life, but they are more likely to deal with relationship problems more positively than you do. They might not be as analytical as you are, so you will be a good balance with their generally optimistic view that "everything will work out." They approach problems with a realistic and constructive attitude. Sometimes it does balance one's natural caution—or pessimism—to be with someone who has a more optimistic outlook.

XBCV (Risk Avoider, Relaxed, Cautious, Seeks Variety): This combination might be a stretch, but it is possible that while you prefer more predictability, you could enjoy being with someone who brings a little change and variety into your life. XBCVs are, like you, cautious and unlikely to be too extreme in what they would like to do. They are also quite conservative in temperament; but they are more apt to experiment to a degree that you might find to be stimulating.

XACP:
Risk Avoider, High Energy, Cautious, Predictable

In general, XACPs are go-getters but they are conservative about their relationships. They could be workaholics who thrive in a fairly traditional relationship or people who channel their energy into raising many children, running volunteer organizations, or simply in juggling many activities at once. Still, the rest of the profile shows what is important to them: being careful about who to love and when to commit, analytical about what should go into the right relationship, putting energy into their daily lives, and trying to build a life stable enough to support a marriage or long-term commitment. An XACP will fastidiously look for "the one" and then eagerly share favorite places, restaurants, and outings. They will invest deeply in their partner and expect the same in return.

Matches to Consider

XACP: With a profile identical to your own, you should find your soul mate if you are drawn to similarity.

RACP (Risk Taker, High Energy, Cautious, Predictable): This person is very much like you except ever so much more romantic! Yet you just might find their romanticism to be irresistible. But you have to remind yourself that just because someone is romantic and goes with their intuitions, it doesn't mean their feelings are superficial. In every other way, this person would feel right for you—and the difference might be a good one for you.

XAOP: (Risk Avoider, High Energy, Optimistic, Predictable) is very much like you except that an XAOP adds a bit more optimism to a personality type that could err a bit too much on the cautious side. Since both personality types are most comfortable avoiding risks and surprises, and well matched for their high energy and verve, this little bit of emotional lift could be a nice touch of support making a couple a little less likely to be too negative or too unadventurous.

XBCP: (Risk Avoider, Relaxed, Cautious, Predictable) could be a nice counterpoint to an XACP. Both of you are equally risk averse and cautious about options, plans, and possibilities. You will respect each other's approach to issues and logic. Your lifestyles will be in sync as well as you both like revisiting and staying with the things and places you have learned to enjoy. The only difference is that an XBCP is a less intense, less driven person and might be a good guardian of the relationship's place in your world. A-types often need B-types to slow them down enough to pay attention to their partner and home. If the energy gap isn't too extreme this could be an excellent choice for you

XBOP:
Risk Avoider, Relaxed, Optimistic, Predictable

People who are risk-averse in romance may have suffered bad experiences—or it might simply be their nature to be reserved, especially when it comes to falling in love. XBOPs have a natural affinity for a slower approach to life, supported by their optimistic point of view that things will work out as they should. Their reluctance to jump right into a relationship or be vulnerable may be more a question of timing and seriousness of purpose than it is of fear. XBOPs can be romantic and they are attracted to the stereotypic ideal of home and family—white picket fence, a golden retriever, the works. But they are willing to wait for it to happen naturally. There are two strong themes in this personality profile: openness and relaxed attitudes, balanced by being risk-averse about both romance and the desire to create a satisfying lifestyle. This may all add up to long dating histories before commitments are made—but at least XBOPs are the kind of people who want to be committed eventually! They are generally oriented toward a serious, monogamous relationship and tend to invest deeply in both people and places.

Matches to Consider

XBOP is the same personality profile as you. If you are looking for a soul mate, and are drawn to similarity, this could be your perfect match.

RBOP (Risk Taker, Relaxed, Optimistic, Predictable): If you like romantic and intuitive people even though you don't consider yourself to be one, this might be a great match for you. Sometimes just a little bit of difference between two people makes the magic in a relationship. An RBOP is your exact type but with somewhat more emotional expressiveness.

RBCPs (Risk Taker, Relaxed, Cautious, Predictable) are more romantic people, with temperaments similar to yours but with a different attitude that is less open, more analytical, and more problem-solution-oriented. Their romanticism softens the cautious part of their character. If you think you sometimes miss things that you should have noticed and want someone else to be the watchdog for the relationship, an RBCP would be a good partner.

XBCPs (Risk Avoidant, Relaxed, Cautious, Predictable) are conservative in the same ways you are—and perhaps a little more so. They might enjoy your disposition and you might like their orientation to problem recognition and solutions. If the romanticism and aggressive pursuit of an RBCP is too much for you, an XBCP might be a good compromise.

XAOV:
Risk Avoider, High Energy, Optimistic, Seeks Variety

XAOVs are not prone to romantic impulsiveness, in part because they have high demands for the kind of person they want to be with and also because they don't want to make mistakes that complicate their lives. Nonetheless, XAOVs are hungry for stimulation, optimistic about what the future has in store, and have a lot of energy to expend in their own behalf. These characteristics may keep them playing the field and lead to their being single and uncommitted longer than other personality types. If a person is risk-averse and also likes variety, the two characteristics can produce someone who avoids a serious relationship or wants to have as many interesting experiences as they can (sexual and/or emotional) before settling down. Put this all together with high spirits and high energy and it might mean avoiding a firm attachment for quite a while. The best kind of partner for XAOVs would probably be someone who can share and maintain the same curiosity about life and the same energy for adventure and change. An XAOV might need a partner who likes variety just so they can help each other stay interested, challenged, and innovative. XAOVs would not want to be with someone who wanted predictability and who held them back: on the other hand, having a partner who was a Risk Taker might help an XAOV get past their natural caution and connect earlier in the relationship.

Matches to Consider

XAOV: With the same personality profile that you have, if you are looking for a soul mate, and are drawn to similarity, this could be your perfect match.

RAOV (Risk Taker, High Energy, Optimistic, Seeks Variety): While you are generally emotionally restrained until you know someone very well, it's not such a bad thing to be paired up with someone who doesn't have those reservations and who puts in the time and the emotional energy to get the relationship off to a passionate start. In every other way, RAOVs are your kind of people—energetic, focused, optimistic, and out to sample the world.

RACV (Risk Taker, High Energy, Cautious, Seeks Variety): More intense and intuitive about love than you are, but not exactly wild and crazy, RACVs are cautious about relationship issues and not likely to be someone you would find to be unrealistic in their outlook. Unless they are depressed or truly negative, you might like the balance they bring to the way you generally look at problems or work through issues.

XACV (Risk Avoider, High Energy, Cautious, Seeks Variety): If you want a more cerebral and careful start to your relationship, XACVs will be on your wavelength. In fact, they are a more serious sort than you, but they share your high energy, focus, and appetite for exploring life's possibilities. If you are looking for a partner who might have a little more grounding than you do, an XACV might be a good match.

XACV:
Risk Avoider, High Energy, Cautious, Seeks Variety

XACV are likely to be tentative about building a committed relationship until they have had a lot of romantic experience and are sure about what they need. They may be very social and like being in a big mix of people. It might look like they are very drawn to creating a relationship, but a great deal of social contact for them is mostly a move away from commitment rather than toward it.

They are risk-averse in starting relationships and cautious about developing something deeper, no matter how things appear at the beginning. Furthermore, they may worry about being bored in a long-term relationship or feel as though they are missing something by making a premature commitment. This type of person can, and will, make a commitment (at least most of them will) but the person they need will have to help keep life interesting. XACVs demand a lot from the world, take on a lot, and probably want someone who does the same—or at least supports their own high-energy, curious approach to life. Occasionally, however, they might want someone who reassures them, centers them, and provides a reassuring stability to the relationship.

Matches to Consider

XACV: If you are looking for a soul mate, and are drawn to similarity, someone with your same profile could be your perfect match.

RACV (Risk Taker, High Energy, Cautious, Seeks Variety): Don't discount an RACV just because they are more romantic than you are in the beginning of a relationship and may push you to figure out what the relationship means to you earlier than you otherwise would. Risk Takers may be a little bit overwhelming to you but you have so much in common with this profile otherwise that they could convince you to take the relationship seriously right from the start. Their openness might scare you, but look at the Cautious (C) in their profile—it means they evaluate circumstances as they go along, just like you do. This is likely to be a good match.

XAOV (Risk Avoider, High Energy, Optimistic, Seeks Variety): Maybe you are just a little too careful about everything. An XAOV shares your drive and your curiosity and wants to live a big life just like you do. But they also bring a positive approach to the relationship. A person like this helps a couple believe in itself and get over issues. This might be just what you need.

XBCV (Risk Avoider, Relaxed, Cautious, Seeks Variety): If you want a big, busy life, but don't want to have to collaborate or compete with someone else who wants a big, busy life, too, then an XBCV would be a great person for you. Sometimes a leader needs another active person to keep up with them, but sometimes they need support from someone who is content to watch them be a comet without having to aspire to the same heights.

XBOV:
Risk Avoider, Relaxed, Optimistic, Seeks Variety

XBOVs are cautious at the beginning of relationships but do not continue to tread softly once they are on solid footing. Their positive approach to relationships and their ability to settle in and enjoy day-to-day life creates good possibilities for love. XBOVs are likely to put love at the center of their lives and need someone who gives love the same priority. They are likely to want to be doing things—traveling, getting involved in outdoor activities, attending cultural events, etc. They will want a partner who shares their overall philosophy of life. They want to be always growing, changing, and adventuresome. XBOV will want someone who helps keep the relationship stimulating—both sexually and emotionally. They are unlikely, however, to seek that stimulation outside of the relationship. They have the personality characteristics that would make it more likely for them to invest deeply in their present relationship rather than look outside it.

Matches to Consider
XBOV: If you are looking for a person similar to yourself in most ways, someone of the same profile could be your perfect match.

RBOV (Risk Taker, Relaxed, Optimistic, Seeks Variety): You are less emotionally open and romantic, less dependent on intuition and instinct than an RBOV, but you might like these qualities in someone else. RBOVs quite naturally prompt a relationship to deepen more quickly than you might like. If you feel pressured, you would back away. If you suspected that the person was being superficial or just attracted to you as the dish *du jour,* you would be seriously turned off. However, if you felt they were sincere and worthy, this could be a good match for you since their style of intuitive risk taking is not necessarily unconsidered or blithely done. They believe they are on reasonably solid ground much faster than more cautious personalities. In any case, RBOVs are very much like you except that they possess a willingness to "do anything for love" when trying to find a mate. If you can handle this spontaneity, or even be flattered by it, this is a very simpatico type of person for you.

XAOV (Risk Avoider, High Energy, Optimistic, Seeks Variety): This is a more intense, "Type A" version of yourself. Whether or not that is good for you is something you'll have to decide. But you might like someone who is professionally or personally ambitious, and they might like someone who is not so much a competitor as a supporter. For example, it is convenient, and sometimes necessary, for couples who want to create a family to have one person who wants to put children before work or other intense pursuits. It's also true that you can have two people who both love their work, but one is happy with an eight-hour day and the other just can't quit. Different degrees of energy intensity in partners can bring overall balance to a relationship, assuming all other things are equal.

XBCV (Risk Avoider, Relaxed, Cautious, Seeks Variety): The only drawback with an XBCV for you is that you may want a partner who shares your level of optimism. An XBCV takes on romance and love carefully, and while they are not as conservative as say an XBCP, they will be more cautious about the relationship than you will be. Still, they share important values and lifestyle choices with you and might make a good balance in decision making and problem solving.

XBCV:
Risk Avoider, Relaxed, Cautious, Seeks Variety

An XBCV is cautious about love and commitment. They will need to know quite a bit about a person before investing in them. Even intense attraction won't make them jump in before they've gotten to know the person pretty well. An XBCV takes things slow and wants time to test character and compatibility and not just act on the intense feelings that motivate people in the beginning of a new relationship. That said, like most people who are cautious about relationships, they usually hold back because of fear of over-involvement before it's called for, or being vulnerable before they know if the other person really cares for them. Caution in the beginning and developing phases of a relationship is often associated with taking things seriously, so these characteristics together generally mean they are not superficial about love. Given this approach, plus their interest in new experiences and places, they tend to want a committed relationship with a partner who has the same appetite for change and exploration that they do. The exception might be an XBCV who has been very disappointed in love, in which case they go out with several people, keeping it light, and investing in no one until they are confident that they've found their perfect match.

Matches to Consider
XBCV: This person has the same personality profile that you do. If you are looking for a soul mate, and are drawn to similarity, this could be your perfect match.

RBCV (Risk Taker, Relaxed, Cautious, Seeks Variety): You might like someone who pushes the relationship, to get serious quickly since by nature you are cautious about first attractions. Still, you ultimately intend to invest in love as one of the most important parts of your life. Perhaps a little romance and passion early in your relationship will make getting to know someone more fun, even if it's not the way you generally approach people. Having someone who trusts their instinct and intuitions might be educational for you, and even endearing. An RBCV shares your cautious approach to problems so there is some similarity in temperament. Another plus: You like sampling diverse experiences in life and this person shares your desire for innovation and exploration.

XACV (Risk Avoider, High Energy, Cautious, Seeks Variety): This type of person brings energy and work-centeredness into your life. This might be a risk factor if you really like more laidback, less feverishly compulsive people like yourself. On the other hand, XACVs might be looking for someone who is more likely to be less intense, more home-centered, or centered on the relationship. This combination might make an interesting balance, and you may admire their accomplishments and industry. The biggest issue between you may be the differences in energy: Will you be pushed to be busier than you want to be? And will you get the kind of relationship time you need? This can work out, but not if you are at the extremes of the energy spectrum.

XBOV (Risk Avoider, Relaxed, Optimistic, Seeks Variety): This is a good match except that XBOVs are more optimistic than you are. This can actually be a great thing for a relationship, since all couples need at least one person in the relationship who has an explicit and implicit belief that you'll be able to work through problems and figure everything out. If a person is blindly optimistic, refusing to see the facts of a situation, you will be disappointed in them. But if they just have a positive attitude, and still are able to see the downside that you see—and be able to collaborate with you when it's appropriate to be cautious—this could be a good match.

Being Different

Flexibility · Decision Making · Emotionality · Self-Nurturing

The preceding chapters looked at situations in which two people who shared personality characteristics were most likely to enjoy a harmonious, long-term relationship. The next four characteristics, however, often work well in couples when each partner brings a different temperament and different habits into the relationship. The result is that each person is complementary to the other rather than wholly similar. In some cases—and I will be very clear about which ones those are—that difference will benefit one member of the couple more than the other. There are many circumstances in which the person who isn't getting what they want out of the relationship (even though their partner is) should consider the option of picking someone who is more similar to themselves in regards to these characteristics. This is particularly true of the last personality characteristic in this group, Self-Nurturing. Whether you share feelings of distress or are transparent about them is a very large issue in many relationships. How you match on this style of communication is critical. But whether or not you should be *similar* or *different* is not always a straightforward proposition.

Overall, you will discover how being different on these next four characteristics might help a couple create a happy team or, depending on what other personality characteristics are present, how difference might create frustration and conflict, or even loss of respect.

8

Flexibility

The following quiz reveals how much people can change at a moment's notice, how much they like to change or, conversely, how attached they are to order. By order, I mean meeting expectations and repeating patterns that have worked for them in the past. Some people may be flexible in some areas of their life yet dig in their heels when it comes to change in other situations. But there tend to be patterns in one direction or the other. In this section you will discover how flexible you are about quite different kinds of personal, domestic, or social habits. Things like whether you are punctual or fashionably late for social events, or follow specific child-raising techniques in which you believe strongly or take a more casual approach when it comes to disciplining your kids, are but two of the many daily activities that reveal your level of flexibility. There is no right or wrong answer here. Some people just need things done in a certain way and at a certain time while others seem to adapt more readily to different approaches and changing plans. And while a pairing that brings together two people at extreme ends of this spectrum might spell trouble, more often than not, people who are somewhat but not radically different in this characteristic can be perfectly happy.

Please mark True or False

T   F   **1.** I like to plan out everything in advance. I don't like plans being changed at the last minute.

T   F   **2.** I like things done a certain way. I'd rather do something myself than let a partner do it their way and have it done incorrectly (or not the way I wanted).

T   F   **3.** Once I have thought a great deal about something I rarely change my opinion. If I do, it usually takes quite a bit of time and/or hard facts to convince me otherwise.

T   F   **4.** I don't think it's a good child-raising practice to be too permissive. I think if you make rules, children should follow them. If they don't, there should be consequences.

T   F   **5.** I believe in being on time. It really annoys me when people are late, and I am almost never late myself.

T   F   **6.** People might label me as a perfectionist or compulsive. I don't believe in "good enough." I have some issues with people who don't do things as well as they are capable of doing them.

T   F   **7.** I get upset when people change their mind at the last minute and don't show up at a party or appointment they said they would attend—no matter how casual the event might be. I think it's rude. It would bother me if my partner simply decided not to do something at the last minute that we had agreed to do.

Scoring

Give yourself one point for every True answer.

If you have more True answers than False answers, give yourself the letter S for Structured.

If you have more False answers than True answers, then give yourself a letter F for Flexible.

The bigger the gap between True and False answers, the more intense you are in this characteristic.

What Your Answers Say About You

---

1. I like to plan out everything in advance. I don't like plans being changed at the last minute.

S (Structured) You like order in your life, you want things to work out as you have conceptualized them, and you invest deeply in seeing your vision come true. This is the case for both small and big plans—from a decision to meet for coffee that you made the day before to a trip you planned out a year ago. While some people might think only the latter was important, you also put the former into your schedule and you arrange time and expectations about it. You don't generally like someone who changes plans often. It might bother you a lot even if it only happened occasionally. Since you can get very upset or disappointed when things fall through or when modifications happen, even if it's no one's fault, it might be nice if you were with someone who didn't care so much and who could comfort you instead of fuming about it.

F (Flexible) It doesn't matter to you if plans change suddenly. You are a go-with-the-flow type of person. You are open to any experience, and it doesn't have to be a prearranged event. You are happy to change most plans at the last minute. In fact, you don't need of lot of plans. You are happy to show up and see what happens. And if it doesn't work out, that's okay. It takes a lot to get you upset. Missing the first five minutes of a movie or having to book a different hotel at the last minute doesn't faze you. If you have a partner who takes those things seriously you would support them—but it could get on your nerves if they always make a big deal

out of every plan that changes. Still, you might like someone very structured especially if you like to delegate the planning, or are willing to have
someone else arrange things any way they see fit. If you find yourself to be
something of a procrastinator, then someone who is more structured
might take the initiative and make things happen.

---

2. I like things done a certain way. I'd rather do something myself
than let a partner do it their way and have it done incorrectly (or not
the way I wanted).

S (Structured) You are the kind of person who has high standards that you
find really hard to compromise. You don't mind doing things yourself as
long as they get done right. So, you need a partner who understands that issue and is either willing to let you take the lead on some things or does
things exactly the way you do. If you are with someone who has a more relaxed approach to how things should be done, it might work well unless
they come to feel that you are taking over on too many occasions. You
would do well with someone who understands the way you like things and
is willing to step aside to let you take the lead, or is willing to do things the
way you'd like them to be done.

F (Flexible) You have a wide range of standards: it's not that you don't care
about doing some things extremely well, it's just that you often see alternative ways in which things can be done and you can accept any one of
them. If you are with a person who has to have things done a particular
way, you can handle it. In fact, you might feel good about supporting
them if you like the way they do things. However, you do want to be
careful not to get deeply involved with someone who has a "my-way-or-
the-highway" approach to life and whose fundamental values differ from
your own. Your flexibility is a great characteristic but you don't want to
find yourself compromising to a degree that is no longer in your best interests.

3. Once I have thought a great deal about something I rarely change my opinion. If I do, it usually takes quite a bit of time and/or hard facts to convince me otherwise.

S (Structured) You don't come to an opinion lightly. You trust your research, your logic, and your instincts. You may, in fact, appear to be intimidating to others who are less sure of themselves or of what they know. You don't think of yourself as being unreasonably opinionated or dogmatic. But the fact that others are that way annoys you, especially if they tend to shoot from the hip or are less informed about an issue than you are. You like having someone whose opinions are either close to yours or who takes the time to research and think about issues as much as you do. You are attracted to people with the same thought processes. As long as they don't hold opinions on values that directly undermine your central beliefs and life choices, you can deal with intelligent dissent well.

F (Flexible) You can often see more than one side of an argument and you pride yourself on being able to read, listen, and change your mind when appropriate. It is likely that you consider being able to change your opinion to be a sign of personal growth and maturity. When you are with someone with an immovable opinion, you may be amused—or irritated—since you normally don't like or respect people who are closed to new information or points of view. However, this may not be a big stumbling block if the person you are with mostly agrees with the way you see the world—or respects your right to see things differently. The very strength of someone's convictions may appeal to you because it causes you to reexamine your own beliefs—and stimulates you in a way that being with someone who shares your "flexible" approach to life may not. Of course, it can be easier—and perhaps equally engaging—to be with someone who will puzzle through a perplexing or controversial issue with you and create a safe platform for discussion and even disagreement.

---

4. I don't think it's a good child-raising practice to be too permissive. I think if you make rules, children should follow them. If they don't, there should be consequences.

S (Structured) Many people, including those who are flexible on many other issues, have strong, even impassioned feelings about how children should be raised. If you are a firm disciplinarian, you probably want to be with someone who shares that approach. Differences on this issue are a common source of intense conflict between parents. Children bring out a degree of emotional intensity that very few other issues in relationships can match. You will need a person who feels the same way as you do on this question—or is willing to follow your lead. If you have a partner who is permissive and you don't believe in that approach, you will either fight for your point of view, or be angry and apprehensive about their conduct and what you see as the consequences of this conduct in your children's behavior. Things can deteriorate in a relationship from a lot less volatile issues. The only way this difference works is if each partner is aware that they are a bit extreme in their approach and respects a partner who mitigates their strictness—or permissiveness—some of the time.

F (Flexible) You may have had a childhood that you considered too strict and don't want to inflict one on your own children. Maybe it was just the opposite: you had parents who gave you a lot of rope—and you think it helped create some of your best qualities. Either way, you like giving your kids freedom and you are heavier on the rewards for doing well than on the penalties for disobeying rules or taking unapproved risks. You might be quite ferocious about a child-rearing philosophy that gives kids some space to think about what they have done rather than coming down hard on them for their mistakes. You may not believe in strong punishments for misdemeanors—perhaps not even for major screw-ups. If you are with a person who gives the kids no latitude, you will probably find both the person and the policy offensive. Unless you are looking for someone to be tougher with your children than you are, this is one area where you may not be endlessly flexible with your partner.

5. I believe in being on time. It really annoys me when people are late, and I am almost never late myself.

S (Structured) The management of time is a big issue in day-to-day relationships. If you are a structured person, you care about being on time, about other people being on time, and about your partner honoring these needs of yours. When your partner is late—or makes you late, you feel disrespected. It might be okay for your partner to have time-management problems in the beginning of a relationship, but if they are almost never even close to being on time it becomes a major source of irritation between you. It is possible that the person who is more flexible about time can teach you not to be so compulsive, and consequently reduce your anxiety that way—but if they can't accomplish that, their lateness will cause anxiety and perhaps build resentment that will transfer to the relationship.

F (Flexible) You understand the importance of being on time for important events—but you don't see what the big deal is, unless the consequences are irreversible, such as missing the last plane out! Especially in social situations, you know that the time something is called for is rarely the time things begin. Even if they do, you don't think you will be missing much. However, sometimes you are wrong, and timeliness does matter! If you are with someone structured they may help you be on time more regularly—and this can be great for you in business or social situations. On the other hand, a highly structured approach to couple time can cause you more anxiety—and not exact much better compliance. If you are easygoing about time, you may resent feeling pushed into a schedule that, in your opinion, takes the joy out of living.

6. People might label me as a perfectionist or compulsive. I don't believe in "good enough." I have some issues with people who don't do things as well as they are capable of doing them.

S (Structured) You tend to be a perfectionist—and you can't help it. Maybe other people can settle for "good enough" but not you. If you are not with someone who has the same drive and compulsion for excellence, they had better at least appreciate it in you. Otherwise it is going to seem like wasted time and effort and it will frequently interfere with your own desire to just get an activity done and over, whether it's planning a vacation, remodeling a room, or picking a name for your new puppy. This characteristic comes up in a lot in relationships because there are daily duties that can be completed at different levels of accuracy, design, or delivery. One problem with a perfectionist is that sometimes things simply don't get completed because the perfectionist in you will keep going at it—and that might mean spending hours or days longer than makes practical sense. So you might be best paired with someone who is more easygoing—or at least has the good taste and good sense to know when something really is good enough. If you can accept their judgment, being with "a closer" might be very good for you. On the other hand, if you are critical of your partner's less fastidious way of doing things, they may become defensive and resentful of what seems to be your endless perfectionism.

F (Flexible) You care about getting things done, but you consider yourself to be a practical person—and a practical person often will figure out what is "good enough" for the task at hand, and feel happy to move on to the next issue or job. You would probably get along easiest with someone who feels the same way you do—but it is also possible that if you both let each other off the hook you will sometimes regret that something was left undone, has to be redone, or, worse yet, causes some lack of confidence in either of you by others. Sometimes people who are more flexible realize that life would be better if they had someone who asked a bit more of them. On the other hand, the search for the "best" parking space, plane schedule, or French tutor can be really tiresome to you. You can see costs and benefits to most choices and you are ready to compromise more quickly to solve a problem than a partner who is a perfectionist. If you and your partner are on opposite ends of the flexibility spectrum, watch out! You are not going to like the constant judging or relentless desire for improvement that an extreme Structured (S) type will exhibit.

---

7. I get upset when people change their mind at the last minute and don't show up at a party or appointment they said they would attend—no matter how casual the event might be. I think it's rude. It would bother me if my partner simply decided not to do something at the last minute that we had agreed to do.

S (Structured) You take people at their word, and you expect them to take you at yours. You are always a bit shocked, or at least dismayed, when someone tells you they will do something and they don't. That is not your way: written contract or not, when you say you will do something, you almost always follow through. You can't imagine telling someone that you will show up at a party and not keep your promise. You are likely to find someone different from you on this issue to be irresponsible and if they repeatedly fail to do what they said they would, you might lose respect for them. You take obligation very seriously. In general you need a partner who supports your feelings about delivering on a promise. If you are with someone who regards these commitments as more flexible than you do, you may feel your reputation—and even your character being compromised. Sometimes, however, a Flexible (F) person's approach might help give you some perspective on what is really important—and what your options might be in any given situation.

F (Flexible) Because you are flexible about most things, you also reserve the right to change your mind, even if it happens at the last minute. You often feel that following convention blindly—always doing what people expect—is not necessarily best for you. You trust your instincts about people and things. You do not consider yourself to be rude, although there may be times when you may not react in time to let people know you are not coming to a big party or event. Sometimes this can also happen with last-minute decisions or complications in your schedule. You may find it un-pleasant if a partner makes a big deal out of carrying through with every single plan exactly as outlined simply because they said they would do so. You consider yourself to be more independent and able to be authentic about your feelings especially as to how they relate to the way you spend your time and energies. If you are with someone who is highly structured, you are going to find yourselves getting into arguments over issues that you consider to be trivial and your partner does not. While the specific issue it-self may be minor, the larger issue of how you conduct your lives when it involves others, or even everyday appointments and responsibilities, is ac-tually quite an important thing to consider. These situations occur contin-ually, and whether you show up late, or show up at all, can create a real rift in a couple. Someone who feels strongly about being on time or going someplace they said they'd go will see your last-minute changes or delays as marks of a lack of consideration for their plans and feelings. Over time, they'll become very angry as they feel discounted, let down, and disre-garded. If you are going to be with someone who feels very strongly about these issues, you need to be prepared to compromise. If you cannot change your approach, it would be better to find a partner who sees things the same way you do.

Romantic Assessment

It's often the everyday things that make a relationship thrive or fail. How you approach the thousands of little things in daily living can make a huge difference. While you don't necessarily choose a mate on whether or not they are on time for a movie, or whether or not they clean up the kitchen after themselves, when people have different ideas about these kinds of is-sues, the accumulated aggravation when things go wrong can be become pretty intense.

If you are a person who likes planning, structure, and fastidious atten-tion to a certain way of doing things, you can get truly upset if your part-ner has a "no worries, mate" approach to the things you care about. While you may not be the most flexible person in the world, that doesn't matter if you are with someone who will support the way you see things or who is so much like you that there is almost never any real conflict. You also will do well with someone who understands how strongly you feel about the way things should be done but doesn't necessarily feel themself to be a martyr. If, however, you try and put together a relationship with someone who feels as strongly as you do—but in opposition to your values—it doesn't take a Ph.D. to predict fireworks—and perhaps a deep sense of alienation from your partner.

If you are flexible when it comes to some of the issues discussed in this chapter, it is axiomatic that you can get along with someone like yourself. Alternatively, if you are able to respect your partner's choices, you can quite happily be with someone who likes to do things differently. However, you have to understand what things are important to them—and may have to do some things according to your partner's preferences rather than your own. Many of these accommodations look deceptively simple—but they may be hard for you. For example, if you are a person who is often late, try-ing to change your pattern is not easy. Likewise, if you like to do things spontaneously and you are with someone who needs activities carefully planned, you may feel frustrated and thwarted. When you first meet a highly structured person, you may be able to go along with them during your falling-in-love period because you are so infatuated nothing about them seems to be a deal breaker; however, ultimately you have to be sure of how much you are willing to change. At some point you may be extremely reluc-tant to live your life on someone else's terms. You need to be aware of what it takes to be with someone with unbending standards and opinions—and make sure you can accommodate them. This circumstance may be most seri-ous when it comes to child-rearing, since people may be very flexible on many relationship issues yet draw the line on child-raising techniques. People who are permissive with children feel that is the best way to raise a healthy child, whereas people who believe in imposing firm boundaries and a clear, consistent disciplinary code get worried about their child's welfare when that code is not supported by their partner. Whether or not you are an F or an S, it's better to check that you both feel the same way about how to raise kids— otherwise there is a lit fuse that will go off sometime in the future.

Bottom Line: Two structured, highly organized, fastidious, and perfectionist people do not always get along if they have different values about how things ought to be done. Two flexible people do well together because it's a give and take relationship. But flexible people can have some advantages by pairing up with a highly structured person, as long as they share the same values and goals and the structured person is industrious and helpful rather than dictatorial. Naturally, a person who really feels strongly about doing things their own way needs to be careful to find someone who agrees that theirs is the way things ought to be done or is flexible enough so that they can accept almost any reasonable approach. Flexible personalities just have to make sure that they are making a bargain they can live with for an indefinite amount of time!

9
Decision Making Style

How you make decisions—your wish for dominance, need to influence, or ability to compromise is extremely critical in relationships. It's all about how you negotiate decision making. To put it another way, it's about how you share or hold power and the style that you use to get your way. You may prefer to let someone else direct parts of the relationship, including major emotional or everyday decisions. Or, you may resist a partner's attempts to be the leader and seek a more collaborative relationship style. It's important to be honest when you answer this questionnaire and say what you actually feel and do rather than what you think the "correct" answer might be. Knowing yourself well on this factor will truly help you find the right partner.

Please mark True or False

T   F   **1.** In most of my relationships, I've been the one who has more money, or at least as much money as my partner.

T   F   **2.** Most of the time I expect to win an argument when there is a difference of opinion. I may not admit it, but I like to be the one who is usually right in my relationship.

T   F   **3.** I may not always agree with it, but I have been described as "controlling" by more·than one or two people in my life.

T   F   **4.** I like being the person who is the teacher in the relationship. I like being the person who shows the other person the wonders of the world. It brings out the best in me.

T   F   **5.** It's not like me to smooth things over or compromise an opinion, just to keep things calm and/or to make my partner happy.

T   F   **6.** I am generally described as very competitive. This character trait shows up in my relationships from time to time.

T   F   **7.** I come to decisions pretty much on my own. I will talk about them, and negotiate if necessary, but I almost never need someone else to help me come to a decision about which I feel very sure.

Scoring

Give yourself one point for every True answer.

Give yourself the letter D (for Dominant) if you have more True answers than False answers.

Give yourself the letter C (for Collaborative) if you have more False answers than True answers.

The bigger the gap between True and False answers, the more intense you are in this characteristic.

What Your Answers Say About You

1. In most of my relationships, I've been the one who has more money, or at least as much money as my partner.

D (Dominant) Being a Dominant type, it is unlikely you want to be in a situation where you earn less or much less than your partner. You know that money brings power, independence, and, if you are a man, you are likely to equate it with maintaining your masculinity in a relationship. You may, under some circumstances, be willing to earn as much but not more than your partner, but in most of the circumstances of your life, you just assume you will be the one who has economic dominance. The thought of ever having to ask for money chills you to the bone. You have to be careful, or you can be heavy-handed about money in the relationship—deciding who can have what and setting yourself up as the person in the relationship who judges if your partner's spending patterns are wise or not. If you are with another person with a lot of resources, you may not have any worries—each of you just does your own thing economically. But if you are with someone whose lifestyle depends on your largess, you need to think about what it takes not to make them feel like a beggar instead of a partner.

While this situation tends to be more male than female, high-earning females have the same issues. For most women it is not an issue of being less financially successful than her partner. But if a woman has substantially more resources than her partner, the same kinds of cautions have to be in place. In fact a woman may have to be doubly sensitive since most men will have no previous experience being with a woman who has more money. A man's expectations might have been to be the senior provider. If a man doesn't feel like an equal economic partner he is more likely to get more seriously offended than a woman in a similar situation and it could threaten the happiness of the relationship if his female partner acts arrogantly or unilaterally.

C (Collaborative) Whether or not you have money, you usually do not base your influence in the relationship according to your economic position. If you are with someone who is dominant and uses money to establish who should do what in the relationship, you may accede to their requests. However, you may not wholly accept their sense of entitlement—to more sleep, less domestic work, or a better car—just because they contribute more income. Still, because you have no great urge to be the most powerful person in the relationship, as long as your partner isn't too far out of line with their requests, you don't get too upset. You could get along with someone who is the major breadwinner because you may appreciate their success in and of itself, and understand what it takes for them to carry the greater economic responsibility for your joint future. You may even be looking for that kind of person because you feel you either can't or don't want to be the only or major provider for the relationship. Someone who needs to be the dominant money person in an intimate relationship will be more drawn to you than someone exactly like themselves. But this could be a problem for you if your partner's economic position encourages them to treat you as an unequal partner and, in turn, you don't feel respected or loved. Sharing or controlling money can be a very sensitive area in long-term relationships and it is essential to watch carefully how it affects the balance of power early on in a relationship.

---

2. Most of the time I expect to win an argument when there is a difference of opinion. I may not admit it, but I like to be the one who is usually right in my relationship.

D (Dominant) You can be quite domineering in conversations, because you often communicate to win rather than just exchange opinions. In fact, you can be so powerful in your desire to be right that you may listen only to catch the flaws in someone else's argument. If you are capable of carrying this off artfully and gracefully, with humor or quiet delivery, you may impress your partner with your logic, knowledge, or articulation. However, if you are a highly passionate person who makes your point with some drama in a raised voice or with negative affect, this can be hard for anyone to take. Dominant types might like the challenge and the game—or they may get frustrated if they find it hard to compete. In a relationship with two Dominants, where each of you wants—and needs—to be right, any situation can escalate quickly to a fight. A better pairing is with someone who is less interested in winning or being right, and more interested in hearing your point of view. A person who is collaborative rather than dominant might be willing to enjoy communication without being competitive, and therefore might make an easier and more enjoyable companion for you. It all depends on how much you like challenge or collaboration in an intimate relationship.

C (Collaborative) You rarely care about *winning* in a conversation—you are generally process-oriented rather than goal-oriented. You don't need to be right all the time, though you appreciate having your point of view heard. You might enjoy someone who is an avid conversationalist because they add energy and intensity to communication. When a partner has something interesting to say, you want to hear it and you don't generally feel driven to make your argument prevail just for the sake of being right. Like anyone, you want to be heard, and if you are with someone who has trouble hearing your other side because they are so convinced of their own position, you could find that approach frustrating after a while. However, because you are a respectful conversationalist and don't usually feel aggressive in discussion, you can sometimes defuse an intensely competitive communicator by not engaging in combat. You are therefore able to be either with someone who is collaborative like yourself in discussion, or with a more dominating kind of personality, if you find that attractive.

---

3. I may not always agree with it, but I have been described as "controlling" by more than one or two people in my life.

D (Dominant) You have trouble letting things evolve. You have difficulty trusting other people to do things as well as you know you can do them. You may be extremely pushy about it or extremely sweet, but your instinct is to find a way to do things the *right way* by doing them yourself. You know this about yourself and other people know it, too. People may have called you controlling—sometimes in an affectionate, albeit exasperated, way. At other times people can become angry with you because they feel that you are micromanaging them or the situation. You might really run into trouble with another person who has exactly the same approach to life: you would both be fighting over little things—like where you go on a weekend getaway or what season tickets to buy—and also over much larger issues, such as where to live or how to educate the children. You might do better with someone who has less of a need to control and finds it easier to concede on at least a number of the issues and activities in your life together. On the other hand, if you find contests of will to be stimulating—or even endearing—another controlling person would certainly make an interesting partner.

C (Collaborative) You may never have been described as controlling because that's not who you want to be and that's not your usual style. You like to think of yourself as consultative, the kind of person who likes others to feel included in decision making and who has no desire to make everything go your way. You could admire dominant personalities or find them too bossy and presumptive. However you feel about them, you have no desire to control other people's behavior. When things bother you, you don't feel compelled to make them right. You are careful about not interfering with other people's agendas and you have a strong sense of respecting personal boundaries. You might like being with someone who takes over and takes care of things even without asking, if you generally like the way they think and do things. In fact, if you like to be taken care of, or have details or plans made for you, you could be a good partner to someone with a controlling personality.

---

4. I like being the person who is the teacher in the relationship or the person who shows the other person the wonders of the world. It brings out the best in me.

D (Dominant) Not everyone likes the role of mentor or teacher. But dominant personalities often like mentoring others, even their own partner. Just because you like to be in control doesn't mean you are unkind or ungenerous—and if no one is challenging you, you are often much better-natured. Being the "guide" in a relationship—the one who opens up the world—may almost be essential in order for you to feel loving. This means you are often attracted to people with less money than you have, are less worldly, or quite a bit younger. While some people might doubt your motivations if you are clearly the senior or more powerful partner, you know it brings out the best in you. This doesn't mean your partner has to be less personally successful, intelligent, or submissive: it does mean that you like to feel needed. If this describes you, you clearly want a less-dominant personality than your own. You want someone who is thrilled to have a partner with greater resources, business savvy, or sexual experience. Be careful though: You may choose someone who is in the student role today but who eventually wants to be more of an equal once they gain experience through you. Ideally, you can be the teacher in some areas but not need to maintain that role in all ways at all times.

C (Collaborative) You are more attracted to equality than mentorship. You are more comfortable with balance in a relationship. This means that when someone has far less experience, business savvy, or education than you do, you will probably find them less attractive. In fact, if there is too much of a gap between you, you feel less able to consider the possibility that this person might be your soul mate. You may find any maternal or paternal roles in a romantic relationship to be a turn-off. You resist being on the other end of that equation as well. In other words, you don't like being the mentor or more knowledgeable one—and you also don't like someone treating you as their protégé. If you do like being mentored and guided in a relationship, you will do well with someone who needs that role to feel fulfilled and special. If you find that kind of treatment insulting, you will need someone who shares your feelings about equality.

---

5. It is not like me to smooth things over, or compromise an opinion just to keep things calm and/or to make my partner happy.

D (Dominant) You tend to believe that most of your opinions are well-founded. It's not that you are unwilling to take in information about things you haven't thought through very well, but when you have done a lot of work on some issue, you stand firm in your opinions and it takes a lot to shake them. You consider it dishonorable and weak to change your opinion just to make someone happy, and you deeply resent someone who asks you to do so. A partner could see you as being bullheaded or rigid, which you think is an unfair judgment. You need someone who respects the fact that you hold on to principles and positions and doesn't try to bully you or guilt-trip you into changing. You want someone who accepts who you are in this way. You don't mind another dominant person who acts the same way you do unless they are too controlling and they try and push you to change. You need someone who will either support your opinions—or respect your stance enough not to expect you to change your position. If you have done something that you think is wrong, you will apologize. But if you are just doing something with which they disagree and feel you have hurt their feelings by not supporting them, you are not going to cave in. You are not the compromiser in a relationship, so unless you are with someone dominant who has very similar sensibilities and values to your own, you will need a partner who can negotiate the compromise in the family since that is rarely going to be you.

C (Collaborative) You want to preserve the peace. You would rather lose an argument or negotiate a position to a compromise than keep a conflict going. You have some principles and feelings about which you would be unwilling to negotiate—but very few. If you are with a person who is defensive about their opinions or actions, you find a way to manage them rather than confront them. You get along with "difficult" people because you've learned how to handle them. This might seem manipulative to some people, and sometimes it is. But it is also just the way you try to finesse a disagreement in order for the relationship to run smoothly. You do well in this way with either dominant types or people like yourself who avoid conflict and tend to think issues are not as important as keeping the relationship stable and happy.

---

6. I am generally described as very competitive. This character trait also shows up in my relationships from time to time.

D (Dominant) Dominant types have a tendency to be competitive. It's just a natural part of your personality. It is hard for you to have just a casual game of tennis, to lose an argument, or not "keep up with the Joneses." This trait also shows up in your relationship and can make things difficult between you and a partner if you aren't careful.

While you might be happy that your partner got promoted, you also feel somewhat jealous or uncomfortable if you haven't been equally successful in some way. If your partner can run four miles, you want to be able to run just a little farther. If your mate is knowledgeable about wines, you want to be equally as educated. You might like someone who is a worthy competitor. Just like some people don't want to play games with someone who is easy to beat, you might not respect someone who doesn't keep you on your toes. On the other hand, if this competitive instinct keeps you from enjoying your partner's own triumphs and lucky breaks, you could undermine the happiness of your relationship. You have to decide whether you want a relationship in which your competitive feelings do not become an issue, i.e., in a relationship with another dominant type, or whether you can enjoy the competition without it becoming mean-spirited and destructive.

C (Collaborative) You don't like competition and the mere sniff of its presence in a relationship may turn you off. You would prefer to jog at your own speed rather than race someone to the end of the trail. You don't generally like being egged on to do things past your comfort level just because your partner thinks you should be able to keep up. In general, you might want to be with someone who is noncompetitive like yourself. On the other hand, sometimes someone who is competitive can bring out the best in you. Some kinds of competition are healthy and as long as they are entered into with the spirit of collaboration, everybody wins. A truly competitive person may annoy you—but someone who makes a valuable game of it might be just what you need.

---

7. I come to decisions pretty much on my own. I will talk about them, and negotiate if necessary, but I almost never need someone else to help me come to a decision about which I feel very sure.

D (Dominant) A central characteristic of Dominant personalities is that they trust their own judgment. While they may take in other opinions, when it comes to a final decision they will go their own way if they think their way is the right way.

You may appreciate honest and even strong input, but if you have a competitive partner who also believes as firmly in their decision, you had better agree fundamentally on most things if you are to avoid always being in conflict. A partner may admire the strength of your convictions, your self-confidence, and the overall power of your personality—but if they, too, have a Dominant personality, they are going to want to influence a lot of outcomes. A Dominant personality might enjoy the sparring that goes into negotiation, but doesn't relish having to compromise on decisions. As a Dominant, you might want to be with someone who simply wants to be heard and contribute rather than prevail.

C (Collaborative) You like to have conversations and it is the interactive part of discussions that interests you. As someone who enjoys the process of discussion you will feel best with someone who you feel listens to you—even if they don't agree. You may need to be with someone like you who prefers to brainstorm or keep an open mind during a discussion. You might like an egalitarian relationship where the two of you constantly counsel over what to do or how to analyze an issue. If, however, you like partners with strong personalities, you will be able to handle this aspect of their character because you are able to interact without having to insist on your point of view. You do want to be careful that you are not with someone who is both opinionated and holds vastly different approaches to issues and values than you do. You could end up feeling disrespected and marginalized if the two of you disagree at lot and you can rarely influence their opinion.

Romantic Assessment

This is a good time to think about what makes a person attractive to you and what kind of match of temperaments is likely to make you feel good now and in the future. Dominant types can be very attractive. Many of them are leaders, successful in whatever they do because they have drive, the need to prevail, and the ego to believe in themselves along the way. In order to win over great odds, or against strong competitors, they have had to rely on themselves more often than not—and this means they are unlikely to be relying on you. Can you take it? Or do you need to be needed in more ways than might be realistic with a Dominant type? Are you willing to be the supportive partner to someone who is used to being catered to or would you find yourself at odds with them most of the time?

It might be worth it. Dominant personality types are often fascinating, competent, and charismatic. Someone like this could easily be captivating for a lifetime. On the other hand, compromise isn't easy for them and they are used to calling the shots. They might be able to share occasionally—especially when the decision is unimportant to them or outside their areas of expertise—but this is not going to be their usual modus operandi. Is that attractive to you or not? It may well be because you want to be with someone who is self-confident and decisive—even if it requires swallowing your opinion occasionally or not being able to influence how things go in your relationship.

On the other hand, if you like compromise and negotiation, you might want to find someone who is willing to approach life in a more collaborative way more often than not. Most people who think of themselves as collaborative will not even imagine issuing an order or feeling entitled to unilaterally plan or veto something.

If you are a Dominant type, you are probably drawn to people who will understand and support your lifestyle, career agenda, and personal perspectives. It is better for you to be with someone who does not contest each decision, especially when you are sure you know what is right, which is often! You might, however, be the kind of person who wants to be part of a power couple; the downside there is a not-infrequent conflict of wills. The upside is that you recognize and respect a spirit as intense and convinced as your own, and when the smoke settles, you admire the person with whom you did emotional or intellectual combat.

Bottom Line: Power and how it is used is an important aspect of a couple's life. You need to think seriously about whether or not you want to be in an egalitarian couple, where each person gets an equal say, or in a more traditional arrangement, where the man is the provider of the family's economic welfare and that, in turn, gives him more decision making legitimacy over more aspects of the relationship. There are also gender reversals of this pattern: where the woman has more decision making clout. This is not traditional of course, but the idea of one person who is the leader and one person who accommodates their needs and supports their right to have more decision making power or veto power, is the same. You need to think carefully of what mixture of these traits—directive or collaborative—you have and what would be the perfect match for you.

10

Emotionality

This quiz reveals how you react under highly emotional conditions—both joyous and stressful. You may be one person in everyday situations but quite another under conditions of anxiety, conflict, or in significant intimate moments. It is important to understand whether or not you react intensely and expressively or are more reserved—and how you feel about this characteristic in someone else.

Please mark True or False

T F **1.** If I feel loving, I'm very passionate and all over the person I want. I don't moderate my romantic and sexual emotions.

T F **2.** I can get intensely moved. I might sob, scream, or express myself in a way that lets people know how strongly I feel. I don't hold this back very often.

T F **3.** If I feel that a partner has intentionally done something against me, I get angry very quickly. I often tell them what I think about what they did at my first opportunity. I don't wait to cool down.

T   F   **4.** When I am very angry, I usually yell and often use some pretty colorful language. I can get pretty nasty when I'm really mad.

T   F   **5.** If I'm jealous—and I can be very jealous—I show it. I don't really understand people who never feel jealous.

T   F   **6.** If there is a crisis, my heart beats faster and sometimes I have an anxiety attack or I panic. I can lose my cool pretty quickly.

T   F   **7.** Even though I know slapping, hitting, or shoving is wrong, things can happen in relationships that hit a nerve. I have sometimes felt the urge to lash out with a partner.

Scoring

Give yourself one point for every True answer.

Give yourself the letter P (for Passionate) if you have more True answers than False answers.

Give yourself the letter T (for Temperate) if you have more False answers than True answers.

The bigger the gap between True and False answers, the more intense you are in this characteristic.

What Your Answers Say About You

1. If I feel loving, I'm very passionate and all over the person I want. I don't moderate my romantic and sexual emotions.

P (Passionate) You are not a laidback lover. When you are really attracted to someone you feel the experience with your whole body. When you feel sexual or loving, your mind, heart, and body are unmistakably involved. This is the experience of love and attraction you crave: anything less doesn't seem worthy of the word *love*. It's also likely that you want the same response back. You indulge your emotions and celebrate passion.

Someone who does not share your enthusiasm might turn you off or make you feel rejected. On the other hand, you might be someone who likes to win someone over and get a cool person to become passionate under your attentions. In fact, you might have enough passion for both of you. Be careful about that, however, since you may have temporarily stoked the passions of a person who usually has a cooler temperament. After a while, they may revert to type. Make sure you are getting what you need and want in this category since it is so central to your personality.

T (Temperate) You fall in love, but you generally take your time doing it. You are a more cerebral type of person—checking in with yourself to see how you feel, gauging the growth of your feelings, and being more careful with your heart. You may like to feel the passion and intensity of attraction of someone for you—but you are likely to wait awhile before you return it—if you ever do. Some people in this category rarely, if ever, become totally swept away with passionate need for another person. You may be the kind of person who doesn't trust those kinds of emotions and rarely experiences them. That doesn't mean you don't feel desire or love; but it does mean you *develop* your feelings rather than have them take over, disorient you, or make you obsessive about the object of your affections. You might envy the abandon and confidence of a passionate lover. A lover who runs hotter than you do might excite you and make it easier for you to cross some emotional or sexual barriers. On the other hand, that might not feel deep or authentic enough for you. You want a love that lasts, and to some more temperate personalities, passionate love can feel too easy, too superficial, and "too fleeting."

---

2. I can get intensely moved. I might sob, scream, or express myself in a way that lets people know how strongly I feel. I don't hold this back very often.

P (Passionate) You feel things deeply so it makes sense that you let those emotions show under most circumstances—at the movies, during arguments, or in lovemaking. It seems right to you to cry if you are hurt or disappointed or to yell if you are furious. You feel that you are reacting honestly, but someone who tends to hold their own emotions more tightly might find your expressiveness indulgent, manipulative, or embarrassing. You need someone who understands your emotional displays even if they have a different emotional style. You can have a partner who is more temperate if they appreciate that you are not. In fact, you might choose someone like this because they are more likely to be able to step back, calm you down, and reassure you since they may not be as visibly upset or out of control. This can be a useful difference between partners as long as the more temperate partner appreciates your emotional nature. You could also be with someone who acts the same way you do because you both understand why the other could explode, sob, or celebrate at a high pitch. The only problem here is that with two potentially intense reactions, no one may be able to moderate an argument or crisis between the two of you. If you have someone just as emotionally intense as you are, you may have to work harder together to find ways to deescalate conflicts.

T (Temperate) Your nature is to consider your thoughts and feelings before you speak, to temporize, to analyze and to keep things conversational and sane. You may have worked at it, but most likely this is the temperament you have had since childhood. You are the person who reacts thoughtfully rather than willfully and doesn't feel the need to jump in the fray when tempers are aroused or people are acting as if nerves have been touched and gut level feelings are called for and voiced.

As useful as your personality is during heated discussions and relationship issues, you may find your own personality a little flat and really enjoy the passionate outbursts and opinions of a much hotter type of personality. You may like it all the more because you can enjoy it as a spectator rather than have it hit a cord in you that makes you angry or tempts you to scream or use strong language. You might enjoy being with someone who has a strong sense of indignation, or is sensitive and lets you know when they feel trampled on; it may seem healthier to you than your own natural, but sometimes, unwanted, restraint. A passionate partner could be very exciting for you.

On the other hand, your restraint might be exactly what you expect of someone else. If you think that it is immature when someone loses their temper during an argument, or somewhat scary when someone's opinions are almost always passionately voiced, then you will need to be with someone who is more like yourself. You might not respect someone who is much more emotional than you are and that won't do in your most intimate relationship. But if you enjoy the fire and spirit of a passionate person, their outbursts or intensity could make them more, not less, lovable to you.

---

3. If I feel that a partner has intentionally done something against me, I get angry very quickly. I often tell them what I think about what they did at my first opportunity. I don't wait to cool down.

P (Passionate) Passionate people feel things deeply, and that includes perceived slights and betrayals of any kind. You may be considered to be thin-skinned or overly sensitive. You may accept that label or just feel that you are highly perceptive and you don't like to let anything go unanswered. If you are sure you are being insulted, you react and are likely to lose your cool. In general you are not the type who turns away and takes time to consider what has happened; you give as good as you get, and then some. If you had a more temperate partner who made you think a bit before you acted, or were with a person who was talented at making you reconsider the situation, it might avoid some high-intensity and potentially damaging arguments. But it is also possible that someone who remained cool while you felt justifiably angry could just enrage you more. Alternately, since you have a hot temper, you might like the emotional honesty of someone just like you. But difference could work well here since most constructive argument is impossible under conditions of intense anger.

T (Temperate) If someone is nasty or inconsiderate, you rarely lash out. Your response often occasions awe in more emotionally volatile people. You step back and either figure out how to moderate the person's response or you find a way to leave the discussion without escalating emotions. You may get your own feelings hurt, but more likely, your ability to step back from the action allows you to create an emotional buffer. You may be one of those lucky people who has learned that when someone attacks you verbally, snubs you, or is in any way mean or impolite, that it is more about *them* than it is about you. Instead of coming back at them, you may show them concern or want to talk, rather than yell, threaten, or slam doors. This response makes you very valuable in a relationship with a passionate person because you can stop the argument from spinning out of control. If you love someone enough to accept and work with their emotional flare-ups they will likely be grateful for your temperate temperament and emotional common sense. Still, this takes a lot of work and self-discipline, so if you consider emotionally intense people too temperamental and unstable, you might just want to be with someone as calm and considerate as yourself.

---

4. When I am very angry, I usually yell and often use some pretty colorful language. I can get pretty nasty when I'm really mad.

P (Passionate) You can't help it. You use bad words when you get mad. Even if you try to curb what you say, you are likely to use some words some of the time that are demeaning or ugly. Of course you know that this is not a good thing, but you will probably need some therapy if you want to retrain yourself. Given the way you are right now, you need someone who has the same style or who is not put off by your all-out fighting style. You might do well with someone or who is more temperate and who can change the rules of engagement to be more civilized. But if you can't accept their intervention, it's going to be a bad match. Someone who refuses to fight down and dirty is rarely going to respect someone who does.

T (Temperate) Yelling, screaming, and using bad language is not your style and you probably don't want to be with someone who does argue that way. It may be something you can handle, but you should ask yourself, "Why should you?" Perhaps if you nip it in the bud and institute certain rules of how you talk to each other, you can get someone to modify their style. But most people who get into a rage when they fight, or have gotten used to using words to knock somebody (or their argument) down have a habit that is hard to break. While you could be useful to someone who is emotionally abusive by helping them change the way they fight, you should think long and hard about why it would be worthwhile to do so. You will feel most at ease with someone who manages their anger the same way you do.

---

5. If I'm jealous—and I can be very jealous—I show it. I don't really understand people who never feel jealous.

P (Passionate) People who love passionately and have intense personalities are also often territorial about the person they love. Maybe it's because you love so fully that the very thought of someone being interested in your partner—or your partner being interested in someone else—tortures you. It could also arise from the insecurity that comes from having a very active imagination; it is not hard to see how someone could want your partner and, as a student of human nature, you can imagine the person you love being tempted under compelling circumstances. If you let these emotions gather momentum, you could be very possessive and even unfair to your partner, doubting their integrity and loyalty. You might need someone with a jealous nature like yourself who understands your sensitivities since they have the same ones. However, it is also possible you might need someone whose calm, cool, and trusting temperament will be reassuring to you. This kind of person, however, might find your jealousy out of line and insulting, since they are less likely to share the same fears.

T (Temperate) Your calm temperament generally keeps you from worrying about every aspect of your relationship. You are less likely to be a very jealous person, unless you have been given undeniable evidence of a partner's infidelity. You may even see someone put the moves on your partner without getting upset if you are clear that your partner is not the kind of person

who is receptive to being seduced. Jealousy is not an emotion that you indulge so if you have a partner who is jealous for no apparent good reason,
you might feel offended. Very few people enjoy a really jealous partner—
except if their jealousy is seen as a validation of love or desire—but some
people are more understanding about jealousy than others. You may understand the origins of your partner's sexual or emotional insecurity. You have
just the temperament to be reassuring, rather than rising to the accusation
and getting angry about the lack of trust. If you don't have a hot, lustful
personality, you may be the right person for someone who does have a passionate self-presentation, provided of course that their sexual or emotional
intensity doesn't cause you worry! If that kind of personality would arouse
your sexual insecurities, you might want to choose someone with a cooler
temperament, someone who doesn't seem like a likely candidate for breaking vows, taboos, or your trust.

---

6. If there is a crisis, my heart beats faster and sometimes I have an
anxiety attack or I panic. I can lose my cool pretty quickly.

P (Passionate) There may be a physiological basis to your passionate nature.
Your body often tells you how you are reacting emotionally. When you are
passionately in love, your palms sweat, your heart races, and you stammer
or lose focus. These same kinds of reactions may also occur under almost
any kind of crisis. If you are the kind of person who starts to panic easily
or, once in a truly upsetting situation, has trouble thinking straight or talking calmly, you may want someone who is quite different from you to help
you through your panic. People who have high anxiety levels can often get
quite nasty when they feel threatened, and if you are like this, you need
someone who helps moderate that tendency instead of feeling it. If you are
with someone like yourself, there may be a feeling of common cause, but
if you are both frightened and out of control, you might lose respect for
one another. Someone who is understanding or who knows how to get you
to calm down and be constructive would be a very good match. On the
other hand, if you are similar on this characteristic the fact that you feel

stress the same way, and react the same way, may make you feel like soul mates—two people who find the same things distressing and react similarly to a crisis. You have to think about how you would react if someone is reassuring you and helping you stay calmer about something really upsetting (like a child being lost) versus someone who might be on your exact wavelength and who feels like your comrade at arms, whether or not that is the most constructive way to behave.

T (Temperate) Lucky you: cool, calm, and focused during a crisis. You are the kind of person everyone would like to be, but not everyone has your constitution or psychological strength. Just about everyone respects someone who can keep their head in a crisis and offer constructive advice. No one likes the smarty pants who dismisses everyone else's fears or distress.

Assuming you are not contemptuous of others during such moments of crises, you are especially valuable to someone who does react emotionally at these times and would deeply appreciate your clear head and steady hand. A highly passionate person will prize you and be grateful for your help. However if you are not sympathetic to their reactions, they may feel disrespected. Of course, if you cannot cope with their behavior and response under pressure, you might need to pair with someone who can take these situations in stride, just as you do.

---

7. Even though I know slapping, hitting, or shoving is wrong, things can happen in relationships that hit a nerve. I have sometimes felt the urge to lash out with a partner.

P (Passionate) You are capable of a great deal of anger, even rage. You do need to ask yourself whether you have—or could get—so angry that it would be dangerous in a relationship, either to yourself or your partner. You feel things so strongly that you know what it means to love someone so deeply that if they hurt you, or leave you, you could feel desperate, humiliated, and vengeful. Most people who feel this kind of fury will never actually act out their feelings, but some of them do, and you need to make sure you are not one of them. Explosive feelings and deep sensitivities have to be watched and controlled—because losing love or feeling betrayed can lead to violent acts. If you have felt your anger go from zero to one hundred in a few seconds, you have probably felt something that Dr. John Gottman, a well respected psychologist and author, calls "flooding"— being so overwhelmed with one's feelings that you quickly become irrational. It takes quite a while to calm down from this—at least half an hour—and for some people, it could be days. If this is true of you, you need to take responsibility for your anger and learn how to control it.

You might also want to think carefully about what kind of partner "presses your buttons" and what kind of person helps you back away from rage. You might think about someone who has strong boundaries, who will not tolerate your bad behavior when it occurs, but who also will not meet your passionate feelings with as equally passionate a response. Someone temperate may be able to help you realize that nothing irreparable has happened, that you have no cause for anger, or that even if you do, getting out of control is not acceptable. If you are a person who can become angry quickly and lose control, it is up to you to control that—but you can help the situation by looking for someone who does not pour fuel on an already burning fire.

T (Temperate) You do not own the kind of rage that causes people to commit crimes of passion. You understand anger and hurt, but you have never allowed your own feelings to reach that level. You would probably be afraid if you were with a partner whose own expression of anger could be so intense. This kind of emotionality is over the top for you, but you need to be aware that it may come with someone who has a particularly passionate temperament to whom you might be attracted or might be attracted to you. People who become irrational or violent if they feel rejected or betrayed usually are pretty insecure. Otherwise if they felt that you had abandoned them or cheated on them, they would blame your behavior on your lack of character rather than see it as a direct assault on themselves.

Everyone needs to be careful about linking up with someone with a weak core self-concept—and a big temper to go with it. Yet it isn't always apparent when you first start seeing someone. If someone has a passionate nature, they may be intense, but well below the line of becoming dangerously out of control. But you need to make sure of that. Your own nature is not combative so you may not look for it in others, but if you feel that someone is going over the line in their possessiveness or anger over your behavior, you might want to cautiously withdraw from getting into a committed relationship. You can be with a passionate type of person or a temperate one—but be sure that the passionate person isn't someone whose romanticism and deep feelings cloak insecurity and a dangerous temper.

Romantic Assessment

Temperament is a major component of our daily compatibility. You might find someone with a passionate, lively, intense personality to be endlessly interesting, sexy, or admirable. Passionate people are often determined, lively people, deeply invested in their work, and deeply invested in their relationships. They may be poetic, charismatic, or charmingly seductive. In bed, they can be mesmerizing, and certainly absorbing. No wonder many kinds of people, even people with much more controlled personalities, are drawn to them. Their vitality is wonderful to be around. But there is, of course, a downside. Passionate people need a lot of emotional feedback. If you are a more Temperate person, the intensity that a Passionate partner brings with them may arouse and inspire you. But you will need to think about whether or not you can sustain this given the way you generally approach your life and your relationships. Do you want to be in a relationship with someone who may easily become jealous, who has strong positive *and* negative emotions and who will be articulate—or just plain blunt—about how they are feeling about you, the relationship, and life in general? This may be a person who will excite you and vivify the relationship—but think about whether the differences in approach are a good match for the long run.

Likewise, if you are a Passionate person there are many good reasons to pick a partner with a cooler temperament—but there are also reasons to think twice about whether this kind of person is for you. Someone with a cooler temper and a less suspicious or territorial nature would definitely be a good counterweight to some of your tendencies, no doubt about that. That alone might make this both an attractive and useful match. But there is another thing to think about: It is possible that some passionate people are attracted to people with cooler temperaments because of the challenge they represent.

If you are a Passionate person you may yearn for the kind of person who does not display emotion easily, precisely because of how exciting it is for you to win someone over. Other Passionate people will show you their feelings right away, but a cooler kind of individual might make you do a lot of guesswork while they are making up their mind. Not surprisingly, there is quite a bit of research on the subject of attraction. Most recently Helen Fisher, in her book *Why We Love*, quite convincingly shows that once we get our hormones percolating with passion, a series of secondary emotions are produced that create a need for deeper emotional connection. The research shows that when we fall in love our bodies produce androgens and dopamine, a powerful elixir of desire and love. If we do not get the continued response we want, our dopamine goes down, but our body's need for it does not. Our craving for emotional reinforcement and more dopamine production ramps up, and we become emotionally hooked, an addiction for love as real as an other kind of addictive response. This is even clearer when we have already begun a sexual relationship, since orgasm produces oxytocin, a hormone that promotes bonding. A cycle of hormone production of this sort can begin with passionate love, and so it is the more passionate personality that may lock on to a quick, deep attachment even though it may turn out to be unrequited.

Bottom Line: If you are a Passionate person, you are likely to know that your intense emotions can be hard on you unless you are with someone who clearly returns your love. Beware of falling in passionate love with someone who does not have the same emotional needs you have—their reticence may be difficult for you to handle. Of course this is not to intimate that Temperate people don't love deeply—but it does mean you may not know how someone more temperate is feeling about you since their style is so much different than your own—and you may end up with someone who, as a recent popular book summed up, "is just not that into you."

Still, there is much to be said for some balance between the two personalities of passion and temperate. Some people who have cooler temperaments need the emotional permission Passionate people can give them. And Passionate people need someone to calm them down when they get too out of control and irrational. Some mix of emotional style here is usually a good thing.

11

Self-Nurturing

This quiz will measure how you communicate your own emotional needs. People usually have a core style and that style is extremely important in intimate relationships. This quiz looks at one very important and central factor: how communication works when one or both members of the couple are worried, hurt, anxious, or needy. When some people are in emotional turmoil they may turn to themselves and "self-medicate" by staying away from their partner and perhaps everyone, until they figure out what is bothering them and what to do about it. This kind of person may resent a partner offering solace, support, or problem solving until it's asked for, which might be never. This personality type needs private time to heal. Other people are just the opposite. They need to be heard, they need to talk, and they want their primary partner to be their sounding board, their pal, and their therapist.

Please mark True or False.

T   F   **1.** I share my feelings with my partner on my own schedule. I don't feel comfortable if he/she always wants to know what I'm thinking or feeling. It bothers me if a partner doesn't respect my boundaries.

T   F   **2.** I don't like big parties. I almost always prefer time alone or time just with my partner.

T   F   **3.** I frequently need alone time. If I don't get it, I can feel trapped or anxious.

T   F   **4.** I rarely share intimate information with friends and if I do, it is only with one or two very close people. I do not want my partner to talk about our life with anyone else.

T   F   **5.** If I am feeling sad or depressed, I need to be by myself. I heal myself by being alone, rather than by talking things over with a friend or partner.

T   F   **6.** I am a very shy person even if I don't appear to be.

T   F   **7.** I prefer conversations that answer questions, solve problems, or discuss something useful. I don't think it's necessary to talk about relationships that much and I particularly don't like going over the same issues again and again.

Scoring

Give yourself one point for every True answer.

Give yourself the letter I (for Introvert) if you have more True answers than False answers.

Give yourself the letter E (for Extrovert) if you have more False answers than True answers.

The bigger the gap between True and False answers, the more intense you are in this characteristic.

What Your Answers Say About You

---

1. I share my feelings with my partner on my own schedule. I don't feel comfortable if he/she always wants to know what I'm thinking or feeling. It bothers me if a partner doesn't respect my boundaries.

I (Introvert) You work through issues and thoughts at your own pace and you don't like being pushed to talk about them before you are ready. This goes even deeper: You feel you are entitled to a certain level of emotional privacy and if you have a partner who feels that personal privacy denies them a truly intimate relationship, you have a problem with that. You may be quite clear that you do not want to talk about certain things right away—or never at all about some subjects. Usually people who are Introverts indicate by words or actions, that they will be respectful of another person's desire to keep some things to themselves—and they expect the same in return. An Extrovert's preferences are not much solace to Introverts. It can be frustrating. Extroverts need to talk over intimate issues and they are not looking for privacy. Another Introvert will really respect and be grateful for your consideration of their privacy but an Extrovert will feel isolated and unloved if you don't want to discuss the issues that were bothering them.

In general you might want to be with another Introvert who feels as you do. But here's one reason why you might not: You may keep too many things inside. There are, however, issues in the relationship that need to be addressed right away, and with two Introverts, these issues may be left to fester and never get handled, or get handled so late that irreparable emotional damage has already occurred. If you do choose an Extrovert as a partner, by definition, they need to talk about issues often. You will have to modify your style somewhat in order to make them feel they can find intimacy in the relationship.

E (Extrovert) You may share your feelings on your own schedule—but sharing feelings is always on the schedule. You need to share anxieties, excitement, and ideas concerning practical issues about which that you feel strongly—and you need to do this often. You need to do this in order to feel close to someone. Furthermore, even if this person listens to what is on your mind and is helpful about your issues, you are not going to feel very close to your partner if they do not reciprocate with their own deep feelings and problems. You will want to probe until you find out what's going wrong, and if you are with an Introvert, this could cause problems. Introverts give up their deepest feelings rarely and not without a good deal of thought beforehand. Your more impulsive approach is foreign to them and emotionally uncomfortable. If you are attracted to the "strong, silent" type, don't expect them to change just because the two of you have fallen in love. You will need to understand their need for serious boundaries and privacy even though this is strange to you. If you want full disclosure and easy and frequent conversation about deeper feelings and important issues in your life, commit to an extrovert rather than an introvert. On the other hand, if you don't want a partner who unburdens themselves to you all the time, and if you want to be the primary person who is the expressive and emotive one in the relationship, an introverted partner may do just fine. Just know their limits. You might get an Introvert to open up more over time, but they are not going to turn into Extroverts just because you encourage them to be more open with you. It is not as satisfying to them as it is to you and they will always need some time to think about how they feel before they can discuss it with you.

---

2. I don't like big parties. I almost always prefer time alone or time just with my partner.

I (Introvert) You are a one-on-one person more than a party animal. In fact, you are just about as far as one can get from a party animal. You like small groups at most, and intimate connections are best had when you are alone with the one you love. That time is precious to you. You may not need a lot of it, but you do need some of it and you can't get it from a group, even a small gathering of close friends. If you are with an extreme Extrovert you may feel you are not getting enough from them and this will be exacerbated if some of the time you are losing is to their needs to interact with a lot of other people. However, being with an Extrovert may bring you out of yourself and you will find a few excellent new contacts or friends. But it will be mostly an irritant unless the two of you are very careful to make sure you get enough alone time together.

E (Extrovert) You love people and you are attracted to celebrations, dinner parties, and big events. If your partner is with you, you will be counting this as partner time, and another Extrovert would agree with you. If you are a party animal and you are with someone just like you, your life could be an unending series of parties or dinner with friends, which both of you will love. It is, however, easy to go over the top when you are both social creatures and you may find that a long time can go by without any real private time together. If the frenetic pace of your social and business lives goes on too long without attention to some "couple" time, you may start to feel your relationship is superficial.

That is why, under some circumstances, someone who is somewhat more introverted than you might be good to keep the relationship at center stage. An Introvert will need more private time with you and will let you know that they aren't happy being out on the circuit all the time. Listen to their needs, and if you cut back at least a little, you will probably help strengthen the relationship. Extroverts do run the risk of being so much about town that they lose track of how much time they need to give to unscheduled time with their partner.

---

3. I frequently need alone time. If I don't get it, I can feel trapped or anxious.

I (Introvert) You need solitude to regroup, to recharge both your capacity to think and to act. You also just need alone time to do your own thing, which is no reflection on how you feel about your partner. If you are constantly in someone else's presence, or they are always talking to you, you start to feel antsy and pressured. You need someone who knows how to give you space, either another Introvert who understands or an Extrovert who learns when to leave you alone. Another Introvert will understand that your silence does not necessarily indicate a darker mood or a deeper thought that has to be shared. It's just silence! An Extrovert will find silence unnerving and may press you to find out what you are thinking, or surmise that some hidden undercurrent exists. An Extrovert needs to learn that silence and wanting to be alone is just your style. They must learn to let you be.

E (Extrovert) You may need some alone time, but not that much. Time and solitude are not generally what you need to energize or think through emotions or issues. Solitude for you is usually associated with loneliness, grief, or depression—not pleasure. You may like it occasionally, but you rarely need it. If you have someone who needs a lot of time alone, it will probably be hard on you. You can do it—after all, you have lots of friends and it might work well to have someone who gives you plenty of time to be with all the other people about whom you care. But this is not how you want things to be, especially if it's obvious that something is bothering your partner. Your natural instinct is to talk it out. If your partner resents what they see as an intrusion, it could be hard for you not to take it personally. Of course you will have to learn that everything isn't about *you*. In general, you might want another Extrovert to be with you as much as you would like to be with them. However, if they are even more extremely extroverted than you are, you could feel overwhelmed. So sometimes, depending on how extroverted you are, having a partner that wanted some private time—or time alone with you—would not be a bad thing.

---

4. I rarely share intimate information with friends and if I do, it is only with one or two very close people. I do not want my partner to talk about our life with anyone else.

I (Introvert) How private each of you will be about the other is one of the main relationship issues between partners. How much should even your best friends or closest family members know about your relationship? Men may talk over problems with a buddy, but it is far more common for women to share their deepest of secrets and feelings among each other. If a woman is having an issue with her partner, it is unlikely she is going to withhold it from her best friend. If she is an Extrovert and has several close friends, they are all likely to hear about it and give counsel or sympathy. If you are an Introvert it makes you upset to even suspect that your partner might be sharing parts of your life that you have only told him or her. Another Introvert might be much more likely to keep your secrets because that is their nature. If an Introvert is with an Extrovert there have to be very explicit rules about what to share. Otherwise, an Introvert will feel exposed and possibly even betrayed.

E (Extrovert) An extrovert feels better about their problems by sharing them with a best friend—or maybe several best friends. Male Extroverts may be more confined by gender norms and be "gentlemanly"—which is to say they do not talk about experiences with women. But the tendency for both men and women Extroverts is to savor, explore, and solve their issues with their closest friends or family. Introverts really want their private life private and they are generally uncomfortable with a partner who tells all, especially if it concerns them. It is very hard for an extroverted partner to edit what they would say if unconstrained by someone else's feelings. But if they are going to choose someone who is quite introverted they will need to understand that sharing personal information is a major emotional violation for an Introvert. If they tell anything significant about their relationship and it gets back to their partner, it could seriously hurt the relationship.

5. If I am feeling sad or depressed, I need to be by myself. I heal myself by being alone, rather than by talking things over with my partner first.

I (Introvert) The worse things get, the more you need private time. But it's not easy if you have an Extrovert partner. Most Extroverts not only gain

energy and solace from venting about their own problems, they want rec-
iprocity; they want to feel needed, and they want to give help the way they
would want it—through verbal intimacy. This is generally not possible for
you. When you are down, you may need a therapist, but you do not want
to talk to a partner until you are in the right frame of mind. You do not like
sharing the recesses of your mind in general, but this is doubly true when
you are truly upset or in a dark mood. Another Introvert would understand but it is also possible you might be left alone so much that you would
have no help getting over your depression or angst—and sometimes people
do need help. An Extrovert might be annoying by offering what you see as
unwanted help. But, over time, their active concern might be good and
something you come to appreciate in the relationship. Some Introverts
(certainly not all) occasionally do need someone to get them out of their
shells and to express fears and problems out loud. Too much similarity on
this trait might not help things get better, and might let genuine depression
gain traction at a time when early intervention could make a positive difference.

E (Extrovert) If you are down, you look to other people to help pick you
up. You may engage friends and families to work through problems, as-
suage grief, or help you understand your feelings. In general, however, you
also want your partner to be your best friend when you are emotionally
needy. In this case another Extrovert is the most likely person who could
help you do that. Another Extrovert will help draw you out, create common cause by sharing experiences from their own life, offer an answer to
your problem, and be the support that you are looking for.

You may be a good partner for an Introvert when they are in trouble:
drawing them out, helping them think out loud, not letting them get too depressed for too long. They might resist this at first, and you might have to
back off, but you are at least potentially very valuable to a person whose first
instinct is to keep things bottled up. On the other hand, when it comes to
sadness and worry, an Introvert may not be the best partner for you. True,
they are good one on one and so perhaps they will be a good partner in intimate circumstances. But an extreme Introvert will not have much practice

sharing their feelings verbally and may have very little skill or knowledge about how to help you work through your problems. Even more problematic, their instinct would be to respect your privacy, the way they might want their own privacy respected, and leave you alone. This could make you feel unloved or uncared for if you still expected them to respond to you as one of your more extroverted friends might. If you understand the limits of an Introvert, you might not take their reluctance to try to draw you out as a lack of love or caring. But you definitely would have to get that verbal support elsewhere to feel better about whatever was troubling you. It might make you sad not to be able to get that from the main person in your life.

---

6. I am very shy when I am around people even if I don't appear to be.

I (Introvert) Introverts are often very shy people, an attribute that is hard to shake. (There is in fact research that suggests that shyness may be a genetic trait.) Sometimes being with a lot of people is literally painful for you, or if not painful, at least not very pleasurable. If you are with another Introvert your social world will be smaller, simpler, and easier for you to handle. If you are with an Extrovert, you will probably find yourself put in situations that are emotionally taxing or even distressing. You can manage this relationship if you and your partner can keep your social lives separate to a degree and you are not put in situations that are so uncomfortable for you. Otherwise, it's a tough match.

E (Extrovert) You love being around a lot of people and you draw strength from your interactions with other people. You have never been shy except perhaps for some fleeting moments in a group of strangers or in a particularly foreign environment. You gain confidence from other Extroverts so if you pair up with one, neither one of you will likely have to be sensitive about the other's shyness. However, if you do fall in love with an Introvert, you need to be sensitive to the possibility that some of their aversion to social situations and large crowds comes from a strong predisposition to shyness. If you drag your partner to the kind of events that make them uncomfortable it's going to be hell for them—and not much fun for you either. Introverts and Extroverts are really in different universes when it comes to some kinds of new or big social situations. Having a totally different reaction to them doesn't have to be a deal breaker, but if you are not aware that your partner is truly shy, you will fail to protect them from averse social situations and unwittingly undermine their happiness, your happiness and ultimately, the fate of the relationship.

---

7. I prefer conversations that answer questions, solve problems, or discuss something useful. I don't think it's necessary to talk about relationships that much and I particularly don't like going over the same issues again and again.

I (Introvert) You do not like the process of conversation—rather you prefer it to be directed and functional. Extroverts may use communication as a way to bond. You want to figure things out, find a solution, and move on. But you do not use language itself as an emotional release most of the time, while Extroverts do. Because Extroverts are sometimes more interested in the emotional journey—looking at an issue from many angles— their discussions may strike an Introvert as being redundant, which in turn could come off feeling like nagging or adversarial. Introverts tend to be spare with language and they may like the same in a partner. Some Introverts, however, are delighted to have an Extrovert partner who takes on the conversational burden for both of them, as long as it doesn't feel like they are covering the same territory that has already been fully explored. You can enjoy a chatty, open partner but they need to know when you are feeling that enough is enough. Another Introvert might share your conversational rhythms more but not be as entertaining a partner for you.

E (Extrovert) Half the fun of a relationship for you is the process of communicating—it doesn't really matter about what! You don't really understand someone who likes to keep interaction short and always to the point. You and your friends can take one subject and discuss it many ways—and even come back to it several times. People and their issues fascinate you and, ideally, you like to bring these stories back to your partner for even more discussion. Another Extrovert enjoys these casual conversations without feeling the need for "closure." In fact, many Introverts might find it a waste of time—gossip in its least interesting manifestation, and not understand why you spend time on trivial subjects. Yet some Introverts would enjoy rambling conversation because they see it as part of the bonding process. With more serious matters, Introverts tend to want to think about things awhile and they would not enjoy being put on the spot to respond.

Introverts certainly don't like going over the same ground over and over; the nuances over which you worry might escape them, unless these details were important in finding some answer. Remember, conversation energizes you—it tires them. It's not that you can't have meaningful conversation with an Introvert, it's just that they may have only so much tolerance for it. You don't want to squander your opportunities. The idea, however, of conversation and communication as a scarce resource in the relationship could be a deal breaker for you. If you don't have other friends you would want to use for some of these talks you may well feel emotionally deprived in your main relationship. You need to figure out how much chat you need with your partner, and how much you can, or want, to supplement that kind of communication with your network of friends. This will not, of course, be a problem if you are with another Extrovert, but it is a definite consideration if your partner tends toward introversion.

Romantic Assessment

Communication is one of the building blocks of intimacy. What constitutes good communication, however, is quite subjective. You are the only person who knows how much you want, under what conditions, and with which people. Introversion/Extroversion is a big character difference—but one also has to consider the whole spectrum from one end of the scale to the other. If you score seven out of seven on either the Introversion or Extroversion scale, you might want to find someone who understands and can respond to your needs, but probably not someone who is your polar opposite. If, however, you score a three, there might be a chance that you could balance each other's needs since there will be occasions when either of you will want to talk and experience other people or need more personal privacy and respect for the timing of communication.

Still, since intimacy is such an important desire for most people seeking a relationship that I would advise you to think deeply about what kinds of emotional support, personal privacy, and collaboration in social situations you will want from someone you love over a long period of time. Many Extroverts are attracted to Introverts and vice versa. Someone who is the private, silent type, who keeps their own counsel, or doesn't need to vent to others can be mysterious, therefore attractive to some Extroverts. Likewise, the open, verbal, and emotionally expansive Extrovert excites some Introverts, making them feel more like a complete package as a couple. But this initial attraction can be a burden if the other person does not have the skills to support your emotional needs. The offices of marriage counselors (and divorce attorneys) are filled with couples who say: "He/she just doesn't understand me." The most common element in these situations is the sense of emotional isolation that results when one partner perceives that the other does not or cannot respond to expectations and needs.

Lack of communication is one of those complaints heard over and over again. The most common and central complaint, from women in particular, is not having a partner who will listen to them when they are sad or troubled or overwhelmed. Not all women have a need to talk about relationship issues, family issues, and personal problems—but most do. Not all men impose limits on how they can express themselves, but many do. This gender difference is so common that it is almost expected and to some extent tolerated, but when it becomes extreme ("He never talks to me!") or doesn't change under stress and crisis ("When I was on trial for malpractice, he never came to court!") it can become the final straw in a relationship.

Fortunately, most partners do want to support each other, and silent, interior-focused people will often rise to the occasion and be able to talk eloquently and emotionally about really important topics or issues. Many Extroverts can realize that their Introvert partner needs time alone sometimes and will not expect attendance at the kind of events that their partner finds painful or boring. They will learn to create more one-on-one time and fewer group functions. They will go a great distance to accommodate a partner's needs. The resulting modification of extreme extroversion or extreme introversion can produce good couple time—and better communication.

However, the importance of this trait in relationships always begs these questions: Am I getting what I need? Would I have to sacrifice a central part of my personality to be in this relationship? Would the accommodations I am making now ultimately make me feel emotionally deprived or trapped?

Bottom Line: How you self-nurture is a critical part of your romantic personality. Your well-being and your satisfaction with your relationship could depend on this one characteristic more than any other of your romantic personality characteristics.

12

Perfect Matches Based on Differences

This chapter looks at how your second set of characteristics—Flexibility, Decision Making Style, Emotionality, and Self-Nurturing—come together into a personality profile. As you read some recommendations for your perfect match, you will notice suggested profiles that are quite different from yours. While similarity, which we discussed in earlier chapters, is generally comfortable, significant differences between partners on some or all of these complementary personality characteristics can be even more supportive of a long-term relationship. You will also see that some personality types have more matches than others; that is because some types could profit from a wider variety of counterpoints to their personalities. However, whatever these lists indicate, all these matches are just suggestions: You know yourself best and so you might know that a certain personality type might be a great match (even if it is not mentioned here) because it has worked for you in the past.

Combinations of
Personality Traits

SDPI:
Structured, Dominant, Passionate, Introvert

This personality profile has a tough shell. SDPIs have well-developed opinions, enjoy making decisions for themselves and for any relationship they are in, and will passionately argue their position if opposed. An SDPI is accustomed to retreating to their own counsel when they have some deep thinking or emotional repair to accomplish. They trust their own instincts more than they trust a partner's and so they are hard to reach when they are troubled or angry. One of the more difficult aspects of their personality is that they do get upset about life, politics, kids, etc., regularly yet probably do not want to talk about these issues as much as an extroverted partner would like them to. If they want a more intimate relationship—and many of them do not—they need someone who will soften the edge on these characteristics and help them express their emotions in a calm, nonaccusatory manner. On the other hand, a person who wants an intimate relationship with an SDPI should be someone who isn't overly sensitive, or easily rebuffed or hurt, since an SDPI will need someone strong. They may not bite, but they will have an intimidating bark. While this personality type expects to have center stage most of the time, they won't respect someone who's a pushover. An SDPI frequently needs someone who respects and understands them, but doesn't have the same need for dominance or privacy. That said, the partner of an SDPI will need to encourage them to share more, or might feel themselves to be lonely in the relationship.

Matches to Consider
SDTE (Structured, Dominant, Temperate, Extrovert): This is a person who is similar to you in some areas but is otherwise your mirror image. SDTEs also seek at least equality, and sometimes dominance, in a relationship. Like you, they have a strong personality. However, they have a calmer tem-

perament, are more open about sharing their feelings and more likely than you to be asking you to share your own. If you want a strong partner much like yourself who might keep the relationship warm without creating intense conflict, an SDTE would be a good choice.

FCTE (Flexible, Collaborative, Temperate, Extrovert): FCTEs would be another good choice for you. They like to get issues out in the open, yet provide a good balance to your more passionate nature. There is a strong possibility that they will go along with a lot of the things you think are absolutely necessary because they don't have a lot of rules and inflexible standards in relationships. If you are looking for a yin to your yang, someone with a comfortable and warm general approach to the world, FCTEs could be a good match. Just be careful you don't mistake their good nature for weakness, or they could perceive your behavior as being hurtful, with unfortunate consequences.

FDTE (Flexible, Dominant, Temperate, Extrovert): You might like an FDTE if you are looking for a soul mate who is a bit more flexible than you. You are such a strong personality that you might need someone who shares your temperament but who has fewer and more flexible demands about how things should happen. This might be the perfect complementary type for you—open, reasonable, strong but flexible.

SDTI:
Structure, Dominant, Temperate, Introvert

This is an exacting and dominant personality in an intimate relationship. However, they possess one quality—their calm temperament—that makes communication and reconciliation relatively easy. In general, they are willing to step back to get some perspective, and discuss most situations. SDTIs do have strong opinions, and do like to win, but they don't anger quickly or become emotionally on edge a lot. They want meaningful discussion and they are willing to lay the groundwork for it. On the other hand, they are very comfortable handling issues just inside their own heads and this can make them seem hard to reach. SDTIs might want someone who is more expressive than they are and who bring issues to the fore, things that they might forget to do—or not really see the need to do. Of course, given that they are opinionated and like to win, they might like someone who also had opinions, but who isn't so stubborn. Someone who is strong but likely to compromise might be an easy fit. An SDTI would be great with someone emotionally open, not too intrusive, flexible, and somewhat restrained.

Matches to Consider

SCTE (Structured, Collaborative, Temperate, Extrovert): In general, Introverts need someone slightly more extroverted than themselves so that important issues do not get buried. Obviously a raging Extrovert might be too much for you, but the temperate approach to life of an SCTE helps balance a gregarious and open nature that might otherwise be too intrusive for you. Furthermore, an SCTE's collaborative approach would ensure that the two of you, who each understand and appreciate a structured approach to living, have a way to deal with issues in the relationship. An SCTE is a complementary enough type for you to make a great partner.

FDTE (Flexible, Dominant, Temperate, Extrovert): Because you are so structured about your life, and you like to dominate a lot of decisions, you might be better off with someone who is quite flexible about how things get done. You might be drawn to someone who has a similar temperament to you, and the two of you would share both an even temperament and strong personalities. But it still might be advisable to work against your tendency to take care of all of your own emotional needs and be with someone who wants more interaction and communication.

FCPI (Flexible, Collaborative, Passionate, Introvert): You might think about trying to find an FCPI. They are more flexible and more likely to compromise on issues in the relationship—but their more passionate and emotional natures might enliven the relationship. If you are going to be with another Introvert because you appreciate their respect for both your personal privacy and their own, you might benefit from a different temperament so that personal responses do get out in the open and so there are chances to increase intimacy and share feelings.

FCTE (Flexible, Collaborative, Temperate, Extrovert): If temperament is what attracts you, and you are more flexible about other aspects of personality, consider an FCTE. You share a calm, steady day-to-day temperament, but an FCTE will encourage more communication on personal issues, will compromise more easily than you do, and therefore will help lower the level of conflict in the relationship. If you are willing to open up a little and also to tend to their emotional needs, an FCTE will be a good match for you.

SDTE (Structured, Dominant, Temperate, Extrovert): This is a chancier recommendation, but you might be the kind of SDTE who needs another opinionated, dominant personality to keep your relationship interesting; someone who is an equal match, will for will, and is as compulsive a planner and executer as you are. However, since you both may be vying for control, it might be a good thing to have someone with a cooler temperament than your own, and with communication skills that would temper what could be a very intense partnership.

SCPI:
Structured, Collaborative, Passionate, Introvert

An SCPI is usually accommodating, so their partner may not know how deeply they feel about things. Of course SCPIs can get angry, but their partner may not know the full extent of their feelings because they keep their emotional barometer rather private, even when they might be seething! In general, SCPIs tend to let things stew and may—or may not— eventually pick a time to talk about their feelings. While they are capable of compromising and often happy to follow their partner's lead, they have a strong internal sense about what is good or bad, right or wrong. When that barrier is trespassed they can become intensely upset. Because they offer the combination of being both passionate and introverted, they might do best if they choose a partner who is an Extrovert and who is able to get them to talk things over before they reach a boiling point. This might not be very comfortable for an SCPI but it will create a release of emotional pressure in the relationship, which promotes intimacy.

Matches to Consider

SCTI (Structured, Collaborative, Temperate, Introvert): You two could be peas in a pod if you agree on general values and how a relationship should work. Your compatibility in this area is extremely important since you both are quite structured and have definite ideas about lifestyle, etc. The one big difference is that you tend to be more dramatic and passionate about issues. The differences in temperament might be exactly what will make for a stable and happy couple. The only danger here is that an SCTI may be so cool and private that you don't know how they really feel about things. Using your more passionate, intense approach to smoke out any distress in your partner could lead to a very simpatico relationship.

SDTE (Structured, Dominant, Temperate, Extrovert): SDTEs can suit you because they may have the same need for perfectionism and planning that you do, but they are also willing to take the lead, allowing you to be the person who is supportive rather than having to take on a more controlling role. An SD is a strong personality combination, but if it is moderated by a cooler temperament and a need for emotional intimacy, the SDTE can be a very charismatic and thoughtful person to be with. Their need to be with people, and to be open with you, is a good counterpoint to your tendency to withdraw into yourself.

FCPE (Flexible, Collaborative, Passionate, Extrovert): An FCPE allows you space on the things that you believe have to be done a certain way and, like you, are willing to compromise their own beliefs or habits, to make the relationship work. FCPEs are easy to be with on a day-to-day basis but will share your tendency to have big reactions to emotional conflicts. Their ability and desire to talk and share emotional issues should be helpful for defusing the escalation that can happen because of your mutually intense personalities.

FDTE (Flexible, Dominant, Temperate, Extrovert): You might like an FDTE, someone who is less compulsive and strict about process and procedures than you tend to be. FDTEs like to be in command of the situation but are flexible about many arrangements. If you like to follow someone else's lead, especially when you think that they are smarter or more profession-ally advanced (or at least at your level) than you are, you might like this kind of dominant personality that is mediated by a more mellow tempera-ment than your own. It could really be a good complement to you to have someone who doesn't get as emotionally intense as you do and is more open about discussing relationship goals and feelings.

SCTI:
Structured, Collaborative, Temperate, Introvert

SCTIs have strong preferences in the way they do things, and equally strong in the beliefs that they hold. However, they do not like conflict, nor do they always need to have agreement on their point of view. They are likely to want to resolve conflict in the relationship just to achieve peace more than they need to get their partner to agree with them. They are a good match for someone who is also structured but dominant, because SCTIs like to make plans and set goals, are compulsive about getting things done, and like closure. However, they are also comfortable with letting their partner dominate a large number of decisions. They mostly keep opinions to themselves, so their partner may not always know what they really feel and they are also less likely to erupt angrily or respond badly to their partner's passionate outbursts. Accustomed to solving problems on their own, they most often formulate their own opinions and determine their own conclusions rather than engage in discussion. This is just the kind of behavior that makes an Extrovert anxious, so SCTIs might be best with an-other Structured Introvert who understands this pattern. On the other hand, if SCTIs feel they would like to be emotionally open, they would do well to team up with an Extrovert who will help them confront some of the important relationship issues they really need to discuss.

Matches to Consider

SCPI (Structured, Collaborative, Passionate, Introvert): If you need someone just as compulsive and organized as you are and you also want a peer relationship where each of you accepts influence from the other, an SCPI ought to fill the bill. SCPIs crave the same emotional privacy that you prize, but because they have a passionate nature you will always know where they stand. (Some Passionate types who are also Introverted may take a while to open up.) If you value someone who can keep certain important thoughts to themselves, SCPIs are compatible because they will respect personal boundaries. On the other hand, if you know from past experience that your reluctance to share personal issues with your partner has hurt relationships, you might skip SCPIs and turn to an SCPE.

SCPE (Structured, Collaborative, Passionate, Extrovert): SCPEs and SCTIs are planners, detail-oriented people who care about how things are done. That said, SCTIs are collaborative so would do well with another SC. An SCPE might, however, create more drama in your life than you are used to, but you are so similar in your general approach to love and communication in daily life, that their emotive, interactional style might be a good counterpoint to your restrained and private personality.

FDPE (Flexible, Dominant, Passionate, Extrovert): FDPEs have strong, emotionally intense personalities and may bring a passionate and emotional intimacy to the relationship, which otherwise might be missing. While they may be controlling in a relationship, they can also be flexible on a number of lifestyle issues, which will make it easier for the two of you to figure out how to make a mutually satisfying life together. They will follow your lead on getting things done but it is not as important to them as it is to you to reach closure. Still, if you want a person who is a strong personality, and who brings emotional vigor into the relationship, an FDPE will do all that and still give you some leeway to do the things you care about the way you want to do them.

FDTE (Flexible, Dominant, Temperate, Extrovert): FDTEs will let you be the perfectionist and the planner but they are not pushovers. Not by a long shot. They have Dominant personalities, but avoid being abrasive since they also have a Temperate quality in their profile. Likewise, their desire to be open with you, and wanting the same in return, is not intrusive. Their calmer approach is good for you, and their extroversion will help you feel welcome and encourage you to talk about intimate issues.

SDPE:
Structured, Dominant, Passionate, Extrovert

Not much gets hidden in a relationship with an SDPE. This is a bold profile. SDPEs have very definitive ideas about the way a relationship and a household should run. They have strong inclinations about the way that decisions are made and how plans are executed. They exhibit a passionate defense of their positions and values and have a lively expression of their ideas and feelings. Plus, they have a demanding need for other people to talk to them *and* listen to them! SDPEs perceive themselves as feeling deeply and want to discuss these emotions with a partner—and probably other close friends or even acquaintances. (Not being your partner's main or sole confidant could really bother someone more introverted, and those with a softer, gentler nature could find an SDPE overwhelming.) If an SDPE finds someone who is every bit as convinced of their own opinions, is just as interested in dominance when important considerations are under way, and is just as volatile and emotionally needy, they might be in for an exciting but exhausting ride! Some SDPEs look for someone who is lower-key and more malleable than they are, simply because it could make life easier.

Matches to Consider

SCPE (Structured, Collaborative, Passionate, Extrovert): This could be your soul mate. Exactly your temperament—the same emotional reactions as you do, the same need to connect—but with one important difference: They are not going to fight you for control of the relationship. SCPEs like the idea of being supportive, considerate, and consultative. It might just be the right kind of difference for you both to run exactly the same kind of life but not step on each other's toes.

SCTE (Structured, Collaborative, Temperate, Extrovert): SCTEs have the same demanding standards you do, but have a gentler nature. They will back off; they will be collaborative, accept influence, and respect your need for more control and decision making power. Their temperament could be the perfect foil to your own as they share your desire to talk through problems and they want to hear what you have to say. But they also have an easy going nature that will not rise to your more explosive responses.

FCTE (Flexible, Collaborative, Temperate, Extrovert): FCTEs could enjoy your strong personality and not feel overwhelmed by it or feel the need to compete with you. If an FCTE enjoys you as a person, they will let you have your way, not get too upset when you get upset, and give you the communication and psychological nurture that you want and need. Be careful with this match, however: You could feel superior just because this person is accommodating and more easygoing than you are. You have to be careful not to confuse goodwill and a less dramatic personality for a lack of self-respect or internal strength. If you do get that wrong, your partner could become resentful and the relationship will suffer.

FDTE (Flexible, Dominant, Temperate, Extrovert): This is a riskier match but it might be intriguing. If you find someone who is strong-willed but flexible enough on daily issues to be able to see and do some things on your terms, it might be a challenging and interesting match. The dominance in their character is modified both by their flexible point of view and their cooler, calmer temperament. Happily, an FDTE is an Extrovert, and is willing to talk over their feelings. This is essential since two dominant personalities like your own will need expressive skills to work their way through the times when perspectives or desires are in conflict.

SDTE:
Structured, Dominant, Temperate, Extrovert

SDTEs are the people who often get elected to be president of things, and who continue to be respected and admired even after their term is over. They are easy to be around, open, friendly and able to hear disparate opinions without getting too hot under the collar. Even if some things they care about are getting roasted. They have an easy leadership quality. They have a knack for getting things done and done right. This overall profile is very attractive to a wide range of personality types. However, a little more flexibility might save them from occasionally erring toward the dogmatic, so their perfect match might be different on that particular characteristic. Their ability to share their feelings and their need for emotional connection is a good modification to the dominant and structured part of their personality. This openness is unexpected in such an otherwise powerful personality and makes them approachable—and for quite a few people, a good partner.

Matches to Consider

SDPI (Structured, Dominant, Passionate, Introvert): If you want to be a power couple, pick another SD, but be sure you share basic opinions, tastes, and habits—otherwise you are going to cause each other a lot of misery! In the case of two big personalities, it helps that you are temperate so you can moderate the exciting, but potentially explosive personality profile of an SDPI. SDPIs have a proclivity for keeping their inner turmoil to themselves—for a while, at least, which is not always best for a relationship. Look for an SDPI who is working on becoming a little less of an Introvert and a little more of an Extrovert. An SDPI can be a combustible type and only your calmer temperament makes it possible to turn this into a satisfying relationship.

SDTI (Structured, Dominant, Temperate, Introvert): This is an exacting personality hidden in a milder package. They have a powerful will and a strong set of standards, but they have fewer expressive needs than you do. They could be attracted to someone like you, who is open and communicative. If you like a strong person who will let you lead the emotional life of the couple, an SDTI could be good for you. (While two SDTEs might vie for all the oxygen in the room, an SDTI will give you center stage and allow you to freely express your big personality.) An SDTI could be too hard to touch emotionally, but if you respect people who are emotionally self-sufficient, you could find an SDTI quite attractive.

SCPI (Structured, Collaborative, Passionate, Introvert): An SCPI might be a nice complement to your personality because you are both planners and both are fastidious in keeping your life orderly. Still, an SCPI will let you take the lead, emotionally and in decision making. The one real downside: An SCPI will not be as expressive as you are, and so you may not want someone who is too acutely introverted. Still, if you want a partner who listens and requires less air time than you do, but holds a strong set of opinions that make them interesting, an SCPI is a complementary possibility.

SCTE (Structured, Collaborative, Temperate, Extrovert): This is an easier-going version of yourself. You share the same temperament and emotional style. If you tend to butt heads with a partner who competes with you for the lead in the relationship, an SCTE might be just the ticket because they will let you be the more controlling partner. Even better news: You will get a person who, like yourself, has high standards, strong opinions, and a reasoned, lower-key approach to everyday life, yet still has the same need you do to be open.

FCTE (Flexible, Collaborative, Temperate, Extrovert): It would be easy for you to be with an FCTE because FCTEs have the same emotional makeup you do, but prefer to be more collaborative than controlling. They might even enjoy handing over the leadership of a relationship. The only worry is that they might not present enough challenge for you, if you are looking for those kinds of sparks in a relationship. They may be too eager to compromise, which might make them less erotic or compelling. However, if you find this rather sweet, open-natured type compelling, this could be an extremely good match for you.

FCPE (Flexible, Collaborative, Passionate, Extrovert): If you want someone who is relatively compliant and supportive, but with a little more flair and fire than a FCTE, then an FCPE is a good choice. This personality type demonstrates some backbone: their essential nature is flexible and collaborative, but they also have strong opinions, and are open and communicative about them. You will always know where they stand. They are good at drawing others out of themselves so this could be a very nice, easy fit.

FDTE (Flexible, Dominant, Temperate, Extrovert): If you are looking for another strong personality with a similar temperament and a mutual need to listen and disclose feelings, an FDTE might fit the bill. The strength of your wills would, however, be modified by the fact that FDTEs give themselves more latitude about how things need to be done in everyday life, which will help avoid quite a bit of conflict between you. You could feel excited yet comfortable with an FDTE.

SCPE:
Structured, Collaborative, Passionate, Extrovert

An SCPE cares passionately about how they live their life, yet are not resistant to influence. They do have rules and values, and can be upset if standards aren't kept up. They are capable of blowing up, showing deep emotions and letting their partner have the full blast of their feelings. Still, when it comes right down to it, they are not as concerned about their point of view as they are about the relationship. They are willing to compromise, which trumps their need, real as it is, to do things their way. They want open communication but if their partner is also needy and passionate, things could become either very inviting and open or extremely trying, depending on the degree of emotional volatility. Their capacity to compromise on their sometimes dogmatic attachment to rules and expectations is an attractive quality and allows for compatibility with more dominant personalities. Still, unless an SCPE loves a good fight—thriving on heated exchanges—it might be best to be cautious about getting into a relationship with someone who has as short a fuse and intolerance for other's values.

Matches to Consider

SCTI (Structured, Collaborative, Temperate, Introvert): SCTIs share your concern for getting things done a certain way and living up to responsibilities and obligations. However, they are less emotionally intense about it than you are. Their cooler reactions to provocations or disagreements might mitigate conflict in your relationship. SCTIs could be attracted to your strong opinions and perhaps your ability to draw them out and create more intimacy. You might enjoy a more harmonious relationship with a person who is calmer and more self-sufficient than you are.

FCTE (Flexible, Collaborative, Temperate, Extrovert): FCTEs are easygoing, and could even be the best possible choice for you. They aren't as finicky as you are about the way things need to be done but, like you, they are looking for someone who is an equal in the relationship, and ready to compromise on day-to-day issues. Their cooler temperament is a nice balance to yours. They also value opening up and sharing important feelings when they are upset or need advice, assuming they like your more intense reactions to subjects. An FCTE could be a soul mate.

FDTE (Flexible, Dominant, Temperate, Extrovert): FDTEs like to take charge of the relationship. They are more forceful and dominant than you tend to be. An FDTE has strong leadership qualities: they are expressive, flexible, and very reasonable—a highly attractive profile for you. They have the strength to balance your more intense emotional reactions and the flexibility to let you win sometimes while still being a powerful presence in the relationship.

FCPE (Flexible, Collaborative, Passionate, Extrovert): FCPEs will understand you because they have the same emotional makeup and needs, but because they are more flexible about a number of issues than you are, your mutual intensity shouldn't drag the two of you into unsolvable conflicts. A little bit of difference can go a long way in making a relationship work, and the FCPE's ability to give way to you could make them a particularly good long-term bet.

SCTE:
Structured, Collaborative, Temperate, Extrovert

An SCTE is a relatively gentle type of personality. While there are some rigid elements of this profile, in general they are the support staff to a relationship. More often than not, they are the soother, negotiator, and communicator of the pair. They don't get upset easily themselves and they don't rise to the bait if they have a passionate, emotionally volatile partner. These instincts modify the more compulsive aspects of their personality. The combination of being both structured in the way they live yet compromising during disagreements produces a balanced, realistic approach to their romantic life. For the most part, they are concerned about their partner's emotional well-being and feel more emotionally stable in the relationship. This profile, in general, describes someone who has good communication skills, is reasonable, and puts the relationship before their individual needs.

Matches to Consider
SDPE (Structured, Dominant, Passionate, Extrovert): An SDPE might be a good and exciting partner for you if you thrive on some differences between you and your partner. With this profile you will find someone with a more dominant streak and more intense emotional reactions. The relationship will work if you share the same values, goals, and habits since both of you adhere very strongly to your feelings about how life ought to be lived. SDPEs have more dramatic emotions about their attachments than you do

and will want to share their feelings and worries with you regularly. You will reciprocate as long as their need is not too overwhelming. You will be a good partner for them because your more temperate responses will help avoid potential clashes. But, above all, you will need to be attracted to their strong, dramatic personality for this match to work.

SDTE (Structured, Dominant, Temperate, Extrovert): SDTEs share your general temperament, but tend to be more dominant. They will quite naturally take the lead in the relationship but will moderate rather than intensify responses to most kinds of events and interactions. An SDTE will be an easy person for you to understand because they will have a similar personality structure to your own. If you are looking for someone who takes the lead in the relationship, this could be your perfect match.

FCTE (Flexible, Collaborative, Temperate, Extrovert): Because you take responsibilities and obligations very seriously and have very specific ways of doing things, someone with a more flexible nature will be a good partner for you—but only if you share basic standards and values. An FCTE shares your temperament and your need for openness. They are willing to negotiate and come to compromises about decisions in the relationship. If you have trouble finding someone with *exactly* the same requirements for daily life as you do, an FCTE would be perfect for you.

FCPE (Flexible, Collaborative, Passionate, Extrovert): If you enjoy someone with a more fiery or intense approach to life than you have, then all the other elements that would make this relationship work are in place. The question is, Are you drawn to people who are passionate in comparison to you, or does that embarrass you or seem too high-maintenance? If you find this quality exciting, then an FCPE is a good match for you.

FDPE:
Flexible, Dominant, Passionate, Extrovert

FDPEs are lively, perhaps charismatic and generally fun to be with. Theirs is a strong type that wears well in a relationship because they are big personalities who still are able to accommodate a partner's needs and wishes. As a result of their ability to change course or accept influence from a partner, they make an ideal match for many different personality types. An FDPE has leadership ambitions and qualities, is intense, likes and connects to a lot of people, and yet is willing to consider other approaches and other points of view. Their flexibility is a great asset in any relationship. They are not rule-bound or particularly compulsive about the way things have to be done, which is an admirable quality in someone who has a dominant personality. It makes them a leader instead of a tyrant. FDPEs are willing to be influenced, even if they try to control final decisions most of the time. FDPEs are willing to talk and debate most issues; they share intense emotions and pour their hearts into the relationship. They are willing and interested to hear the problems and feelings of a partner.

Matches to Consider
SCTI (Structured, Collaborative, Temperate, Introvert): Structured (S) types are going to come looking for you and you are going to need to consider how you will fit with someone who has strong opinions about the way they want to lead their lives. While this may sound daunting, as long as you share the same values and goals, the person who does what they say they will do and lives up to what they believe in might be very attractive to you. An SCTI has a more temperate way of going about negotiating needs and desires in a relationship, which means that differences can be dealt with without ruffling too many feathers—yours or their own. If you find people who keep a part of themselves private an appealing quality, an SCTI could be an interesting partner. If you like this general temperament but need someone who talks and shares more, then consider an SCTE, someone with the same basic traits only more extroverted.

FCPE (Flexible, Collaborative, Passionate, Extrovert): FCPEs are open and flexible and operate pretty much the way you do, adapting to life and not getting their backs up too readily. The fit is particularly good because they can handle your more dominant personality and not try and compete with you. They are similarly intense and opinionated but, like you, like to be open and discuss issues and feelings, which makes for a very close, positive relationship.

FDTE (Flexible, Dominant, Temperate, Extrovert): If you are attracted to some challenges in a relationship, you might consider an FDTE, whose way of reacting to issues is more contained than your own. You would respect their restraint because they also have a dominant personality and would indeed resemble the strong, silent type, you could find attractive. This is a difference that can easily be accommodated in the relationship because FDTEs are flexible and expressive about issues, so clashes of wills can be handled constructively.

FDPI (Flexible, Dominant, Passionate, Introvert): You may feel that one powerful personality is enough for a relationship and you don't want a partner as dominant as you are. But in case you would find someone strong attractive, or in fact need that constructive collaboration between two alpha types to stay interested, an FDPI is a good profile match to you. You both are Dominant, but because an FDPI is also Flexible, there should be some give in the relationship, which will help resolve conflicts when you disagree. But because you want and need emotional sharing, which does not come naturally to an introverted FDPI, you will want to make sure that the passionate side of their nature will allow things to get out in the open. You don't want to be frozen out entirely. If you like challenging relationships, this one could work out.

FCTE:
Flexible, Collaborative, Temperate, Extrovert

An FCTE is the universal connector, or as close as any one personality type comes to being at the hub of most wheels. They get along with just about everyone. There are some matches that would be less organically sensible. For example, since they are the soul of negotiation and communication, with fairly predictable emotions, they might be seen as weak or boring by a person who wants someone more dominant and emotionally expressive. While a temperate, extroverted personality is a very pleasant person indeed, this is such a "nice guy" or "sweet gal" profile; it could be uninteresting to someone looking for an edgier, challenging, or even high-maintenance partner. However, for most people, an FCTE has the tools to be a great partner. They are secure in relationships and like to work with someone to create a good life together. They seek an intimate union, open up their hearts readily (but not aggressively or inappropriately), and don't get upset easily. They are endearing sorts because they are actively trying to be loveable and likeable. They have to be careful, however, that they don't act so nice that their goodwill and desire to mitigate conflict are judged by some dominant types as a sign of weakness rather than love.

Matches to Consider
An FCTE can be with almost anyone. The following are five good choices, but don't rule out SDPE, SCPE, SDPI, or FDTI, since they would do very well in a relationship with you.

SDTE (Structured, Dominant, Temperate, Extrovert): You are a very easygoing person, and SDTEs are looking for you to complement their more dominant, structured personalities. You might like this kind of strong personality since you are flexible and like to compromise to consensus rather than try to win unilaterally. An SDTE would add some pizzazz to your life but not be too hot to handle. Like you, they want an expressive, open partner and that, plus a calmer approach, might be enough to keep the relationship vital and intimate.

SCTE (Structured, Collaborative, Temperate, Extrovert): An SCTE has strong opinions, but like you is lower-key and willing to work things out through conversation and disclosure. You could hand over a lot of the everyday organization of the relationship if you didn't like to do that kind of planning, without sacrificing too much power or participation in decision making.

FCPE (Flexible, Collaborative, Passionate, Extrovert): If you want a partner who is more emotional than you are, but who otherwise shares your general flexibility and collaborative approach to the relationship, an FCPE would be a very good choice. An FCPE would add some interest because they would address issues at a more fervent pitch than you normally do. An FCPE is unlikely to get nasty even if they feel passionately about an issue. But the addition of passion would not negatively affect the collaborative way you two would discuss issues. This added depth of feeling could enrich the intimacy of your relationship.

FDTE (Flexible, Dominant, Temperate, Extrovert): An FDTE mirrors your personality except that they want to direct the relationship more than you do. If you want benign leadership rather than tyranny, an FDTE is flexible, reasonable, and empathetic, but still takes charge of the way the relationship grows. FDTEs will communicate openly the whys and wherefores of what they want yet are unlikely to get out of control even over issues of great importance to them. If you particularly like a partner who can evoke your admiration, or you are willing to have someone else take responsibility for the biggest decisions, an FDTE is a great person for you.

FCTI (Flexible, Collaborative, Temperate, Introvert): If an FCTI wants someone like you to help bring them out of their introspective tendencies, you may enjoy guiding them into deeper communication and sharing. That "if" is really important, however, because sometimes introverted people are more expressive and open when they first fall in love but don't sustain that feeling for long. You would need to be confident that the lines of communication were going to stay open. Otherwise this could be a very disappointing match.

FCPE:
Flexible, Collaborative, Passionate, Extrovert

FCPEs are open to negotiating most partner differences, and they don't have immovable positions on how their life together should be run. They are more likely to be spontaneous than many of the other personality types, which makes them fun, and sometimes creative. They are pretty easy to be with, unless their hotter temperament is disturbing to someone with a low threshold for drama. They need someone who will work with them when things get rough, which means talking things over until an understanding has been reached. FCPEs are particularly sensitive to passive-aggressive behavior that is unconsciously or consciously aimed at hurting others. In general, anyone who is a CPE has no tolerance for camouflaged nastiness. They need someone direct and honest, even if they are highly emotional. An FCPE might be good for someone who has a quieter, more private nature since they may help them to be more open. This could help deepen the intimacy of the relationship.

Matches to Consider
SDTE (Structured, Dominant, Temperate, Extrovert): You are a passionate person, a supportive extrovert, and you probably want someone who will enjoy and encourage your affectionate nature and not shut you out. Being with someone who is unable to have a deeper emotional connection would be painful to you.

On the other hand, you might want someone who is more Dominant who will take care of practical and perhaps even emotional issues for both of you. An SDTE might be a good choice because this is a person who is a natural-born organizer and leader, but is not going to conduct a relationship in an aggressive manner. They have the same commitment to emotional healing through intimate conversation as you do. (If you like a partner with well-honed planning and organizational capabilities, but want consensual decision making, then you might like an SCTE. This personality type retains an expressive, nondramatic temperament, but also accepts a partner who wants to be collaborative rather than directive in the relationship.)

FDPE (Flexible, Dominant, Passionate, Extrovert): This is a very easy match if you want someone who has a more dominant personality. Many people are drawn to strength and charisma, and because you are flexible about daily issues and ready to compromise on areas of disagreement, you can accommodate someone who is passionate like yourself yet who also is clearly the leader in the couple. When a Dominant personality is also able to be flexible and expressive, they are not likely to be abusive, unreasonable, cold, or punishing. This means they can be a loving partner, and differences can be worked out.

FCTE (Flexible, Collaborative, Temperate, Extrovert): Of course you will get along with another person who shares your need for a consensual and expressive relationship. In addition, if they were less emotional when it came to sorting out issues, you might find yourself in a low-maintenance, low-conflict, and ultimately, very satisfying position. The difference in temperament might be very pleasing to you since you may need a partner who is more analytical and able to maintain some perspective and calm in the situation when you cannot.

FDTI (Flexible, Dominant, Temperate, Introvert): You might be the kind of person who likes to be the follower and peacemaker to a partner with a strong, dominant personality as long as that person isn't so rigid about the way things ought to be done that you feel ignored or disrespected. You may have enough intensity and communication skills to bring out someone more private than you are. An FDTI can appear as if they don't really need anyone, which some more passionate and more expressive personalities see as a challenge. If you feel that you can "complete" a more temperate personality, then an FDTI may be right for you. However, sometimes, it is hard for Dominate types to accept these kinds of encouragements. If you don't want to take on the challenge of an FDTI, but you do like a moderate temperament coupled with personal charisma as part of a partner's profile, than a good compromise would be someone more extroverted, like an FDTE.

FCPE (Flexible, Collaborative, Passionate, Extrovert): In general the suggestions in this section focus on complementary factors; that is, differences in some part of your profile. But you might discover that all the difference you need lies in the intensity of your emotional natures. Another FCPE, being a similar personality type, might help create a very warm, collaborative, and deeply intimate relationship, which could be an astounding match.

FDTE:
Flexible, Dominant, Temperate, Extrovert

FDTEs have commanding personalities. They like to take the lead, but they are not compulsive about how life should be organized. They do not have a lot of specific requirements for a relationship. In general, they are easygoing, confident, and quite content to do everyday things in new ways, some of which might be on their partner's terms. Dominant but temperate and flexible personalities don't need to be control freaks; they are quite at ease negotiating day-to-day decisions. It is only when really important decisions or lifestyle choices are at stake that their personality asserts itself and allows their natural inclination toward leadership to take over to make sure everything is done right. They are willing to talk, share, and often accommodate a partner as needed. They are likely to instigate a conversation when necessary or to give the relationship the time and room to grow. While they do seek collaboration, the dominant streak in their temperament means that they are used to doing more than their partner (or anyone else) in most areas of their lives. Women tend to find men with this temperament quite compelling: the mixture of dominance and compromise in their character and their stable, nonaggressive temperament will strike many women as having just the right balance. In particular their willingness to share their feelings, increases their value as mate material. Men who like stronger-willed mates will be attracted to partners with this personality. Women, in general, will see an FDTE as warm, competent, low-maintenance, and emotionally stable.

Matches to Consider
The FTDE type could enjoy a wide range of matches. There are five good types described below, but FDTI, SCPI, SCTI, SDPI, SDTI, or FDPI are

also possible matches if they aren't too emotionally introspective and with-holding.

FCTE (Flexible, Collaborative, Temperate, Extrovert): This is an easy match. You have very similar temperaments and needs, but FCTEs will be happy with letting you be the leader. You both have even temperaments and flexible approaches to everyday issues, and unless you need a more aggressive personality as ballast, an FCTE could make you very happy.

SCPE (Structured, Collaborative, Passionate, Extrovert): You are more inclined to hang loose than an SCPE but because some of their concerns don't really bother you, you probably won't get in their way on the issues that may preoccupy them. If you do pick ways of meeting responsibilities that they don't find appropriate, the SCPE is the type of person who will let you know it but be willing to find a mutual solution to the problem. This is an expressive and collaborative type of person, all characteristics you understand and appreciate. They need emotional intensity, and so do you, even if you conduct yourself at a lower pitch. There might be some adjustment here but it seems like a good match.

SDTE (Structured, Dominant, Temperate, Extrovert): This is another dominant type of person, but if you are looking for your equal, or perhaps someone to look up to, this is an intriguing profile for you to consider. SDTEs share your even temperament and your expressiveness, so you ought to be able to talk things over, bond with close confidences, and depend on each other for emotional healing. SDTEs will be sticklers for some of the traditions and habits of the relationships, but you probably don't mind bending on those sorts of things.

FDPE (Flexible, Dominant, Passionate, Extrovert): This is a good match if you are attracted to a strong, charismatic type or at least someone with the same flair for leadership and decision making that you have. The nice aspect of an FDPE is that the two of you could be a power couple because you are both flexible and expressive enough to work through issues. You might also benefit by the counterpoint to your temperament; in this case, someone emotive and perhaps dramatic to enliven the way you experience the world. The complement of a more passionately expressed nature than your own could ramp up the romance and intensity of your relationship in a positive way.

FCTI (Flexible, Collaborative, Temperate, Introvert): You are a reasonable person who is willing to change plans, see things in a new way and in general, be calm, thoughtful, and open with a partner. Yet, you are also inclined to take the reins in a relationship and have your opinions prevail. An FCTI is an easy person to be with because they prefer compromise and know how to work with a willful or forceful partner. They will keep their cool while you might be losing yours. The only significant area you might have to consider is their tendency to be introspective and keep their emotions to themselves. This could be a problem. But an FCTI is such a genial type of person that it probably wouldn't be that hard to have them modify their emotional style enough to be more open with you about important psychological issues. Their inclination is to try and create a harmonious relationship and so they would be a good bet even if it means they had to expand their emotional range.

FDPI:
Flexible, Dominant, Passionate, Introvert

FDPIs can be very exotic creatures—passionate, dominant, but hard to really know their deepest selves. They feel most comfortable when they are the dominant personality in the relationship and often claim some of that space by having strong, instant emotions. However, this person can be hard to read, because they are quite private and keep many of their deeply felt emotions inside. This can be frustrating to an extrovert who will sense some emotional turmoil and will want to discuss those feelings openly. But an FDPI is going to resist. They are emotional, but they don't feel compelled to express or explain those emotions. FDPIs might be better off with an Extrovert who could eventually draw them out of themselves. An

FDPI, however, might be more attracted to other Introverts because they are both naturally uncomfortable with emotional openness. A potentially difficult pairing might be another FDPI. Both would feel passionately about things and if they have conflicts they might burn each other up fighting. They would be unable to delve into the origins of those problems, and likely to be unable to find solutions. A better match would be with someone on the more expressive side of the Introvert scale (or the more private side of the Extrovert scale). However, even if an FDPI isn't emotionally accessible all of the time, they have a flexible nature that allows them to rethink positions and not become overly attached to their initial positions.

Matches to Consider

FDPE (Flexible, Dominant, Passionate, Extrovert): Even though your general inclination is to go inside of yourself to deal with trauma, anger, anxiety, or other kinds of troubling emotions, a good relationship really needs someone who is at least somewhat willing to encourage communication and emotional exchange. The need to have one partner carry the burden of this emotional work for the couple is especially true for FDPIs. You are a strong and challenging personality so you will need a more extroverted partner if you hope to be able to mediate problems effectively. You don't want feelings of resentment or misunderstanding to gain traction, especially between two people with strong wills and deep emotions. Both of you need to be flexible enough to make changes, so this might be a really terrific match.

FDTE (Flexible, Dominant, Temperate, Extrovert): If you have found that the pairing of two intense personalities has undermined your relationships in the past, you might look to strong but flexible profiles, but choose one that is more Temperate. While this choice of partner shares your strength and flexibility, they also have the kind of temperament that is unlikely to inflame disagreements. Their general inclination to discuss issues will help to create more intimacy than you might be otherwise inclined to initiate.

FCPI (Flexible, Collaborative, Passionate, Introvert): If you find that you really don't get along with Extroverts, or rather, they just don't get enough out of you, then look for another Introvert who has a Passionate nature. While each of you is inclined toward emotional distance and the need for privacy, even if it takes some time to work out issues at least you will know where each of you stands. Furthermore, FCPIs are good for you because they want to be supportive of the relationship and their inclination is to find a way to solve problems rather than insist on their own path.

FCTE (Flexible, Collaborative, Temperate, Extrovert): This might be your best match if you want a partner who likes to follow and support rather than be the dominant partner or even the coleader. An FCTE is the epitome of a partner who tries hard to please and keep the peace. They are willing to be conciliatory and flexible about plans, opinions, even major decisions, and they act in moderation in most instances. They only thing they ask in return is a high level of intimacy about things that matter. If you pick an FCTE, they will need to talk to you about how they are feeling and they will need you to reciprocate. If that is too high a price for you to pay over a long period of time, pick an FCTI. You will get the same great nature but in a person who is as private about their deepest feelings and worries as you are. This might be more comfortable for you but be careful: FCTIs are such easygoing, private people, you might miss the signals that things are going sideways.

FDTI:
Flexible, Dominant, Temperate, Introvert

An FDTI has a personality that can surprise any partner. They may appear very easygoing because they generally eschew drama or passionate declarations about values and beliefs. They are flexible about lifestyle issues and collaborative on day-to-day decision making. On the other hand, they have a strong streak of independence and do not depend on others for emotional comfort or validation. Their quieter nature and tendency to keep their feelings to themselves plus their ability to accept influence from their partner in many areas may lull their partners into thinking of them as compromisers rather than as dominant decision makers. This would, however, be a mistaken picture. The FDTI fits the stereotypical description: still waters run deep. In their own understated way, they may prove to be the most dominant person—but never less than equal—in a relationship. They are reasonable and controlled in conversations, but rarely initiate discussions about things that really matter to them. When important life-changing decisions are being made, they will tend to stand their ground and eventually get their own way. They need someone who recognizes their need for a powerful position in the relationship and who is content with no more than equality. FDTIs will need a Flexible partner, and in general, an Extroverted mate who will encourage positive exchanges on important issues.

Matches to Consider

FCTE (Flexible, Collaborative, Temperate, Extrovert): Almost anyone can get along with an FCTE. If you are looking for someone who will do the emotional work that creates intimacy and staunches percolating problems, then look no further. This is a great match for you because FCTEs share your quiet and easygoing temperament but they will defer to your will much of the time if that is what you need or enjoy. They are definitely more consistently supportive than Dominant types and they are not intensely emotive. They do, however, have a price for their goodwill in that they need their emotional needs to be recognized and tended to by you and they will want some entry into *your* emotional life as well. This could be too high a price for you if you are not able or willing to give them access. You may, therefore, opt for a more introverted person. But if you can open up enough and listen well enough you could gain new intimacy skills and create a great partnership.

FDTE (Flexible, Dominant, Temperate, Extrovert): If you respect people with strong wills and leadership capabilities then you might want a partner who is as aggressive as you are in search of their goals and vision for the relationship, but with the same kind of temperament as you. This would feel comfortable when issues arise; discussions would take place in a way you like and understand. Best of all, given that two strong people will be trying to configure the relationship, each with strong ideas about how things ought to go, an FDTE will have the communication needs and skills to make sure their thoughts and issues get brought up and dealt with. If you like a partner with a strong personality but a low-key and flexible style, and you are willing to respond to their need for regular communication in the relationship, this would be a good match.

FCPI (Flexible, Collaborative, Passionate, Introvert): If you really need to be with another Introvert because you just can't take all that emotional digging and exposure and chat, then look to a very companionable and flexible kind of person who, while introverted, still shows their emotions in a visible way. FCPIs may still be private people, but unlike you, they are not moderate about expressing their values and opinions. While being collaborative and compromising as they are, they still feel things deeply, and you will hear their reactions almost immediately. At the very least, this will help the two of you to stay in touch even though your partner may not come to you for sympathy or to solve problems. Only in exceptional cases will an FCPI seek a great unearthing of personal data. Still, because they are more Passionate and Introverted than Temperate and Introverted, you will have some more emotional reckoning in this relationship. If this situation is handled well, however, you will have more opportunities to sympathize or at least reach an understanding on important issues.

SCTE (Structured, Collaborative, Temperate, Extrovert): SCTEs have the same kind of compulsiveness, and expectations about values and habits as you do. You will appreciate their attention to time and detail. Even if there are some differences between you, an SCTE is capable of a great deal of compromise and has the temperament to discuss issues and work out concessions in a way you understand. Their temperate, moderating style will also make it easier for you to engage in discussions when they need your counsel or seek comfort from you. You will need to be able to talk with them—the need to talk is one of their defining characteristics—but they can pick the time and place better than a Passionate Extrovert. This capacity may help you adjust and even come to like these kinds of conversations. In general, SCTEs will not challenge you but the *S* in their profile means there will be things they need to have a certain way and they will resist a competing idea. And even if they don't challenge your leadership or your authority to make some final decisions for the relationship on important issues, you will have to learn to deal with their strong convictions.

FCPI:
Flexible, Collaborative, Passionate, Introvert

An FCPI needs someone who is not too intrusive but understands, and accommodates the fact that they have strong emotions, even if those emotions are not on the surface or shared. Once they have a partner who understands how deeply they feel things, FCPIs are easy people to get along with. They have very accommodating and flexible personalities. They tend to be oriented to their partner rather than to many friends or an expansive outside social life. They will do a lot to keep their partner happy. As strong as their opinions may be, they are more likely than not to modify their own desires to make sure that the couple can go forward, that the bond remains strong, and that their partner is content. Their partner, however, needs to remember that not everything an FCPI feels is being openly expressed. Even though the FCPI may have agreed along the way to solve problems or deal with issues, it might not always reflect what they really want. Over time the FCPI may become quite unhappy always accommodating and compromising. The relationship could get into trouble. An FCPI has mastered the art of negotiation without betraying their innermost feelings. Then, seemingly out of nowhere, they show their displeasure, which can come as a great surprise to a partner who has missed the signs.

Their partner may have had no idea that they had been offended, or thought things in the relationship were unfair. Someone who has a temperate nature may not understand that anything is amiss. In some ways, an FCPI either needs someone with their own temperament who understands that things may be percolating under the surface, or someone with the sensibilities of a Passionate Extrovert who can help them get their feelings out before resentments build up.

Matches to Consider

SDTI (Structured, Dominant, Temperate, Introvert): You are a bit of a puzzle to a lot of people. You can go with the flow but you have intense reactions that can erupt quite unexpectedly. Since you are more of a private person, others may not realize how passionately you feel about certain things. An SDTI would understand your need for personal privacy and have the temperament to soothe you when your emotions overflow. Moreover, they are strong personalities with the presence to counteract your more emotional temperament. You would complement an SDTI because your more flexible and collaborative nature would work well with their more structured and dominant traits.

SDPI (Structured, Dominant, Passionate, Introvert): An SDPI shares your emotional intensity, which means that they probably would understand you more readily. This has its good and bad points since emotional similarity makes you feel more understood, but in this case, two of you with this same strong emotional response on issues of great importance might create more fiery arguments than the relationship could endure. Still, your mutual understanding of each other's need for privacy, plus your respect and sensitivity to each other's strong emotions, could create a relationship that makes you feel like two soul mates. (Since a calm or temperate approach to relationship issues may not even be something of importance to you, alternatively, an SCPI might be an exciting partner.)

FCTI (Flexible, Collaborative, Temperate, Introvert): FCTI is about as mellow a profile as you can get. You will not need to have an extroverted partner if you have someone this low-key who is also collaborative and flexible. It is very easy to be with someone who has the same approach to negotiation, planning, and adjusting to everyday issues as you do. An FCTI will be very unlikely to crowd your space or create drama of any interpersonal kind. You will need to observe your partner carefully, however, because they may not *show* distress or bring up deeper issues. Because you are naturally emotive, you might not appreciate your partner's reticence. If you are with an FCTI, you'll need to make sure that you check in enough to make sure your partner is happy and feels that the relationship is going well.

FCTE (Flexible, Collaborative, Temperate, Extrovert): If you believe that romance is enhanced from more self-examination, an easy choice for you would be an FCTE. FCTEs are easygoing in all ways, but they need to talk to you about their problems. They want to give you the blow-by-blow of their daily activities and concerns, and expect to hear the same from you. Their temperate style may help you open up and process what you have been doing or thinking. This may seem like a lot of work to you, but an FCTE should make it feel more like sharing and storytelling than being psychoanalyzed. This kind of person could help you move seamlessly into a deeper, more intimate relationship.

FCPE (Flexible, Collaborative, Passionate, Extrovert): This is another type of person who could be your soul mate, if you felt you needed someone to be the relationship "specialist." To be a good match, you would need to welcome at least a reasonable amount of talking about the relationship. You would need to develop a taste for using each other as a sounding board in exploring feelings about all aspects of your life and relationship. An FCPE and you would operate as equals and would probably appreciate each other's inclination to look for compromise in most situations. You would also both be very passionate about life in general and each other in particular, which could create a strong, intimate bond. The only question here is, Can you extend emotional access to your deepest self in times of stress, when you are most inclined to turn inward? An FCPE wants to get in deep: You would need not only to permit it, but to utilize it and come to enjoy it.

FCTI:
Flexible, Collaborative, Temperate, Introvert

FCTIs are easy to get along with because of their natural inclinations to be flexible. They are always willing to compromise, but are reticent to express or share all of their thought processes or emotions. These qualities may prevent some important issue from being brought to the fore when talking straight from the heart is necessary for the health of the relationship. An FCTI is a high-functioning person who easily inhabits a relationship without much drama—and also with minimum exposure. They keep issues to themselves, and like to keep things running smoothly—but perhaps not always to their personal long-term advantage. They might need someone who will shake things up a bit because they could let things go on that should be examined and changed. They will mull things over for quite a while, which keeps a relationship pleasant and placid but if issues or feelings never surface, this lack of confrontation or soul-searching may suck the vitality out of a relationship. If the relationship is on track, and there are no critical issues to be dealt with, then this is a terrific personality type to maintain that happy state of being; it's just not as functional when change is necessary. An extroverted personality will take an FCTI at face value—never questioning their partner's unexpressed feelings, unhappiness, or even depression. On the other hand, some Extroverts will, if only because of their own needs, draw out an introvert, which could ensure that things are humming along below as well as above the surface. If you are an FCTI you need to make sure your deepest feelings are being expressed in the relationship *as well* as inside your head.

Matches to Consider

FCTE (Flexible, Collaborative, Temperate, Extrovert): An FCTE is probably exactly what you need. They share your general approach to love, are easy to please, and fast to compromise. They are less likely to be high-maintenance, but they differ from you in one important way: they are Extroverts, which is probably exactly what you need. A FCTE will want to have an intimate and in-depth exchange of feelings, especially when things are tough. That may be exactly when you choose to be quiet and gather your own thoughts about what you feel. An FCTE may seem wrong for you at first blush, but you would profit from someone who brings you out of your usual self-sufficiency. And this kind of person would definitely help you create a deeper connection than you might otherwise find comfortable.

FCPE (Flexible, Collaborative, Passionate, Extrovert): If you are attracted to a more passionate temperament than your own, an FCPE would be a great person. You have the same approach to relationships but they have more intense opinions, more dramatic delivery, and possibly a bigger, quicker temper than you have. Fortunately, their extroverted nature makes them able to share their feelings fairly easily with you—and you should be able to more readily discuss any discomfort you might have with their behavior. If you want someone to add some excitement to a relationship, and some additional intimacy, an FCPE would suit you.

FDTE (Flexible, Dominant, Temperate, Extrovert): While an FDTE shares your temperament and will seem easygoing because they are flexible, if you look a little deeper you will see that this is a strong personality, both expressive and dominant. This is someone who wants to direct the relationship and will demand a lot of emotional openness. If you let yourself follow this person's lead, you will find yourself in a much more intense relationship than if you were with a more Collaborative person, such as an FCTE or certainly with another FCTI. If you like to have someone who takes on the leadership of the relationship, and who gets you to share emotionally in a way that both profits you and the relationship, then by all means, choose an FDTE.

FCPI (Flexible, Collaborative, Passionate, Introvert): If you find that you are not comfortable with a true Extrovert, that you need to keep more of yourself private or you feel annoyed, or even worse, violated, and pushed beyond your natural desire to share, what you might want is someone with a moderately different temperament than your own but who is an Introvert like yourself. Sure, you could pick someone just like you, an FCTI and probably be just fine, but it might be better if you had someone who was able to foster a valuable emotional exchange. While a relationship with two mellow, flexible, and collaborative people can thrive, if they both take too long to get to the emotions they are feeling, the relationship is put at risk, which is why you might want to mix things up a bit and pick someone like an FCPI, who has an emotional style that will encourage the two of you to share feelings right away.

Part Three

Love and Lifestyle Issues

As important as personality characteristics may be to determine perfect matches, there is more to compatibility than personality. Couples also need to make sure they are in sync on important lifestyle choices. You could be just right for each other as personalities—and so wrong when it comes to your fundamental values, hopes, and dreams. People have to do more than simply fall in love, or even continue to work at staying in love. They have to find a way to live that is satisfying and comfortable for both of them. In the following chapters you will find a series of short quizzes that will guide you to think about what aspects of day-to-day living are essential in order for you to be happy with a partner. At the very least these quizzes will give you questions to ask in any serious dating relationship. They are especially important if you are considering living with or marrying someone. These may be, in fact, the questions to ask before you say "I do."

It is extremely important to be able to talk about what your expectations and feelings are in these five areas: money, sex, children, core values, and social life. These questions and the commentary that follows should encourage you to take each of them seriously. And, as much as the personality profiles from the previous chapters, your responses to these questions will not only guide you to a better understanding of yourself but will put you in a much stronger position to choose a compatible partner. These questions may not cover every issue that pertains to your core values and desires. Using these as a starring point, I think that you'll be motivated to add your own questions to evaluate whether a person is the right long-term partner for you. In any case, this is a starting place. If you can find someone whose answers to these questions are similar or complementary to your own, you have gone a long way toward being in a strong and compatible relationship.

The Challenges of Money

Why Money Is So Important

Money is not the most romantic topic we could talk about—but it could have the most impact on the choice of partner you make. Money (either earned or inherited) determines where you live, what you buy, how you spend your leisure time, your network of friends and acquaintances, even the way you view yourself and others. Unfortunately, it is one of the least discussed premarital issues. Even if it is talked about, couples tend to skip over some of the harder issues: how much money do they feel they need to be happy; how would they spend money on luxuries versus necessities; how much money is appropriate to save; and to what extent are they responsible for each other's debts and charitable commitments.

Some serious couples will discuss their entire sexual history with one another—even being graphic about it during counseling, and work to change things for the better if the situation warrants it. But these same couples who can be so frank and open with each other concerning one subject will react quite differently when asked about how much money they have in the bank. A couple's financial situation is more often than not viewed as the most intimate aspect of their relationship—and they hardly discuss it with each other, much less an outsider.

Money creates and expresses status, freedom, prestige, and control. Some people try to resist its seductions, while others embrace them without guilt or ambivalence. While it is unseemly and perhaps offensive in most modern Western societies to admit that you are marrying for money, many societies across the globe base marriage on exactly that premise. While we seldom hesitate to use jobs and education as measures of present and future success and prestige, we rarely have the guts to declare how important money can be when it comes to love matches. You need to know what your economic agenda will be inside a relationship, and what you can and cannot do without. Again, there are no right answers to the questions that follow, but your answers will provide a good diagnostic about your financial habits and values and help you to determine the ideal economic profile of a future mate. which you and a partner should agree.

Money and Economic Aspirations and Evaluation: How will you mix love and money?

Please answer True or False to the following questions. Calculate your score according to the guidelines provided at the end of the quiz and then read the explanation section for your romantic analysis.

T   F   **1.** I could not love a person who doesn't make enough money to help me live the lifestyle I need in order to be happy.

T   F   **2.** All other things being equal, I tend to respect people who make a lot of money more than people who have modest incomes.

T   F   **3.** I have often spent more money than I really can afford.

T   F   **4.** I have, or want to have, the "best of the best" on some high-ticket items such as cars, a house, and vacations.

T   F   **5.** I need economic stability in my life. I don't overspend and I would be extremely upset if I was with someone who overspends or doesn't have a plan to save money.

T   F   **6.** I would very much prefer to be with someone who makes more money than I do.

T   F   **7.** I would very much prefer to be with someone who did not have major economic responsibilities to children or parents unless they had a lot of money and these responsibilities did not affect our life together.

Scoring

Give yourself one point for every True answer.

0-2: Money is not particularly important to you in your choice of a partner.

3-5: Money is moderately important to you in your choice of a partner. It is something you have to consider carefully.

6-7: Money is extremely important to you in your choice of a partner. You will not be happy unless you have a partner who has enough money, and has similar values about money that you do.

Romantic Assessment

The answers to each of these questions reveal important aspects about money acquisition and management, which affect relationship satisfaction and stability.

1. I could not love a person who doesn't make enough money to help me live the lifestyle I need in order to be happy.

How you answered this question reveals your expectations of your partner's ability to earn enough money for the lifestyle you want. If you answered True to this question, it means that you will be extremely disappointed if you have to become the major wage earner or your partner does not reach the economic level of success that you expect. Alternatively you may have answered False because you are sure that you are the one who will be economically successful and you believe in yourself and don't need any help. But if you are depending on someone else to help achieve the lifestyle you want, you better make sure that you are looking at people whose economic success is relatively predictable. This leaves out many entrepreneurs where although the possibility for success may be high, the probability of failure is not to be discounted. And you might be cautious about those in highly competitive fields in which few people reach a high level of compensation such as artists, actors, architects, teachers, and professional musicians. Of course, many people have surprising successes and failures—there are no completely accurate predictions: Even highly trained professional people can lose their jobs, get depressed, or change ambitions over the life cycle. Success is relative, so you will be judging someone's financial potential on your terms. If your happiness is really dependent on economic success, you have to make as safe a choice as you can in order to keep your love alive. This statement may sound calculating, but it's actually the most thoughtful course you can take. Not everybody cares a lot about money and many people can be perfectly happy no matter what their economic situation. But if you want and need the sense of fulfillment and security that only money can bring, you will have to consider your partner's economic solidity so that you never want to have to leave an otherwise viable relationship because of "insufficient funds."

Be realistic. If you care about money, make it key to your emotional and marital decision making. Don't kid yourself. You might have been tempted to answer the questions in this chapter to create the impression that money doesn't matter to you. Okay. You will get points for being politically correct but if your partner is an economic disaster, you won't be happy and your relationship will suffer.

If, on the other hand, having or earning a lot of money really and truly is not an important issue to you, and your respect and love for your partner will not be affected by economic instability or failure, picking a partner suddenly becomes a lot easier. Just make sure that the person you are picking has the same values you have or you are capable and willing to be the person who meets their economic expectations.

---

2. All other things being equal, I tend to respect people who make a lot of money more than people who have modest incomes.

Respect is one of the key elements for long-term love and if you tend to give people who are economically successful more latitude then you obviously need to be with someone who fits that profile. If you believe that a high income is a clear indicator that a person is special—able to survive in a cutthroat business environment, obviously bright, savvy, or hard working, talented to get so far in life, etc.—you really should be with someone whose economic success lives up to your standards and expectations. Many women—and some men—will accommodate many personality quirks and differences if their partner is economically powerful; not just because of the money, but because of the strong personality that often goes with it. If respect and income go together for you, admit it and act accordingly in your choice of partner.

On the other hand, if money has little or nothing to do with your respect or admiration for a partner, and your partner feels the same way, then the need to pick someone who is economically secure becomes less critical. You do, of course, have to make sure this feeling is mutual, or again, be in a secure economic position so that their feelings for you will never have to be tested. Many partners have had a rude awakening about the nature of their relationship when the couple had to face unexpected economic hardships. Even if those times were eventually weathered, the fact that one's spouse didn't believe in them, or that they were cold and fretful and couldn't be emotionally supportive during the challenging period, could have some long-term fallout that affects one or both members of the couples' commitment. It is hard to forget that when money did become an issue, your partner voiced disappointment or loss of confidence in you as a person.

---

3. I have often spent more money than I really can afford.

If money just burns a hole in your pocket, it's going to be hard for you to live within severe economic limitations. (Granted, one can overspend no matter how much money is coming in but if you are dangerously over-spending, you will need to control it or it could destroy any relationship.) Even if your overspending is not of catastrophic proportions, you need to be able to earn enough yourself to cover this habit or be with a partner who can offer some shelter and repair.

If you answered False to this question, you probably watch your dol-lars carefully and can be disciplined about how much you spend and save. You most likely want someone who is as cautious (and as good a planner) as you are. If you have other characteristics that show control, such as being a Risk Avoider and being Cautious, you have a fairly consistent profile: You are conservative in many areas of your life and your partner's approach to monetary matters should be reasonably similar to your own.

---

4. I have, or want to have, the "best of the best" on some high-ticket items such as cars, a house, and vacations.

If you answered True to this question, you are going to need some big-time money to indulge your tastes. Some people look for good value; oth-ers like you, want the best—the most beautiful or most prestigious items. In general, those are very expensive. If you can provide such preferences for you and a partner, and feel good about being able to do so, no problem. But if you cannot do it for yourself, or you can do part of it but will need a partner's contribution to help make it possible, you need to take that into consideration.

On the other hand, if you find that the insatiable desire for living the high life to be a preoccupation of the shallow-minded, you might want to find someone else who shares your distain for labels, five-star hotels, and "name" restaurants—even if you can afford them.

5. I need economic stability in my life. I don't overspend and I would be extremely upset if I was with someone who overspends or doesn't have a plan to save money.

Money isn't just important for people who live the "high life"; it is also important for people who are very worried about economic stability. If you answered yes to this question, you may not need someone wealthy, but you do not want much volatility in your economic world. You would be very worried about having a partner who spends money they did not have, who has suffered economic ups and downs in the past, or who carried large debts or made risky investments that could have a negative impact on your basic lifestyle. In this case it is not the level of money that is important to you. Rather, it is the style of spending, investing, and maintaining money about which you need to be aware. If you risk finding yourself in an unstable economic situation, you might want to look for someone who can help make your financial life more predictable. If you answered false to this question, however, you probably have more of an entrepreneurial or adventurous spirit that allows you to deal well with the ups and downs of financial fortune. You don't worry about getting in trouble over money; it may have happened and you lived through it! You might need a partner who is willing to live on the economic edge; and who can absorb economic uncertainty without it affecting their feelings about the relationship.

6. I would very much prefer to be with someone who makes more money than I do.

Economic success is always relative. No matter how much money you make, if you feel that your respect and satisfaction will be substantially increased by being with someone more economically successful than you are, then you need to look for someone who not only makes more money than you currently do, but is almost guaranteed to do so in the future, still economic success is notoriously unpredictable. If you were to become the senior earner, then you need to be quite sure that you are picking someone with a very good chance of staying as successful.

One caveat here: Since economic success is relative, there is always the chance that the person you meet will continue to earn as they have but that you will become much more financially flush than you are now and earn more money than your partner. While you may both be at a level that satisfies you now, relationships do get tricky when the balance shifts. While modern men are becoming increasingly comfortable having a high-earning female partner, they may have expected to be the lead earner. If this changes, it can be an issue with some men whose pride is hurt by not fulfilling the role of chief breadwinner. Finding out how important being the main provider is to someone could be important in predicting future problems.

---

7. I would very much prefer to be with someone who did not have major economic responsibilities to children or parents unless they had a lot of money and these responsibilities did not affect our life together.

Let's face it: The older people get, the more economic responsibilities they accumulate. By the time people are in the mid- to-late twenties they may already have educational or other kinds of debt. Our lives continue to get more and more fiscally complicated because the older we get, the more we find ourselves having to take care of other people besides ourselves—children, parents, spouses no longer able to work. Even by the age of thirty many people have taken on all sorts of obligations: child care, child support, medical issues, care of a sick family member, mortgages, among a large list of other possible economic drains.

It is hard to avoid monetary baggage—yours or someone else's. Even if you are adamant about not inheriting someone else's money problems, it is often hard to get an accurate reading on someone's personal finances. Even people who have nothing to hide are often very private about their economic status. It may be almost impossible to find out how encumbered someone might be. If you are very worried about being dragged down by someone else's debt or don't want to sacrifice your own standard of living because of a potential partner's financial obligations, you do have to pay special attention to their circumstances. You need to talk about money to find out if you share the same values, habits, and priorities. Questions such as how much you both think is right to spend on a child's education or when economic responsibility to children ends—if ever—could become crucial areas of disagreement. If you are seriously interested in getting into a long-term relationship, you need to discuss issues such as savings, charity, mixing funds, and a myriad of other financial matters. Money management is a day-in, day-out challenge, and unless you see money in similar terms you are going to have problems.

14

The Importance of Sex

Okay, you think: well, of course, sex is important! But sometimes people who are attracted to each other and/or love each other's souls are willing to overlook the fact that they may be a sexual mismatch. I cannot tell you how many letters and questions I have received from people who were engaged to be married who intended to go through with the marriage even though there was evidence of some pretty serious sexual problems. Men and women who have written to me about these serious problems often confessed that they felt themselves to be superficial for even bringing the issues up. Very few wanted to reconsider the partnership, even though sometimes the issues were so serious that sex was aversive, absent, or unsatisfying. Oddly enough, many people have asked me if sex would get better after marriage even though it was clear that there were deep-seated personal problems with one or both of the partners. To marry and hope that the change of "status" will solve the problems is never a good way to approach the situation—even though it appears that many couples buy into this myth.

It really is important for sex to be good; or even better, to be great. For men, sexuality is often the way they express love—or learn to love— their partner. For many men, the intimacy starts with sexual behavior and then blossoms into affectionate feelings, and ultimately into disclosive and intimate conversation. For women, it is often the opposite. If women feel loved, respected, truly listened to and understood, this feeling of being bonded and committed is the best aphrodisiac they could ask for. Even if men and women are starting from different places, sex does the same thing for both sexes: it helps them break boundaries, reach out, say loving things and make themselves vulnerable. Without sex, forgiveness, reaffirmation, and emotional attachment are a lot harder to achieve.

Many studies show a correlation between sexual frequency and satisfaction, and relationship satisfaction. In their studies, Vaughn Call, Susan Sprecher, and Pepper Schwartz Call, (*Journal of Marriage and Family*, Volume 57, No. 3, August 1995) used National Opinion Research Center data to show that sex was important for relationship happiness and longevity. In fact, every behavioral science study has revealed the same conclusion: Intercourse is associated with emotional attachment and sexual and relationship happiness.

Intercourse and frequency of intercourse is not the only, and perhaps not even the major fact I wish to use to prove that sexual attraction and sexual pleasure are important parts of relationship success and longevity. The following questions help delineate critical areas of sexual functioning and suggest how they might directly attribute to relationship success.

Mark T for True and F for False for each of the following statements:

T   F   **1.** I care a lot about sexual technique. I want my sex life to start out and stay superlative.

T   F   **2.** I need a physically attractive partner to be sexually turned on. I have very specific requirements of what my partner needs to look like, and if these requirements aren't met I can't respond sexually in the way I would like to.

T   F   **3.** If I see my partner admiring someone else at a party or on the street, I get jealous and can feel offended.

T   F   **4.** I need lots of hugs, kisses, and plenty of foreplay to be happy and feel loved.

T   F   **5.** Sometimes I feel like covering my emotional bets—like having a sexual relationship on the side in case the person I am with disappoints me or leaves me. If I feel neglected I am likely to seek sexual and/or emotional comfort elsewhere.

T   F   **6.** I believe in quality over quantity, but if the quantity goes down too much it can't be a quality sexual relationship.

T   F   **7.** I need a sexual relationship that has a lot of experimentation and fun in it. My partner and I should enjoy trying different things together and be open to new ideas.

Scoring

Give yourself one point for every True answer.

0–2:   Sexuality is a very low priority of yours. You would want to be with someone who agrees that it is pretty unimportant.

3–5:   Sexuality is an important part of any romantic relationship you are in. Make sure it is also important to your partner.

6–7:   Sexuality is a central concern and desire in your relationship. Do not enter a serious relationship with someone who doesn't give it the same primacy you do.

Romantic Assessment

1. I care a lot about sexual technique. I want my sex life to start out and stay superlative.

If you care about how someone makes love with you and you want it to be great from the beginning, you are looking for a perfect sexual match. That is hard to find, because sexuality is something that is learned together, and in the most fortunate of relationships, keeps getting better. Nonetheless, there are people who are so well-suited to each other that their sexual desires and techniques mesh immediately, and that can make for an immediately passionate and satisfying attachment. Fabulous as that might be, you need to be careful about how that makes you feel about someone. If sex and sexual satisfaction is very important to you, you might be swept away by someone who is a good sexual match and not want to look more critically at what else comes with the package. Great sex is a powerful bond and for someone like you, who cares a lot about it, it can become the central focus of the relationship.

Good sex can sustain a relationship when it is having troubles or help keep it from getting boring. A great sexual match is not as common as the movies would have us believe, and if it is instantly present it is a fortunate benefit not to be overlooked. Obviously you are making half the contribution to the magic but as the old proverb says, It takes two to tango. You would be fortunate to have one another.

However, if sexuality is important to you and it is not immediately successful, don't despair. It can get better. Many people need time to relax, explore, communicate, and modify their approaches to one another in order to create a special sexual connection. I would urge you not to give up immediately on someone if your sexual styles are different, unless neither one of you is willing to talk about it or work together until you are both in sync. Techniques such as how a person touches you or wants to be touched can be customized if someone is interested in learning what you like and vice versa. Books, movies, and just plain trying out different approaches and positions can create a new and more satisfying sexual relationship.

As your relationship continues, if the magic never seems to materialize, you have to take serious stock of whether or not this is the right match for you. If there is a sexual mismatch that doesn't positively respond to your repeated attempts to make it better, you have to acknowledge that the two of you have a problem that might never be fixed. If you scored over a 4 or 5 on this quiz, then a lack of sexual fulfillment probably should be a deal breaker. This is especially true if you are paired with someone who has told you, by words or actions, that sex isn't very important or to them.

Don't indulge a dangerous fantasy—that eventually seductive and sexual powers will make your reluctant partner much more enthusiastic about sex. More likely, the opposite will happen. People who start out less sexually engaged more often than not decrease in sexual appetite, not increase. Don't get into a situation where you see that lack of interest from the beginning but choose to ignore it or imagine you could change it over the course of a committed relationship or marriage. Usually that just doesn't happen.

---

2. I need a physically attractive partner to be sexually turned on. I have very specific requirements of what my partner needs to look like, and if these requirements aren't met I can't respond sexually in the way I would like to.

Some people have a very exacting template for sexual arousal. Psychologist John Money describes this phenomenon in his book, *Lovemaps*. While there are many theories about why someone might like blonds rather than redheads or tall people versus shorter ones, there is no explanation that can predict much in the case of any individual. Furthermore, we don't really know why some people might prefer someone slim but be able to fall in love with someone who is stocky while another person simply cannot be attracted to someone who isn't the embodiment of zero body fat.

No matter why we are attracted to certain people, the fact is we are attracted to some but not others. If you need a certain kind of person to be aroused, you just have to accept that fact even if you wish it were otherwise. Sometimes tastes change naturally, but they never change on demand. You don't want someone to suffer by falling in love with you when you are trying to eroticize their looks because you think they are a swell person, but just can't quite be truly aroused. The more stable and specific your visual needs are, the more you have to honor that fact, and make your selection within the physical parameters that work for you. If on the other hand, you turn on to people more because of their personality, or accomplishments, or a twinkle in their eye, you are lucky; you have a much bigger field to choose from. People who have a narrow zone of eroticization may be forever on the hunt for the perfect example of those looks; if you turn on to someone because they have a loveable personality and then that loveable personality makes you feel sexually attracted, you are fortunate because those characteristics last while looks may not. If you have a partner, however, who falls in love with you in large part based on your looks, be careful you understand the source of their desire and maintain the, so far as you are able, the look that drew him or her to you. Otherwise, the relationship may not last, or a painful alternative: it may last but be passionless.

---

3. If I see my partner admiring someone else at a party or on the street, I get jealous and can feel offended.

Jealousy can be hard on a relationship. Few people like to feel distrusted and even if someone is flattered that you care so much that you are protective, there is a time when the flattery ends and the feelings of not being trusted or respected begin. Jealousy has to be controlled; otherwise you could end up in a grizzly headline. People have done some terrible or embarrassing things when they thought they were being left or cheated on— and many times their fear and anger were totally unjustified. All things being equal, it would be a better choice for most people to pick a partner who is so secure in their love and own worthiness that they never—or almost never—get jealous.

That said, if you are prone to jealousy, you need to be with someone who doesn't act seductive to other people. Some men and women need the approval of others so much that they flirt a lot, sometimes without consciously knowing it (or admitting it to themselves). If you do tend to be insecure, do yourself a favor and stay away from any woman who likes to show her body off a lot, or any man who enters a party and makes a beeline for the prettiest woman in the room. If a person feels they have to put on the charm and make an impression all of the time in social situations, it's going to make a jealous person crazy—which is not a fun way to go through life, or a good foundation for a relationship.

Sometimes, of course, a partner is absolutely loyal and unflirtatous, but so attractive or charismatic that the world beats a path to their door. You have to decide if you can handle having a partner like that without becoming paranoid. Remember, if you are jealous, you have to either be able to change (believe you are loved and your lover is completely faithful and beyond reproach) or control it—or avoid circumstances that provoke it. If you are not jealous and you have a partner who is prone to jealousy and who can't or won't take steps to deal with it, then you might think twice about getting more involved.

---

4. I need lots of hugs, kisses, and plenty of foreplay to be happy and feel loved.

Sometimes your sexuality is more about sensuality and affection than about intercourse. What you really need is to be lovingly stroked, hugged, kissed, and touched. If you need this, don't settle for someone who doesn't do it naturally—you will find yourself begging for crumbs of affection and never quite feeling well-taken care of.

This isn't something you can usually teach someone to do. There are affectionate, huggy people—and there are people who do not need constant physical affection themselves and so consequently dole it out rather sparingly. Over a long period of time you might feel quite deprived if you are almost always the one who initiates a snuggle or a cuddle or a kiss.

On the other hand, you might be the kind of person who finds it annoying to be touched and hugged all the time. Some people find it downright cloying, even creepy. This is a characteristic you really want to be matched on—otherwise one of you is always moving back as the other person is moving forward. It doesn't matter whether you like affectionate touching or not—it does matter that you both feel the same way about it.

Foreplay, however, is quite another thing. If you have a female partner, you better like foreplay. Without it, you will never have a steamy hot lady—or she won't stay steamy after the newness of the relationship wears off. The fact is, most women are not orgasmic—or not as excited as they could be—if there is not a luxurious amount of touching and/or oral sex before intercourse. Getting it right is also important! This doesn't take going to school to get a master's degree in foreplay—but it does require communication—and some indication that you enjoy doing this and it's not just a job you do to get your partner ready for intercourse.

While foreplay is essential for 99 percent of women, quite a few men will not be happy without it as well. While many men are quite content to just have intercourse, many more men want variety in their sexual life and will be much more delighted with their partner and with their sexual life together, if all kinds of sexual play is encouraged and enjoyed. Dating couples may take their time before becoming sexual and everyone has their own morality concerning sexual matters in a relationship. But remember, you get a lot of information about someone's sexuality just by the way they kiss—how much they like to kiss, touch, or receive pleasure from you. All of this can produce critical insights about what your future sex life could be like even if you never make love before marriage or commitment.

---

5. Sometimes I feel like covering my emotional bets—like having a sexual relationship on the side in case the person I am with disappoints me or leaves me. If I feel neglected I am likely to seek sexual and/or emotional comfort elsewhere.

If you are someone who can feel emotionally insecure relatively easily you need a person who is steadfast and likes a lot of time with you. Obviously it would be better if you could accept that you are loved and not worry about it, but if you start to go sideways when you feel neglected then you need someone who gives you lots of affection and attention. If you get a lot of reassurance in your relationship you may be less likely to feel that you will be left, and less likely to be calling up old beaus or being flirtatious with a co-worker who happens to be in the right place when you are feeling lonely, unloved, or uncertain.

All things considered however, you need to control some of these insecurities because you could easily undermine a perfectly good relationship. If you cut and run at the first hint of relationship boredom or the preoccupation of your partner, you are probably helping to foster the very problem you are afraid of. You have to be careful not to create a self-fulfilling prophecy: fearing a betrayal, you become involved with someone else, and your partner, sensing your absence and fearing the worst, also gets involved outside the relationship. None of this needed to happen.

The answer is communication and picking someone who can give you the time and centrality you need.

On the other hand, if you become involved with a partner who needs this kind of reassurance, you need to think about what it will take to keep them happy and secure, and whether you are prepared to do the work. Another person's needs can make you feel important, wanted, and necessary to their happiness. Or it could drain you as you try to satisfy their hunger for security. It all depends on your personality—but you need to figure out whether a partner's demands for your physical presence and emotional focus are pleasing or frightening to you.

---

6. I believe in quality over quantity, but if the quantity goes down too much it can't be a quality sexual relationship.

How much sex is enough is a very subjective issue. The difficulty of figuring out how much sexual contact is "right" or "enough" was famously caricatured in Woody Allen's film *Annie Hall*. In the movie the heroine (Annie, played by Diane Keaton) complains to her therapist that her partner (Allen) is pestering her for sex three times a week—and it's too much. On the other side of the split screen, Allen is also confiding to a sympathetic listener that he never gets any sex! Why, it's only three times a week!

Of course there is no specific amount of sex that is correct. People who have been together for less than two years tend to have sex three or more times a week, and the first year will be the most intense, sometimes involving sex every day and night! Over time, and as people age, sexual intercourse (or sexual contact of some sort to orgasm) declines slowly and becomes less regular, diminishing from three times a week to two times a week to once a week, or less. This doesn't necessarily mean satisfaction goes down—unless one or both partners are getting a lot less sexual contact than they want and expect.

While some people believe that quality sex is more important than quantity of sex, ideally there is some balance between the two that works. For example, another classic joke has an older man all excited about his sex life. His friend asks him how often he and his wife have sex and he says once a year. The friend, shocked, asks him how he can be happy when he has sex only once a year and the old man says, "Because tonight is the night!" Like other classic jokes, this one has a point—it's rather ludicrous to think of having sex only once a year and be happy about it. Quantity in and of itself is not a predictor of satisfaction—on the other hand a very spare sex life is rarely an exciting or happy one.

The other fact to consider is different levels of desire. Someone with a very strong libido really does want a lot of sexual contact, usually to orgasm. If you are a very sexual person, you will have a lot happier life if you pick someone who is just like you. Being rejected is no fun. Neither is being pressured to have sex much more than you want to have it. Being in sync about the importance of sexual intercourse or other kinds of lovemaking can be a critical element of a relationship. It usually is a difference or similarity present right from the beginning of the relationship, and it usually doesn't change dramatically. Thinking you can take a cool partner and make them into a hot one is usually a futile hope or a temporary transition.

7. I need a sexual relationship that has a lot of experimentation and fun in it. My partner and I should enjoy trying different things together and be open to new ideas.

If you are an adventurous lover, you need someone who shares your vision of sex, or at least wants to learn it! On the other hand, some people find comfort in what they know and things they have done before. (You can review the differences between those who want predictability (P) and those who seek variety (Vs) in the first part of the Duet® Total Compatibility System in chapter 6 for more insight into this characteristic.) They make love the way they always have and it never bothers them that they have had intercourse or foreplay the same way for twenty years. Other partners mix it up by trying new positions in new locations, with new toys, or with new visual stimuli. They are drawn closer together by the fact they are both up for almost anything.

Sometimes people start out one way and mutually decide to get a little bolder. It can take quite a while to become comfortable enough with each other and with sexual expression to feel like you can handle something that you might have previously thought of as taboo or disrespectful. Many people can go years and years, for example, without sharing sexual fantasies because they think of them as too personal and/or embarrassing. However at some point in the relationship one or both partners feel close and trusting enough to exchange fantasies or use them as a scenario to include in their lovemaking. They may not have brought either the ability or the desire to do play-acting or sexual imagery into the beginning of their relationship, but as they become more confident with each other's love, they feel safe to explore their psyches in their love life.

Not everyone needs to swing from trapezes to have an exciting sex life. For many people, the spiritual connection of sexuality will be all they will ever want or need. Again, the importance here is linking up with someone who is like you, and not which choice is right or wrong.

15

And Baby Makes Three, or Four, or More . . .

The Importance of Children

Many people think the whole point of being together is to create the kind of relationship that is an appropriate and solid foundation for having children. Other people want to concentrate on the adult relationship and don't want to dilute their intensity and freedom by adding a family.

Somewhere in the middle are large numbers of people who want to have kids but only if the relationship is in great shape, their career is in order, and the timing is "right." Even if someone wants children, it is easy for one or both partners to be ambivalent about when to have children, and whether or not they are ready, as individuals and as a couple, to make the sacrifices required and to be able to parent effectively. A very common problem in relationships occurs when one person feels the time is right and the other person does not. Whatever the choice, there are few topics about which people feel stronger than *if* they should have kids, *when* they should have them, and after those decisions, how to collaborate on child raising. Because this is a basic building block of the future health and satisfaction of the couple, understanding your own agenda about children is critical because it will help you know what to look for in a partner, should you get serious enough to start looking at them as daddy or mommy material.

Please mark each of the following statements True or False.

T   F   **1.** When I get serious about someone I always think about their parent potential. That is one of the most important evaluations of someone I do.

T   F   **2.** I am happy to consider someone who already has children as a mate. I just love children in general.

T   F   **3.** I think it is important to have children while you are young.

T   F   **4.** I want a big family.

T   F   **5.** I want a fifty-fifty partnership in raising kids, or as close to that as possible.

T   F   **6.** I think once people have children, they should not break up unless there is abuse or violence.

T   F   **7.** I would not want to leave my children alone with a sitter for the first couple of years, maybe longer. I think it is important for parents to spend most of their "free" time with their young children.

Scoring

Give yourself one point for every True answer.

0–2:   Children are not your highest priority.

3–5:   Children are very important to you and guide many of your choices.

6–7:   Children are extremely important to you and you need to be with someone who has prioritized them in the same way you have.

Romantic Assessment

1. When I get serious about someone I always think about their parent potential. That is one of the most important evaluations of someone I do.

If daddy or mommy potential is the first thing you start thinking about when you are getting interested in someone, you may be on a coparent hunt as much as on the hunt for a romantic partner. This is fine—but since it is such an important part of what you are looking for, you really want to be looking for someone who is doing the same thing.

There are plenty of men, as well as women, who feel their biological clock ticking. Men's issues about time are often not so much about fertility as about being a father at the age they feel best about the role. But for many, the lack of a biological imperative makes them less sensitive to this issue than many women of the same age. If you look at some of the online ads it is clear that some men and women are only looking for someone who wants to get serious and start a family. If this is where you are at in your life, be up front about it. The only thing you have to be careful about, once you find someone who is at the same level of readiness as you are, is not to let your eagerness to start a family totally eclipse the romantic relationship. Your family will only be as stable as the relationship and if you don't give adult love its due, you will find the whole dream slipping away from you.

On the cautionary side, if you are not focused on children—and might even be concentrating on being free and unfettered as a couple either for the time being or forever—find out where your potential partner's head is at on the issue of children. If you are at opposite ends of the continuum this isn't going to be a good match.

2. I am happy to consider someone who already has children as a mate. I just love children in general.

A person who adores children tends to love more than just their own biological or adopted children. If you are a single mom or dad, you are looking for someone like this. You will need that kind of attitude, because it is notoriously difficult to integrate two families (even if on *The Brady Bunch* they supposedly did it seamlessly). People might love their partner's children—but most of them love their own children more and tolerate someone else's children's foibles less.

At the beginning there are dating issues when you take up with someone with kids: when (if ever) you can stay overnight in the same house as the children, or how much affection you will allow yourself to show in front of the kids. Most important, there can be struggles about how to preserve the essential culture of the family that existed before the two of you got together. Additional stressors happen when the children are older and more protective of the status quo. They can make it painfully clear to you that you are an unwelcome intruder. Loving kids unconditionally is necessary if a new couple is going to forgive the children some of their thoughtless or intrusive acts.

If, on the other hand, you are not a big lover of children (either any children or any children not your own) you might be very aware of how difficult children can make things, or how your lack of interest or ability to interact with the children will doom the relationship. If you have kids or are considering getting serious with someone who has kids, you need to be honest with yourself about how much effort you are willing to put into a romantic relationship with a person who has a preexisting family.

3. I think it is important to have children while you are young.

Timing, as they say, is everything. Perhaps when you say you love children and you would like to have some, you have an idea of when in the future you might want to put that plan into action. What you might not have figured on is that some of the people you meet will have had children very young—by choice or not—or want to have a child as soon as possible.

So much has been made of the ticking clock of a woman's fertility that men think that a childless woman in her mid to late thirties is probably on a major hunt to find a daddy. This makes them exceedingly nervous because they might fear being seen as a sperm donor—and be trapped into an unwanted relationship. A man in his forties or fifties who may have already had his family and is not too crazy about starting over again can be fairly sure that there are many women who are hoping to change his mind about having another child immediately.

It can be a wonderful, exciting adventure if both people have the same desire to conceive a child. But it is certainly an upsetting situation if a man does not want to even think of having a child for an unspecified amount of time. Then what happens is a tug of war over whose needs are going to win out—with the possibility of "contraceptive error" and potentially a very angry difference in opinion about what would be the next best act.

Dating with a deadline to conceive is not for the faint of heart. It puts a lot of pressure on any young relationship to have that goal front and center. Because of that, some people may underplay their eagerness to become a parent. But it is very important that you find out what their timing is—and how it meshes with your own. This can be a sticky issue even in middle-aged couples if the woman is younger than the man and still wants a family or if both of them might consider a child with each other and time is of the essence for one or both people. If this issue is at all relevant to the time of life you are in, it needs to be discussed honestly and thoroughly.

4. I want a big family.

There is the issue of when, and then there is the issue of when to stop! If you come from a big family and want to create your own large family, or if you come from a big family and want to avoid it at all costs, you will need to find the person who shares your vision. Having come from a big family doesn't at all tell you what a person will want for themselves, and sometimes people who are only children or one of two will want a big family themselves. The issue you need to think about (besides the obvious one of not having children, or saying you will have lots of children, just to please a partner) is whether or not you will want the impact on your relationship that comes along with the needs of so many babies, toddlers, and eventually adolescents. It may sound romantic to think of a big family when you are head over heels in love. It's another thing entirely when there are bills to be paid, houses to be rented, and clothes to be bought. All the research on children shows that they are hard on all but the most blissfully matched of relationships; children's needs distract from parent's needs. But lovers can only take so much of that before they are not lovers anymore. If someone wants a big family and you have no feelings about it one way or the other, think about it this way: If someone wants a really big family, will there be enough of their time and energy left for you? In fact, even if this is just a fantasy and never comes to pass, it still might be a good diagnostic tool to determine what their priorities truly are. If that is where your priorities are, too, it's a great match. But if you are more couple-centered than family-centered, then your partner's desire for a big family might be a warning signal that the two of you will be aiming at different relationship goals.

5. I want a fifty-fifty partnership in raising kids, or as close to that as possible.

How much participation should each person have in raising children? Most couples never discuss this essential question. Many men assume that they will have a small percentage of time spent compared to the mother of their children, but not every woman wants that traditional division of labor. Many modern women, especially those who work outside the home, fear becoming "single" parents because the father takes on minimal child care responsibilities. Conversely, quite a few men do not want to be marginalized as much as their fathers were, and want to have more participation and authority in children's activities and care. Women who say they want equal participation of fathers often don't take into account that that means they will not have an unrestricted directorship over their child's welfare.

If a woman has a partner who wants to play a major role in parenting, she would have the benefit of his help and his devotion as a father. But she might have to compromise on child-raising policies and give ground on everything from toilet training to curfew time. Given that the cultural pattern of child raising in western societies has been to grant women expert status and almost complete directorship of a child's education, daily habits, and interactive conduct, learning to share that authority and control would be an unacceptable loss for many women.

Likewise, men who want to be fully engaged in child raising do reap the rewards of this involvement. But the relationship with their spouse changes since both people will be doing some of the other person's "traditional" job. This kind of interdependence means that since both people will have to compromise schedules, shared child raising may be somewhat less economically beneficial than traditional parenting which releases one partner (almost always the man) to focus on earning money. On the other hand, research, including my own book on egalitarian couples, *Love Between Equals: How Peer Marriage Really Works*, indicates that shared child raising is really good for love and intimacy and probably, durability. In the case when both partners want to participate, the overall effect on their relationship is to be equally vested in the children's welfare and affections. In general, this is a great thing for a relationship if parenting doesn't eclipse partnering.

6. I think once people have children, they should not break up unless there is abuse or violence.

It is important to know how each of you feels about divorce. And it is another thing again, equally important, to think about how having children modifies or exaggerates that position. People who believe that having children cuts off the possibility of divorce no matter what, are quite different from people who believe that they are not doing children a favor by staying in a troubled marriage. There could hardly be two more different, and more antagonistic, positions. If one of the people in a couple believes that marriage is a sacred act, and the other partner sees the vows as something that has only as much power as the relationship itself warrants, the possibility of a future cataclysmic conflict exists.

When dating, the idea of divorce seems foreign, unreal and perhaps, irrelevant. After all, no legal commitment has been made and young relationships in the throes of physical attraction and excitement can hardly be expected to sit and calculate emotional risk. But divorce does happen, children can be involved, and there are several lessons to be learned from the demise of past relationships before you make a commitment for yourself. The important consideration here is to think about each other's philosophy of commitment, and how that is affected by having children.

If children are at the center of someone's life, their decision making will certainly be affected by the desire to protect those children. If personal fulfillment is at the center of a person's values then the relationship itself may dictate their behavior, whether or not there are children present. This is an important difference to think about as you get serious about a partner.

7. I would not want to leave my children alone with a sitter for the first couple of years, maybe longer. I think it is important for parents to spend most of their "free" time with their young children.

How much of your life is going to be changed by having children? There is quite a range of personal parenting styles that work for any relationship. Many couples do have caretakers with whom they feel their children are safe and take quite a bit of time back for themselves. They go out on "dates" or even trips while trusted sitters (often parents or relatives) give them the security to enjoy couple time. The polar opposite of this approach are couples who will not hire a babysitter, and will not leave their child at home for five or more years of the child's young life. They find their fulfillment in family time rather than couple time.

Each of these choices or circumstances present strengths and weaknesses but they don't coexist very well with one another. A person who wants to take their child with them everywhere does not feel comfortable with a partner who insists on significant private time as a couple. Likewise, if one partner never wants to leave home because, in their opinion, that is where the child is safest and functions best, a partner who wants to take the child with them or a parent who wants alone time with their partner are both going to be stressed about their loss of fun or romance.

How a child is incorporated into the adult relationship makes all the difference in the world to that relationship. When you start to get serious with someone you might want to explore how those beginning years of child raising are envisioned, and how far away or close you are to each other's perspective. This is one of the most challenging periods of a couple's life and if enough attention isn't given to the relationship, the couple's communication can change in quality and quantity and their connection can become fragile. Some couples can draw strength through family life—others need more of each other. This is not a small difference—but there is no reason it can't be discussed when the relationship becomes serious enough to warrant this kind of conversation.

16

Core Values

What's *Really* Important to You

There are a few values that each of us hold dear. They may be our belief in God, or in the political process, or about environmental issues and our responsibility to the natural world or to other human beings. In any case, these are the values that we try and uphold in our daily lives. Often we use these values not only to judge whether or not we admire someone, but whether or not we even want to be friends with someone.

These values are obviously important in the deep, intimate relationship of marriage or long-term commitment. However, there are areas in which a couple might differ from each other, and they risk losing respect for each other if their ideas or opinions are dramatically divergent. For some feminists, for instance, it would be critical that their partner believe in equality for women in the workplace and in personal relationships; for someone else who was deeply religious and observant, a partner's beliefs and involvement in a joint life organized around religious community might be nonnegotiable. Everyone has their own closely held values and in a relationship, it is less important what these values are than whether or not they are shared or if a compromise on them is possible. Often, when people say they have found their soul mate, what they are really saying is that they have found someone with whom they are totally comfortable—and that comfort level often means that their most important values are in sync. The couple sees the world in the same way with the same judgments, and this makes them feel a deep kinship with one another.

The list of critical values could be quite particular to a given person, so the statements in the following quiz are not meant to be inclusive but rather to make you think about these and other values that are critically important to you. Therefore, this list is meant to be suggestive; use it to create your own list of values and which, if any, you would be willing to modify for the sake of a partner who disagreed with you on these core elements of your life.

Check each statement about which you feel strongly, either for or against. If you do not hold a particularly firm opinion one way or another, go on to the next statement.

☐ **1.** I feel sharing religious traditions is extremely important in a relationship. I believe that the best-case scenario is a couple who has the same religion and same values about religious education.

☐ **2.** I care about politics and want someone to either support the same party I do or support the general platform of that party.

☐ **3.** Education is extremely important to me. I would sacrifice to educate my children, and I want someone to have a similar educational background and concerns to my own.

☐ **4.** Health and fitness is very important to me. I care about my health and physical well-being and I want a partner who cares as much about their own well-being as I do mine.

☐ **5.** I believe in giving to good causes or doing volunteer activities that make the world a better place. I want a partner who also shares my level of commitment to these values.

☐ **6.** I care a lot about the right to individual freedoms and civil liberties. I would have trouble being with a partner who was strongly opposed to my views on abortion, homosexuality, military action, gun control, etc.

☐ **7.** World peace and other global issues (such as the environment) are extremely important to me. I believe our planet is in grave danger.

Scoring

Whether or not you agree or disagree with these statements, give yourself one point if one *or* the other side of each statement would be important to you in a relationship.

0–2: You do not hold strong opinions on many core values; you could probably get along with someone who disagreed with you.

3–5: There are a significant number of these core values that you hold dear and it would be dangerous to get into a relationship in which you had widely divergent approaches from your partner. You would probably be very attracted, however, to someone who felt strongly and similarly about these areas.

6–7: You are a person of many passionately held values, probably not limited to the ones above. You will definitely need someone who has similar core values to your own—or terrific negotiating skills. Sometimes passionate people respect passionately held differences of opinion. Still, this probably means a lot of conflict throughout the relationship that could endanger your sense of being soul mates, and ultimately undermine your love for one another.

Romantic Assessment

1. I feel sharing religious traditions is extremely important in a relationship. I believe that the best-case scenario is a couple who has the same religion and same values about religious education.

Most people come from some kind of religious tradition, which they may or may not have adopted as their own. If they are very observant, they often feel they need to be with someone from the same group or someone who at least supports common values and activities. This can also work in reverse: that is, some people have rejected certain religious traditions and this rejection is a very important part of who they are and how they want to live. This is especially true if they consider themselves escapees from a specific orthodoxy. It took a lot of effort and perhaps grief from their family, to separate from their background and they don't want to be seduced or dragged back into it.

For many people, religious background and religious beliefs are so important that they won't even consider being with anyone who doesn't share both, and so it may never be a problem. But it is not uncommon that people underestimate the importance of their religious background and it surfaces only when the relationship starts to get serious, or when a couple starts discussing the possibility of having and raising a child together. This can occur pretty far down the relationship road and reveal some unsettlingly strong feelings, which may be difficult to modify. Religion, it has been observed, has a strong emotional component, unreachable by simple rational discussion. It is wise to talk about it, and talk about it honestly, early on in the relationship.

2. I care about politics and want someone to either support the same party I do or support the general platform of that party.

Some people are very politically savvy and involved. They wouldn't miss the morning newspaper; in fact, they often read three or four papers to make sure they are up to date on all the political gossip and commentary. Other people find politics, and especially politicians, boring and depressing—and they really don't want to let the national or global picture enter their life any more than is absolutely unavoidable. Of course there are plenty of people in between, but it is the extremes of feeling and involvement we are interested in here. Politics may be irrelevant to many, but to those who care about who is in office, what are the current government policies, and what social and military legislation is affecting their lives, the issues raised by these subjects can be inflammatory.

James Carville and Mary Matalin are a couple who seem to be deeply committed to each other but who are also committed to diametrically opposed political parties and are political operatives at the highest level. As entertaining as they are when they disagree about politics on talk shows, one wonders how two people who have such strong beliefs in opposite directions are able to get along, much less have the intimacy and comfort of a happy marriage. Many people who care deeply about political issues can get so angry with people who do not share their political beliefs that they have trouble holding their tempers. They may even regard the other person contemptuously. All the hot-button issues: abortion, Supreme Court appointments, military policy, gay rights, civil liberties, etc., come up again and again. For most people, this is incitement to argument and frustration. Only the most rational and respectful of partners would be able to navigate comfortably through these controversies without getting mad at each other. Conflict isn't always avoidable in relationships and may not be such a bad thing if it is constructive and helps people to sort out their beliefs. But political loyalties are rarely plastic (polling suggests, in fact, that they are notoriously steadfast) and the values that each party represents may be so different that arguing about politics is really a challenge to one's most deeply held values.

3. Education is extremely important to me. I would sacrifice to educate my children, and I want someone to have a similar educational background and concerns to my own.

Most people believe in good education—but the degree of importance it holds in their lives varies greatly. The area of greatest disagreement happens when one person is in favor of spending a great deal of money to send their children to four years of college—and possibly beyond—while the other person thinks it's a waste of money, especially for a very expensive private school. Views about education often originate from a person's own experience, and if one person has a lot of postsecondary education and the other does not, the arguments about the importance of education often represent different backgrounds. Educational similarity might not sound important, but it does represent a kind of training. It's the respect for that training that literally affects the way partners look at things. People who have been to college, and enjoyed that experience, are taught to do critical thinking, that is, to think about how the material or findings they are presented with were derived and look for holes in the validity of information before accepting it. Non-college-educated people (or people who went to a high school that didn't encourage critical thinking) often find their college-educated spouse picky, critical, and tiresome; non-college-educated people often look to the values underlying a statement rather than the research—although of course that is not always the case.

The bottom line on this difference is that education is a surrogate for class background. Educated people may have learned how to argue better, use more sources to underscore their point, and feel that the weight of academic opinion is important in shaping their viewpoint—all positions that a less educated partner may not share—or respect. In general, people with a similar educational background are going to understand each other's worldview a bit better.

4. Health and fitness is very important to me. I care about my health and physical well-being and I want a partner who cares about their own well-being as much as I do mine.

Western countries in particular have become very health- and fitness-conscious—but that doesn't mean that every citizen exercises and watches what they eat. People who aren't fitness-conscious don't make it one of the ways they select a partner, but for people who are disciplined about exercise and try to eat healthy foods, a difference of opinion about how to live a healthy life can create serious problems. Health and fitness regimes really work a lot better if you have a partner who supports you. If your partner overeats, especially junk food, or doesn't practice any health regimes, it can create conflicts about how the day should be organized or how fit each of you should be. If you are someone who is unconcerned about dieting or disciplined exercise, you may resent the amount of time a partner spends on these pursuits. If one person is a serious athlete, quite a bit of time will be spent exercising and perhaps preparing for games or competitions. How much time a couple spends together is an elemental part of a relationship, and if one person is athletic and the other is not, the amount of time expended on exercise could eat up most of the couple's discretionary time. If someone is very committed to their physical program, the two people need to discuss how much time can be dedicated to sport or fitness. Only extreme differences create a problem, but this issue is not rare in relationships.

---

5. I believe in giving to good causes or doing volunteer activities that make the world a better place. I want a partner who also shares my level of commitment to these values.

Many people feel their existence on this earth is justified by the good works they do while they are here. They admire others who are charitable and who give back to the world, and they feel best about themselves when they are doing something that improves other people's lives, building affordable housing, lobbying for children's rights, or some larger cause than their own happiness. People like this have been part of the Peace Corps, Mercy Corps, or similar organizations. They may be very active in their church, be a board member of a group that has an educational or philanthropic purpose, or serve as occasional volunteers at hospitals or charitable organizations. Sometimes their passion to help others becomes the main and driving force of their lives and they want a partner who has the same calling as they do, or at least does not resent their own need to be of service. This can become an issue between couples who don't place the same weight on charitable giving or charitable acts when precious time or resources are involved. Most important, someone who sees giving as extremely important may lose respect for a partner who does little or nothing in this arena.

6. I care a lot about the right to individual freedoms and civil liberties. I would have trouble being with a partner who was strongly opposed to my views on abortion, homosexuality, military action, gun control, etc.

A couple needs to be in agreement when it comes to fundamental beliefs about social issues. When two people have strongly held views on opposite sides of a social policy platform, usually these differences are enough to stop courtship in its tracks.

But occasionally couples will agree on most but not all of these issues. They may, for example, agree on everything except whether to respect a picket line in a union dispute or to support gay marriage. And while people do not usually break up over their differences on social issues, heated disputes can make a couple feel less respect for one another than they otherwise would. Liberals who have a partner who is conservative on these issues might feel that their partner had a lack of compassion or humanity; conservatives could feel that their partner has lost their moral compass is unpatriotic or simply is being foolish by protecting one group's interests over the population in general. A strong difference here between partners is almost always alienating. Some of these issues may not arise in the early days of a relationship so it is important that you be aware of how a potential partner feels about these and other important social concerns before you find yourself at loggerheads.

7. World peace and other global issues (such as the environment) are extremely important to me. I believe our planet is in grave danger.

Many of us look at the newspaper or watch the television news and see the daily damage of war and environmental pollutants and other problems but don't become activists. However, there are a large number of people who take on the world as their project and work hard at being global-minded citizens. Usually they are concerned with subjects like population growth, world health, world peace, and preservation of the environment. If this activism is at the center of someone's value system, they are likely to be impatient with or disappointed in someone who either doesn't care, or who cares but doesn't do anything. If they are heavily involved in these kinds of concerns, it shapes the way they live their life. How it affects their relationship depends on how passionately invested they are, how tolerant they are of the differences between themselves and their partner, and how polar or modest their differences of opinion really are. However, even great differences in commitment and opinion are not necessarily toxic in a relationship. Some partners like to clash on issues. They like having different worldviews or supporting different political candidates and they spar with each other, hoping that over time they will change or modify their partner's stance. Still, the more common stance is to want a partner who shares your worldview. Many of these values form a person's deepest identity, that is, they are the values by which they judge themselves and what they do. If a partner does not understand how important these feelings and commitments are, and furthermore, cannot personally support them, their partner can feel emotionally isolated and unloved. If a person's deepest values are not respected, and in the best case shared, only the strongest of romantic connections will be unaffected.

17

Your Social World

Why Your Social Life Is Important

Unless you and your partner live in a remote region, depending on only yourselves and your dogsled team, you are likely to be interacting with other people regularly. Of course there is a huge range in how much you interact, with whom you interact, and for what purpose. Your involvement with others will be a large part of your life as a couple. Many people know that living near parents or in-laws, staying in the community they grew up in, or having a large group of friends and extended family, will affect their relationship. And certainly other social commitments that arise from business or other networks may have an impact on the couple's relationship. Who you are with will definitely affect how your social networks expand or contract, and for some people, this becomes more than they bargained for. People who prize privacy may interact for a while with someone who has an intense social calendar, but when they come to realize what this means for their own life, they may abandon the relationship altogether. Often, however, people don't realize how intertwined their social lives will be until they are well into a relationship. For many, this becomes an unexpected area of growth and satisfaction. For others, it is an unwelcome responsibility that dilutes the pleasure of the relationship. The following quiz gives you a chance to look at the complex social world couples can create with one another so that you can decide which version of social interaction, and what balance of privacy versus sociability, you want in your life.

Many of the issues raised in this section are related to those personality characteristics reviewed in chapter 11, "Self-Nurturing," which discusses introversion and extroversion, and which play a significant part in shaping your social life.

Please mark the following statements True or False.

T   F   **1.** I love and look forward to big family gatherings and vacations.

T   F   **2.** I have many close friends and intend to give them serious time even if I am married or in a committed relationship.

T   F   **3.** I love having friends over for dinner parties, casual gatherings, or just to talk. I also like having out-of-town friends visit and stay with us.

T   F   **4.** I want to help close relatives when they are distressed. I would feel duty-bound to do something for them if they were in economic or emotional trouble.

T   F   **5.** I like it when people just drop over.

T   F   **6.** I count time with friends and my partner as couple time. I don't feel that I need to be alone with my partner a great deal of the time to feel connected.

T   F   **7.** I need close friends. I need to confide in them and I would want my partner to understand that some of those confidences would be about our relationship.

Scoring

Give yourself one point for every True answer.

0–2: You are moderately social and could probably accommodate someone who is more private than you.

3–5: You are quite social and you would have to be sensitive to a private
person's needs, which would probably include modifying your social life.

6–7: You are an extremely social person. It would be very hard for you to
be with someone who wanted you mostly for him- or herself. There
would have to be many compromises.

---

1. I love and look forward to big family gatherings and vacations.

Some people who grew up in a big family loved it, while others felt op-
pressed by always having that many people around. There is no telling how
family size or family ties will affect someone but the fact is that some people cleave to their family. Others try to separate by moving away or limit-
ing family time and see family outings as a duty, not a pleasure. While this
attitude may apply only to their own family, it could also apply to their in-
laws as well. The idea of meeting Uncle Morty at the hotel bar and hearing
another story about your childhood is a dreaded scenario. . . .

But sometimes people are extremely attached to their families. They like
to take vacations with their parents or brothers and sisters. Family gatherings
can become huge affairs. Yet even on a day-to-day basis, some people just like
to stay connected—in person, by phone, or e-mail. They love to gossip, deal
with every little crisis, or simply pass the time of day together. Spouses or
significant others are usually expected to get with the program and at least
pretend to be happy to be involved. Ideally, if you both like the family connection, each partner will appreciate the other's participation and pleasure in
the people they love. Even here, however, there are pitfalls since families

tend to be territorial and there are the inevitable issues about where to spend the holidays or what to do when two important family events coincide.

At the beginning of your relationship, it may not occur to you to discuss how you would deal with your own or your partner's family. But how you handle familial obligations can become an increasingly important aspect of your dynamic as a couple.

---

2. I have many close friends and intend to give them serious time even if I am married or in a committed relationship.

Friendship is a mainstay of many people's lives, but what percentage of time and emotional space it should take once people get in a serious relationship is negotiable. Some partners believe that once you are with them, all other relationships should be minimal and only attended to in time that could not be filled with each other. They have expectations, sometimes gleaned from their parents' lives or from the movies and books they have read, about how much they are willing to give up time with a spouse. Alternatively, others need time with friends, family, or many others outside the relationship, or they will feel isolated and lonely. This makes some partners feel less special, and lower on the priority list in their spouse's life. Yet, the opposite response could arise since some people seek lots of personal quiet time and welcome the opportunities to be alone when their partner is engaged with other people.

You may get an inkling of your partner's preferences when you are dating, but once a commitment is made, the reluctance of one partner to give up friendships or outside commitments for the other may become more intense.

But possessiveness over a partner's time is more than just a response to a practical issue like filling up one's time or resentment at being left with all the chores. It can also be a jealous response: Many people want to be *everything* to their partner: friend, lover, confidant, and sole support for their physical and emotional needs. Or they want to be taken care of and they don't like having other people take their partner's attention.

They see their partner as a scarce resource and they simply don't want to share. They may also be somewhat worried that certain friends will lead their partner down a path that is dangerous to the relationship or shared values. Quite often they are worried that the privacy of the relationship will be invaded.

How you see friendship, how deeply one invests time in platonic relationships, how private or shared friends should be, what kind of time as well as how much time is reasonably invested in them, and whether or not time in a group counts as time together for both of you, really affects how happy people are in a relationship. While the specific philosophy of how you value and organize time inside and outside your relationships doesn't matter, what does matter is that you share the same notions of how to apportion time with each other, with family and friends, and other social obligations.

---

3. I love having friends over for dinner parties, casual gatherings, or just to talk. I also like having out-of-town friends visit and stay with us.

One great way to pay homage to friendship is to have friends into your home. Provided your partner likes your friends, is willing to help with the work (or you really don't mind that they don't help), and doesn't feel that their privacy is compromised, things will work out fine.

People who are very private (those extreme Introverts from chapter 11) do not throw dinner parties, or have them only once in a blue moon. They prefer to meet people outside their homes. The idea of weekend guests fills them with dread. It does not energize them to have friends over—especially large groups or new people—or, in fact, anyone who will upset their daily routine or disturb their peace and privacy.

If you are a very social creature, you like putting out the effort because people energize you. But this is not true for everyone, and what you see as a delightful and celebratory event could be seen by your partner as a painful intrusion of valuable couple time. Where, when, and how often you socialize could be a great bond in a relationship—or it could be divisive.

4. I want to help close relatives when they are distressed. I would feel duty-bound to do something for them if they were in economic or emotional trouble.

If you answered True to this question, you are tightly connected to your family and you feel a sense of ongoing responsibility. This is admirable, but it may not be shared by all partners. Many people have broken their ties to home either because they feel it is natural once a person becomes an adult to concentrate mainly on their own household, or because they have ambivalent or angry feelings toward their own family. Sometimes these two feelings fuse—the anger or disappointment a person experiences about their own family background helps support a general philosophy that everyone is on their own as an adult. They don't feel this obligation to their own family and are probably not crazy about the idea that you would support yours.

This can be a big issue especially if time and resources are tight. If there is a significant sacrifice involved, the struggle between two people who don't share the same vision can devolve into the question, "Who do you love most?" Furthermore, if your spouse feels that your family and friends are constantly needy, they may also feel that the needs of the relationship have become secondary to your other emotional commitments. Relationships have broken up on this very issue, and finding a mutually acceptable policy about the needs of family members is important. Family loyalty is a powerful emotion and any impediment to being a good son or daughter—or even a friend—is a challenge to a person's estimation of their own integrity, honor, and goodness. Figuring out how to set priorities and limits in the relationship and still satisfy your own or a partner's sense of their responsibilities can be tricky if your values about duty and love are very different.

5. I like it when people just drop over.

This statement taps into *how* permeable you want your life to be. If you are a people person you welcome the surprise guest—you are almost always happy to see friends. You want people to feel that they can drop in anytime and will always be welcomed.

However, for more introverted people, an open house is a nightmare. The last thing you would want is to have people interrupt the peace and privacy of your home, unless you have expressly invited them. You want to feel that you have created an island of intimacy and that you can control the way you experience your environment. If you were with someone socially open to the world, you would have to have an explicit discussion about your physical and emotional boundaries early on in the relationship. People who are very social rarely understand the cost of unexpected visitors or household guests to someone who is private. Moderation would be essential but depending on the gap between the two partners, there might have to be considerable revision of one, or the other's, tolerance level for company.

---

6. I count time with friends and my partner as couple time. I don't feel that I need to be alone with my partner a great deal of the time to feel connected.

A very social person can get most of what they need from their partner during larger social occasions. They feel together as a couple when going out to a movie in a foursome, being at a dinner party together, or just watching television with their children. They don't necessarily distinguish friend time, family time, and couple time. Of course, they want some alone time, but they will rarely feel deprived of their partner if they have had a week in which they saw each other a lot but only occasionally without other people around.

This group interaction would not satisfy someone who is very private or couple-oriented. They could be with their partner every day and night, but if there isn't one-on-one time, it doesn't count. A more social person may not realize that all you really want to do is be alone with them, and that you are not counting all of this social interaction as couple time.

This situation can become really upsetting for a private person if it goes on and on and especially if it is exacerbated by heavy work schedules. Then, partner time for intimacy is extremely curtailed with one or both partners starting to feel neglected and unimportant. If you are someone who gets absorbed in your work, your colleagues, and friends, you have to be careful that you really have given enough to your relationship.

---

7. I need close friends. I need to confide in them and I would want my partner to understand that some of those confidences would be about our relationship.

While many of the statements in this arena of couple relations may be more applicable to one gender or the other, this one is likely to be extremely different for men and women. Women tend to have more friendships built on the exchange of confidences in which intimacy is measured by how much is being shared. Withholding information about one's relationship or other important issues is considered proof of the limits of the friendship. The deeper the friendship, the more likely nothing is held back.

Men are less likely to do this, although some men have a best friend who can listen and will protect these secrets. More often than not, a man's confidant is a woman—and often their spouse—since men learn early in life that other men are their competitors and that to expose their vulnerabilities is dangerous. This explains why most men consider the intimate conversations they have with their partner to be very special, probably unique, and definitely not appropriate to be shared with anyone else.

This puts women in an untenable situation. In order to keep female friendship profound, they must exchange secrets and talk about their relationships. But to be true to their partner's wishes, they should keep most things (perhaps all things about them) private. Caught in this dilemma, most women solve the issue by lying or omitting what they are sharing with their family and close friends.

But this is not exclusively a woman's issue. Many couples have differences of opinion about how much information is private and how much is shared. If a woman knew that her partner was sharing details about their private life with another woman or another man, she probably wouldn't be too happy about that—even if she was doing the same thing! It is not clear what is fair to talk about and what is disloyal and potentially harmful to a partner, but whatever the finer points, some partners would consider anything, even their shoe size, to be no one else's business. Setting up boundaries of mutual protection, and then observing them, is the safest and most loving way to proceed. This is especially true in the beginning of a relationship, when commitment is fragile. When someone feels unsafe and vulnerable they may be inclined to bolt in favor of a safer harbor. While privacy may be the best option in any relationship, sometimes one needs to seek advice and perspective from a friend to help solve problems or determine the course of a relationship. Finding the balance between getting advice and maintaining your partner's privacy and dignity may be harder than you might think but it is essential in the long term.

Part Four

*What to Do with What
You've Learned*

How to Search for a Perfect Match

Now that you know a lot more about yourself—and more about the kind of person you should be with—you have to go out and meet people! The intention of this book has always been about *finding* someone, rather than just getting to know yourself better or creating an idealistic vision of your perfect match.

Just like you wouldn't go hiking without checking out the weather, your equipment, the trail, and your physical ability for the path you've chosen, you shouldn't start looking for a partner unless you have the equipment and information you need to be successful. The checklist in this section will help you determine if you have the emotional skills and psychological readiness that you need. There are eight questions to answer, a dating health inventory if you will, that will help you to understand if you are ready to find someone to love.

Once you've gone through the readiness drill, this chapter continues with the action steps you need to take, including a review of basic dating skills—and lots of pieces of advice to help you along the way.

The Dating Readiness Checklist

There is really no reason to go to a dance if you don't want to dance with anyone. Yes, I suppose there is a certain enjoyment to be had by watching from the sidelines, but at some point you have to get involved or you might as well not be there. So, the overarching question to yourself is, "Am I ready?" If you are not going to give it your best effort, who knows what really good opportunity you are going to mess up! You need to ask yourself the questions that will determine both your present attitude *and* your availability—because you have to be ready *and* open if you want to meet your perfect match.

1) Are you optimistic about finding a relationship?

If you feel dating is probably a waste of your time and you are only going to meet losers, this is not the time to start looking. People who are convinced that one bad date, or even ten bad ones, means that no one good is out there, will broadcast their bitterness and disappointment in every word and gesture. It will discourage people from even trying to engage with you. You need to come to the party full of optimism, determined to have a good time, and be open to new—and potentially thrilling—opportunities. Granted, you have to kiss a lot of frogs to meet your prince or princess, but so what? Who said it would be easy to find true love? Furthermore, if you expect frogs, frogs you will get. But, if you go forth hopeful to meet people who have at least an interesting story or two to tell, you will be collecting experiences, and you don't have to care if they are exactly right for you. You will be expanding your horizons—and opportunities—even with the most froggy of dates. A positive attitude is not only welcoming—*it is essential*.

2) Are you too needy?

It is possible that one can be *too* enthusiastic, too ready to love. It is really not a compliment to someone for you to be ready to move in with them when all you have shared in life is an appetizer. Moving too quickly can turn many people off. They might be left with the impression that you want any relationship you can get. Everyone wants to feel special.

There are many clues that a potential partner can pick up from you. How wise is it to talk about money problems, or loneliness, or how hard it is to be a single parent or how fast your biological clock is ticking down? These are signals of desperation. And for most people, they signal "Stop!" While it might seem obvious, most people are looking for a happy, self-confident, well-adjusted person, who is looking to augment their lives with love. Most people seeking a serious relationship want someone who has something to offer them—good character, happiness, curiosity, wisdom, and energy. If you are not feeling good about life, you need to get your act together *before* you go out or you will certainly defeat yourself in your quest.

3) Are you defensive?

Dating can be hard on the ego, and feel like a series of dashed hopes and expectations. You have to be prepared to be rejected—and to reject. Over time, people can construct a shell to protect themselves from disappointment and the judgments of others. It is understandable. But ultimately the worst thing you can do is to build an impermeable wall around yourself in order to withstand letdowns—or repel overeager inappropriate suitors and seductresses.

The challenge is to stay open and reasonable no matter what the last date was like. Being open means that you avoid rushing to judgment. Your first reaction to someone's looks, age, body type, or other potentially superficial characteristics. It also means making the effort to charm a new acquaintance whose immediate response to *you* may not be positive. After all, you have to spend some time together even if it's only a few minutes at a cocktail party, so make the best of it.

You might find that with a little bit of charm your initially uninterested coffee partner can become quite enthralled. No kidding, it happens.

Finally, don't rule out anyone because you think they have too much "baggage" and you aren't interested in dealing with people's past lives. *Everyone* has some baggage: debts or children, or family feuds, or a chronic illness. On the other hand, I think it's a fair position to take if by saying you want to avoid "baggage" you mean you don't want to get entangled with people who are bogged down with past experience and who are still angry or sad about perceived injustices from the past. You want to be with someone who is happy living in the present and has made their peace with past difficulties.

Take your cue from this thought and if you need to, convince yourself to let go of expectations formed by previous experiences.

If your last boyfriend was on your case for being heavy, don't assume that this new guy cares so much about your weight. If your last girlfriend left you because you dropped out of school to become an actor, don't assume that the next woman will consider that an unattractive choice. Don't overexplain, and don't start out on the defensive. Figure out who you are, what you like about yourself and your choices, and present them in a straightforward and confident manner. If you spend time trying to protect yourself, or worrying about what people will think of you, you will seem insecure, which will make it harder for someone to trust and respect you.

4) Are you feeling warm and friendly? Do you feel physically comfortable and attractive?

We all need to make peace with how we look and feel in our skin. We need to feel confident that we own something that the right person will find attractive. This self-confidence is hard to achieve because we live in a culture with very demanding standards of beauty. There is no denying it: People who are classically good looking—slim, fit, and young—attract a bigger group of people who are interested in dating them. But look around you:

when you see couples together, are all of them gorgeous? Are only great-looking people paired up? The answer is, of course not. People fall in love with other things besides looks. They fall in love with intelligence, a smile, twinkling eyes, expressiveness, articulate discussion, body language, achievement, cleverness, kindness, any number of attributes that enliven personality and give character to faces and make a person attractive in the broadest sense of the word.

We have to remember that we will be very attractive to someone. That doesn't mean we will be everyone's ideal type. When you are ready to date, you need to feel good about how you look without being unrealistic. You are prepared to have some people pass you by because you know eventually someone will be captivated by you and you will be captivated by them. You need to be strong enough to realize that this selection process is not personal in the deepest sense of the word. It just takes time for people to find their perfect match.

5) Are you over your ex? Are you over being angry?

You are not ready to date again unless you are open to love. You are not ready to be loved and love if you are still in love with someone who doesn't love you—or someone who is unworthy of your love. If you are still grieving over the one who got away, the one who left you, or even the one who died, you are not ready to begin again. On the other hand, it is unwise to wait *forever* just because you feel some vestige of hurt, regret, or guilt. If it's a serious problem for you—and only you can really determine if your lingering feelings are hurting your chances at future happiness—see a therapist.

Too many people in the dating market have a huge well of anger inside of them, some of it bubbling up to the surface with the slightest of provocation. Men talk about how much their ex-wife "took them for," women talk about their husband the rat who had an affair with the babysitter. Both sexes can have a laundry list of nasty things their ex-partner did to them. It hardly makes for a sexy picture. You may have been with someone who hurt you deeply, who was dishonest, unscrupulous, and did you wrong.

But as understandable as it might be for you to be angry, it is not in your best interests to try to meet a new person while you are still feeling abused or vengeful. Your anger will make someone else think about what it would be like to have that rage turned against them. They will not see the light, happy person you know you can be.

6) You cannot be found if you hide yourself. Are you ready to get yourself out where there are people to be met?

The truth is that after high school, college, or the first years of employment, finding eligible partners becomes harder. There are so many choices in the years between eighteen and twenty eight because people are staying single longer and longer. While it may always be difficult to find the love of your life, the fact is you will easily bump into many eligible contenders during those years. However as people pair off, the pickings get sparer. This doesn't mean, however, that there is no chance to find a lifetime partner after age thirty. Many western countries have a divorce rate of 30 to 50 percent of all marriages: this sad cloud has a silver lining; divorce creates a lot of recirculation of single people back into the mating pool. That means there are other single people looking for a lifetime partner at just about every stage of the life cycle. The challenge though is how to find them since they are scattered all over the world and your perfect match might not be someone you would have any chance of just bumping into. Certainly people get fixed up by well-meaning friends or coworkers, but meeting enough single people to help increase the odds of finding your perfect match is difficult. Fortunately, some churches, affinity groups, and now the Internet and other commercial enterprises make it relatively easy to introduce yourself to men and women who are looking for a partner. The relevant question then becomes, are you ready to get out there and work to find a partner, or are you going to wait in your house or apartment doing nothing to find your true love except think about it?

This book can only be used if you apply it. The theory of the Duet® Total Compatibility System, guides the website Perfectmatch.com, for which I am the relationship expert. Obviously I think PerfectMatch.com is a great place to go to find someone compatible. But there are other sites as well, speed dating exercises, personal matchmakers, singles cruises, religious retreats, gallery walks, and pub nights— you name it. You need to find out what feels comfortable for you and pick *something*. And if that doesn't work, pick something else. You are only ready if you are willing to put yourself into the mix of people who are serious about meeting someone. And if you do, eventually, you will.

Your Basic Dating Skills

So, if you have decided you are ready to find true love, it's time to make contact with eligible and serious candidates. Once you have made contact, you need to be able to find out who they are—and, if you like them, convince them that you are worth knowing. As part of your dating preparation, you need to do an inventory of your self-knowledge and see if it's in working order. You also need to think about what approach, what personal information and presentational style represents you well. You want to be sure that the way you talk, and what you talk about, authentically shows who you are, and helps someone open up to you. Charming someone (or, as a friend of mine used to say, putting the spotlight on yourself so that you look like a star) is a talent but it can also be a learned skill. You need to review your dating techniques to see if they serve you well or are so rusty or offensive that they will doom you to be alone unless you change course. I take it as part of my duty to you, to give you some pointers and positive dating skills that will enhance your chances of being loveable. Consider the following guidelines—along with a healthy dose of common sense—to be a good foundation you can build on to create a romantic and meaningful relationship.

Listen, Listen, Listen

One of the most common dating mistakes people make is that in their rush to make themselves interesting, they talk the ear off of the other person. If you find that they have finished their dinner and you haven't touched yours, you can be sure you are talking too much. There has to be an ebb and flow in the conversation or it will be boring to the other person. Likewise, you have to do your part of the positive word flow—being a great listener is essential, but you have to build on what you hear, and further the conversation—otherwise, how will they know you have really listened? Don't pretend to listen; consider what the other person is saying, think about what is interesting, and carefully choose questions about what else you'd like to know. Don't stop listening just because you aren't immediately attracted to this person. Dig deep and you might learn things about them that increase their appeal to you.

Always try to be likeable and sympathetic. If you have listened enough you will have learned something—and that will make almost every date worthwhile. Remember, you are not only learning about someone else on these dates, you are learning about yourself—what you like and what you don't. (And you'll be able to refine the lessons you've learned from the Duet® Total Compatibility System.) If you thought, for example, that you wanted to be looking for another A type like yourself, and you find yourself more attracted to more laid-back B types, take that as information and select your dates based on this new insight. Almost no date should be considered wasted—even a date with a total mismatch can tell you something new about yourself or your relationships—and as a bonus, you'll probably have material for a good story to share with your friends!

Be Present

Almost the worst thing you can do on a date is make someone feel you would rather be anywhere else. You may be tempted to look at other people at the party, in the restaurant, or next to you, but that will kill more first dates than you can imagine. You need to be rapt, which means sustained eye contact, a quick follow-up on an interesting point, and an energy flow that supports every second of the interaction. Likewise, keep your conversation in the here and now. Don't concentrate on your past or all the reasons you are back in the market. On the other hand, do a reality check from time to time when you talk about your work and other things that matter to you. Don't be so present that you forget that the other person has a story, too.

Be Discreet

For some reason known only to themselves, some people feel the need to air every piece of dirty laundry they have on the first date. This is a big mistake. The same information on the fourth or fifth date might just make you a sympathetic character, but in the beginning, people would like to think they have found a gem, not a bruised peach. You have to avoid including any number of topics in your first conversations (bankruptcy, personal rejection, divorce lawyers, miscarriages, betrayals, gallbladder operations—you get the idea!)—and while you won't purposefully withhold information that might be vital to a continuing, happy partnership, you want to err on the side of discretion. The acronym TMI comes to mind—Too Much Information can derail even the most positive encounter.

Seriously, forget the following topics for quite a while:

Economic or credit issues
Fertility problems
Children with behavioral issues
Mysterious or serious illnesses including STDs
Divorce proceedings
Bad wife, husband, or lover stories
Extremely technical descriptions of your work
Hot-button issues about which you can be extremely passionate
Sexually explicit stories
Rabid political opinions

Be Honest

Don't exaggerate and don't reinvent yourself. Remember, there is Google and there are countless other ways someone can check up on you. If this relationship gets serious, your partner will be meeting your family and friends, and sooner or later any one of them is apt to spill the beans.

The art of omission is a more acceptable tactic than invention (or less politely, lying). If you didn't finish college, you don't have to confess that you got kicked out. Claiming that you have a BA in pharmacology—then getting caught in the lie—will make someone believe that everything you say might be false . . . and that alone will make most people pass on a second date. Even if they don't find out the lie, you may forget what you told to whom—and live in fear that you are going back on something you stated as fact. You are in this for the long run, so why start out with something that could potentially undermine the relationship. The occasional white lie—or omission—doesn't seem to bother people (such as not mentioning that you are a lousy dancer after your date has rhapsodized about how much he/she loves to dance) but bigger variations on the truth (such as saying you are ten years younger or older than you are) are going to get you in big trouble. (In particular, avoid the most common prevarication committed by so many people, especially on the Internet dating sites by putting in a picture of yourself from much younger and thinner days. Be truthful and honest and you will find someone to love a whole lot sooner.)

Be Careful

Many first or second or even third dates happen without one or the other person checking on whether what the other person said on the Internet or at a bar or at a friend's party is really true. You cannot assume that just because you have been fixed up or because someone is a paying member of a dating site, that they are representing themselves accurately.

No matter how you meet someone you have to do your due diligence: Google them on the Internet. Follow up to see if they really graduated from the university when they said they did. Check to see if they know people they should know given where they worked, went to school, etc.

Start your first date in a public place in daylight, and do not let someone walk you to your car until you know them pretty well. Don't give your home phone number until you have been going out awhile: if you give your cell you can change that number a lot easier than your home phone if the person turns out to be a stalker or just obnoxiously tenacious. Don't let anybody manipulate you when it comes to trust. People who date these days know that because we come from all over the place and few people are located in the same circle of friends or industry, it's perfectly reasonable for someone to want a few verifiable references or pieces of information. You really do need to remember that it's better to be safe than sorry. Most people are honest, but you have to be aware of the few unscrupulous or unbalanced types—and know how to get them out of your life if you need to.

Conversation Starters— and Killers

While there's many a taboo subject, some of which were listed in the section "Be Discreet," there are many good ways to get a conversation started and keep it rolling.

Establish a Connection

Finding common ground is important. It might start with the interesting details you have exchanged in your e-mails about the friends who introduced the two of you, or the school you both attended. Start from a positive place. Have you already established a common interest in sports or literature? What is it that has drawn you together? Find out more about it and establish some joint interests or some reason it seems like a good idea for the two of you to get together.

Share the Things You Love to Do

People's faces light up when they talk about their grand passion. It doesn't matter if it's riding horses, making fine furniture, fishing, or bookbinding. If you have a passion, figure a way to bring it into the conversation. Show yourself as you are when you are happy, excited, creative, and totally engaged. But don't get bogged down in technical details or become too heated about those controversial issues that don't need to be addressed during your first dates. Once you know each other more, "hot" issues could be fun and interesting to discuss. But in the beginning emphasize the positive and those things that bring out your best, happiest, and most interesting self.

Market Yourself, Discreetly

Share stories that show the positive things about you—without bragging or exaggerating. Think of a traditional salesperson. He doesn't say, "See this shirt? It's last year's design, its kind of a hard-to-wear color, you need to be slim to make it fit right in your jeans and you can probably get it cheaper next door." No, he says, without lying, "This is a traditional color I love that isn't widely available this year and we only have a few left. It is form-fitting, which looks great in jeans, and while other versions of it might be cheaper elsewhere, our workmanship speaks for itself and we back everything we sell."

See the difference? Surprisingly, many people who date start out with a list of their flaws, disasters, shortcomings, you name it. This is dating suicide—unless you are looking for someone who has a Mother Teresa complex. You are selling yourself, and you have to sell the best version of yourself that will stand up under scrutiny. If you are a bit overweight, sell your love of the good life, fine food, and sensual living. If you appear too busy, talk about how you are when you relax and the great vacations you have had and the ones you would like to go on. Show what is fun about you, deep about you, spiritual about you, caring and selfless about you, ambitious, or accomplished—whatever the things are that you think will make someone you want to know want to know you, too.

Show What You Care About

All of us have a noble side to us. Maybe it is our charitable work in soup kitchens or maybe it is the way we helped our child through their dyslexia even when the teachers gave up. Or it could be just introducing deeper discussion about the meaning of life and how to use the time and gifts we have been given. We need to reveal our hearts, not just our actions. We also need to reveal our character: what we believe in and the stuff we are made of. Just don't feel the need to get all of this out on a first date. Reveal something about your soul a little at a time.

Help Others Reveal Their Character

You also need to know what this person is made of. Using the eight characteristics from the personality profiles as a guide, you can determine if they fall in love quickly, intuitively, or consider it a careful, slow process (Risk Taking or Risk Averse). You can discover whether they lead a high-energy life or one that is more laidback (High Energy A type versus Relaxed B type).

Get a sense of their temperament. Are they cautious or analytical in the stories and life experiences they tell, or are they enthusiastic, hopeful, joyful, and even impulsive, expecting the best and minimizing the worst? Do they bring light and happiness to the table, or do they make you think deeply and somewhat more analytically about life's possibilities (Optimist versus Cautious)?

What about their general approach to day-to-day life? Have they been in the same job for twenty years, or worked their way up in the company, or had their own business for a long time? Or have they changed jobs a lot, been many things, almost had many different lives? Have they been in very few intimate relationships, or have they had many marriages, or live-in relationships? Do they seem like a player or a stayer? Get a sense of how much variety or predictability they want in their life (Predictable versus Seeks Variety).

How about finding out whether your date is accommodating or needs things exactly their way. Do they describe themselves as compulsive or a perfectionist? Listen to how they describe their work history or their expectations for themselves and others. If they are talking about a challenging situation (say, whether to move for a job) how do they describe the way they handled it? Did they consider many options or just feel there was only one good option? Are they dogmatic? Does this seem to be a theme in the way they talk about things (Structured versus Flexible)?

How much do they dominate their life story? Is it always about them or do the supporting players get some credit? Are they a leader in their work or in the way they describe their interactions with friends or children? Do they seem like a team player or someone who needs to structure, organize, and control the discussion or enactment of each part of your time together? Are you comfortable with their style, which may be Dominant or Collaborative?

Look at their speech patterns. Are they animated? Are their opinions intense and dramatic or calm and moderately delivered? Does their animation turn you on or get you tired? Does a calm delivery make you relax and enjoy the conversation or put you to sleep (Passionate versus Temperate)?

Finally, do they seem to want to open up to you, or do they play their cards very close to their chest? Are they showing you emotion or appreciation, letting you know how they are enjoying the date or not? Do they tell you nothing really personal, or do you leave that first date feeling they have shared some vulnerabilities or with some at least a little as to how their heart works? Is their style of Introversion or Extroversion acceptable or attractive to you?

If you use the eight keys in conversation, you will leave this date knowing if you want more from this person. At the very least, you will know a lot more about them than whether or not they like to take long walks on the beach. You will gain some confidence in your "interviewing" process by discovering really interesting things to observe and talk about. Your time will not be wasted. Now you just have to get out there and do it!

19

Keeping Love Alive

So you've found your perfect match . . . what about happily ever after? Falling in love is only the beginning of the story—keeping love alive, weathering the inevitable misunderstandings and conflicts of daily living are continuing challenges for long-term relationships.

Even highly compatible partners will have differences of opinion and failures in communications at times—and many couples that everyone else thought were perfect for one another, break up. What went wrong? What guidelines, if followed from the beginning, would give you the best chance for keeping your soul mate for a lifetime?

Pay Attention

To begin with, the most important advice I can give you is to keep your eyes and ears open. What starts many couples on a decline is that they let other preoccupations such as careers or family obligations take over, and they leave their relationship on automatic pilot. While this might work for a short time, it is a guaranteed recipe for failure if it becomes the dominant theme of the relationship. There is no relationship that can prosper without attention. Someone, but preferably both people, have to be watching the relationship to monitor the everyday mood, the unresolved issues, or whether each person feels connected and fulfilled. Medical doctors recommend a yearly checkup to promote and sustain wellness, but a yearly relationship checkup is not even close to enough to maintain happiness. Even a few months is enough time for hurt feelings, resentment, anger, or loneliness and feelings of rejection to gain firm traction. The best prescription is vigilance: each partner has to pay attention to how they are feeling, what is being said—or not said—and take it upon themselves to check out the mood of the household and each other. If something is amiss, someone has to say so and not accept a partner's evasiveness as an answer. Sometimes people are just so busy they don't want to take on another responsibility—like talking about the relationship. They may express impatience about little things, give annoyed remarks, smirk at comments, show they are unhappy through words or gestures, but still not own up to the deeper feelings. Nonetheless, what linguistics call the "metamessage" (unspoken feelings conveyed by body language or facial responses or passive-aggressive language) is something to recognize and take seriously. Once these negative energies appear, communication is necessary, since the metamessage is a part of larger negative feelings about the partner and the relationship. Ignoring these moods, statements, or cutting remarks is tantamount to aiding the unraveling process.

Refine Communication Strategies—Early and Often

So how do we prevent a relationship from losing its resilience and positive passion? As clichéd as it may sound, the key is good communication, and there are a few essential rules to follow. The most important rule is to get things off your chest sooner than later—but not before you're ready to have a constructive conversation. When feelings are suppressed, they tend to fester. If partners wait too long to discuss an issue they may even forget what caused their concern, yet they somehow retain the angry or disappointed feelings that were a part of it. If you can't trace where the negative feelings come from, it becomes increasingly hard to solve problems. You know you are unhappy, but you have forgotten the original impetus for those feelings. That makes it hard to fix anything.

People in good relationships talk a lot. They talk early in the process of a problem, and they talk often. As we have noted, there may be different styles of communicating—everything from quiet whispers to full-out screaming—but the style is not as important as dealing with problems so they do not recur and so that each partner feels they have had a part in decision making.

Another communication tactic is "active listening," a technique pioneered by Harvel Hendricks. This simple but effective technique requires each person to repeat what they thought the other said to them. Each person checks each exchange of feeling or information to make sure that of misunderstandings are not accumulating. This all has to be done, however, in a context of respect.

Because communication is so important, there is a great deal of research on the topic. Psychologist John Gottman is among the most famous of clinical researchers who have videotaped couples' interactions in order to identify and analyze continuities in communication that are functional and dysfunctional for the relationship. He looked at four types of communication that were devastating to relationships: shows of contempt; personal criticism rather than critique of the act or the situation; reacting to feedback with defensiveness and countercriticism; and stonewalling, withdrawing from the conversation, or creating an icy, nonresponsive face that effectively cuts off any possible exchange of opinions or feelings.

Criticism might be the most ruthless of these communication pitfalls. It is hard not to be defensive when we feel we are under attack. If someone says to us, "You never" or "You always," there is hardly room for improvement, discussion, or apology. The attack is such a complete wipeout that our poor scared and scarred ego puffs itself up in a counter-strategy to save itself. The response is basically an, "Oh, yeah? Well, you are always . . ." Alternatively, one partner abandons the interaction—physically, emotionally, or both—and keeps moving away from what they perceive as their partner's attack on their identity and character.

The cure for this is to start talking about feelings early, openly and often in order to discover what hurts our partner and how we can negotiate changes without destroying each other. People have different communication styles, and sometimes constructive communication is difficult, but that still doesn't let anyone off the hook by offering *no* communication at all as an option.

Resist the Slide from Equality and Respect to Efficiency and Hierarchy

When you first fall in love, you are pals and lovers. Research indicates that you will never be more equal, more like peers and friends again as you are at the beginning of a relationship. Why? Why would you fall in love one way, and conduct the rest of your relationship another way? As I have written about extensively in my book *Love Between Equals: How Peer Marriage Really Works*, the slide happens when work gets going, children are born, and traditional sex roles kick in. Men leave most of the parenting to women and women often have a job that is subordinate to her partner's in favor of child raising and child health issues. Partners who used to do everything together start allocating "his" and "her" jobs to make more efficient use of their time and talents. Jobs of lower status, such as domestic chores, start to be primarily allocated to women, and lowly duties begin. The high earner, especially if it is the man, starts to expect certain privileges, such as getting to sleep through the night when the baby is crying, because their job supports most of the couple's lifestyle. Resentment starts to build if this slide isn't noticed and corrected.

Some couples weather this transition because they agree with the idea of a relationship organized by traditional gender norms or because they see these changes in domestic labor as merely a temporary necessity, having nothing to do with the influence of each partner in couple decision making. Many couples try to share what domestic jobs they can as a way of stopping this slide into hierarchy in the relationship. They focus on staying pals, avoiding unilateral decision making, and ensuring that each partner feels equal goes a long way to keeping love alive.

Avoid Parallel Lives

It sounds simple, but it isn't. Doing things together gets harder as your life together gets more complicated with friends and family responsibilities, extended work hours and travel, household maintenance, children's needs, etc. Couples that always used to run together just sneak in twenty minutes alone whenever they can. Saturday-night dates start to fold into necessary dinner parties or just individual rest time. Evening times are devoted to catching up on e-mail, bills, or personal phone calls. Arlie Hochschild, in her book *Time Bind*, shows how work has so permeated private life that friendship and camaraderie start to be associated more with the office than with family or a partner.

In the interests of efficiency, or just because of fatigue, couples start to do less "dating" and spend more time just to get things done! Giving up the time to romance each other, have an adventure, do a project, or go on a trip, takes so much of the joy and friendship out from the relationship that a couple may forget just why they are together anyhow. Guarding couple time and couple activities, keeping that bond sacrosanct, is really important if you each want to keep the image of best friends and playmates front and center in your minds and hearts.

Keep Your Optimism

Everyone knows that relationships ebb and flow. Longtime married couples will often talk about tough times in their relationship and how difficult it was to get back to love and happiness. During tough times it is often easy to tell yourself that there is too much damage, too much neglect, or too many differences to go on. But couples who maintain an optimistic vision, even when they are undergoing stress, have a huge advantage. What therapists Tobey Hiller and Philip Zeigler advise in their marital therapy book, is that every couple could construct a good or bad story of the early and best days of their relationship, and how that is constructed creates either hope or despair when things aren't going well. The "Good Story" is the narrative of how you fell in love, what it was you loved about each other, what were your greatest days, events, adventures, and triumphs, and what makes you so special together. The good story may have some rough spots but has a solid core. The "Bad Story" on the other hand, reveals a relationship that was never really fundamentally good but had a few good moments.

Maintaining a belief in the core goodness and integrity of your relationship allows you to acknowledge problems, anger, and disappointment, but never forget how solid the foundation of who you are together, and why you would want to save it.

Be Affectionate, Seek Passion

Unfortunately, one of those things that can go on automatic pilot are words and touches of affection. It's hard to believe that the people who couldn't keep their hands off each other in the beginning, have to remember to touch and kiss and compliment each other. But life goes along faster and faster, stress builds up, and it's easy to forget affectionate gestures. Even sexuality can get back-burnered because the couple is busy, tired, trying to do too many things at once, or focused elsewhere. Our over-scheduled lives make it hard to have a spontaneous sexual connection, and memory of the early days of making sex happen anytime we could start to fade. As time goes by, some of the bonding and connection that a couple established through passion gets eroded. But this is not inevitable. While sexual frequency does go down as people and the relationship age, that doesn't mean satisfaction has to go with it. Long-term couples can have better sex lives than new couples because they become very sensitive to each other's state of mind and desires. Still, the best relationships also make sure that some of the original passion gets maintained by thinking of new ways to please each other, saving quality time for lovemaking, and stoking romance through kind gestures, hugs, and kisses. Bringing little gifts, dressing up for a date, and cuddling up to each other for a movie all pave the way for a hotter private encounter. Couples that continue to woo each other, long after a wedding band has been placed on their hands, will keep a deeper emotional and physical connection.

Mercy and Forgiveness

There is no partner who doesn't eventually make some dumb, insensitive, or seriously hurtful mistakes over the course of a committed relationship. Some of these acts can be serious violations of the couple's vows or of an individual's dignity or feelings. Sometimes it can just be nasty words, but those words leave a welt that doesn't go away easily. John Gottman's work with troubled couples shows that there needs to be a ratio of five compliments to every bit of criticism, however slight in order to get the relationship back on track. It is hard to be criticized by one's partner and it takes quite a bit to get over it.

Satisfied partners do not take pot shots at each other. They have a realistic understanding of each other's sensitivities and weaknesses and they try and avoid confrontations or language that will push nerves and egos to the breaking point. Over the years they see the real person they committed to, as well as the idealized person they first fell in love with. As long as there were not wildly exaggerated expectations of their partner, they can slowly accommodate their partner's shortcomings.

But there are acts that no one can or should simply accept and move on. Some fights are full of cruel accusations, and some relationships break apart or are reduced to continuous pain and fury for a while if one or both partners has had a continuing flirtation or an affair with someone else. This is the time when people have to dig deep inside their psyches, get past the agony of betrayal or profound disappointment, and see if they can forgive their partner and reestablish love and trust.

All relationships eventually need forgiveness. It is hoped that most apologies will be for small trespasses, not for excruciating acts. Still, even relatively small offenses can be extremely upsetting. For a relationship to prosper, partners have to face situations where one or both behaved badly, and find a way to get over them. Apologies have to be made—but they also have to be accepted.

Goal Sharing and Building a Future

Finally, there has to be something to keep the two of you together. The world has plenty of forces pulling us apart, and it's up to the two partners to figure out how to resist it. Work will eat up all your spare time if you let it, and dinners will start to be quick affairs, wolfing down a sandwich or bowl of cereal rather than taking time out and preparing a proper meal together. It's not that hard to get to feeling "Is this all there is?" Couples bond over building a business together, creating a house, raising a family, doing voluntary activities as a couple, being the hub of their social group. Whatever it is, it brings you a sense of teamwork, of creating and contributing to shared values and goals, and builds your admiration of each other as you work toward something both of you care about you will grow closer, achieving dreams that seemed quite impossible at one time.

These are the activities that make two people into a couple, and a couple into soul mates. You need shared goals, projects, and mutual help to create then sustain a perfect match. But even more than pulling together, you give each other reasons not to pull apart. Over time, as your dreams come true, you are grateful to each other, and finally come to and other place in your heart and mind where the relationship is bigger than you are as individuals that you cannot imagine life without each other. It's not impossible to have a perfect match for a lifetime. But it will take conscious purpose: creating a relationship that is a priority in your life, understanding yourself and each other very well, and a continuing high standard for intimate communication. I hope this book will help you accomplish all of that, and more.

Acknowledgments

All books have a team behind them. Mine starts with my family, who gives me optimism, energy, motivation, support, and love. Their understanding and encouragement gives me permission to do what writers do: disappear into a computer for long periods of time. Likewise, the people I live with, or have lived with, at Rosebud River Ranch, Linda Cobb, Tom Estes, Alicia Bemeerleer, and Christy Matvizek, made this book possible by superbly handling the ranch and Rosebud River Ranch Experience and loyally protecting my privacy and time. Not enough thanks could ever be given to my dear friend, business colleague, and all-around advisor, Julie Blacklow, who makes my life richer and easier every day.

I am indebted to my colleagues and friends at PerfectMatch.com: the awesome Duane Dahl, Cindy Dahl, Ed Winn, and the rest of the team. I wish everyone could find such a creative, industrious, and honorable group of collaborators. Duane, in particular, has given me the creative license and space to develop Duet®, the Total Compatibility System, and Cindy has helped me shape Duet® into its present form. I am grateful for their tireless pursuit of excellence, their superb and fair corporate values and team-building, and their true dedication to creating the most effective and scientifically based relationship site on the Internet. We have been together for many years now and they have always made me proud to be associated with PerfectMatch.com

Of course, I also want to express appreciation to my colleagues at the University of Washington for supporting my mix of academic and nonacademic work. I am particularly grateful to the American Sociological Association for recognizing the importance of getting social science data and thinking to the public and for giving me the 2005 award for Public Understanding of Sociology. Academia has traditionally been cautious of popularizing findings, fearful of distortions that might occur during translation from a scientific paper to a talk show or trade book. The ASA, mindful of this problem, has validated my efforts, and by extension, encouragement to many other academics, by saying, with this award, that translation is a worthy thing to do, even if some accommodations in style and content are inevitably made during the journey from journal articles to a general readership.

Certainly in my list of those to whom I owe gratitude I give a high position to my longtime editor at Perigee, John Duff. In a changed publishing world, John remains a gentleman, the kind of person one could safely make a book deal with in five minutes in a car phone conversation—and not regret it later. He has done yeoman's work editing this manuscript, invading sacred weekend and vacation time to help the book stay on schedule. Thank you, John, for hanging in there!

Finally, some thanks to amazing friends and advisors. David Deetz was the first person to introduce me to the Myers-Briggs system and help me realize what a good model it would be for a romantic assessment instrument. He is a brilliant psychologist who just happens to be a physicist by training and an entrepreneur by temperament. He taught me a lot. Another friend, Kiman Lucas, selflessly helped me understand all the iterations of personality profiling, and colleagues Barbara Risman, Judith Sills, Graham Spanier, Ross Koppel, John Gottman, Peter and Patti Adler, and Sandra Leiblum looked Duet® over and gave me feedback and validated the utility of the system. Thanks also for support and my last-minute emergency help on quote citations from Hadley Iliff Adams, Rebecca Adams, Dominic Cappello, Mark Clark, Stephanie Coontz, Cynthia Epstein, Rhonda Gates, Kathy Gerson, Phil Graves, Megan Hildebrand, Susanna Hansson, Vivian Horner,

Judith Howard, Nancy Klopper, Karen Lawson, Linda Morgan, Virginia Rutter, Herb Schwartz, Susan Sprecher, and Tobey Hiller Ziegler.

I'm sure I am forgetting some important people who helped make this book possible. I hope they will forgive my lapses; it feels like the concepts in this book have been percolating in my head forever, and important details get lost over time. Please know that I am mindful of all the subtle ways friends and colleagues help me be better and smarter than I would ever be on my own.

Index

Biological clock, 217
Bonding
  through sex, 142, 205, 207
  through teamwork, 28, 65, 266
Boredom, 20
The Brady Bunch, 218
Breadwinner, chief, 202
Bridget Jones's Diary, 14
Briggs, Katherine Cook, 7
Burns, George, 16
Businessman, self-contained, 27

Career
  investment, 17, 51
  obsession, 49
Carville, James, 228
Catering, to another's preferences, 24
Cautious Type, 60
Cautiousness, 15
Chaos, 22
Characteristics
  complimentary, 8
  different, 105
  Duet™ sixteen combinations of, 10
  interaction of, 82
  similar, 8, 37
Charisma, 52, 209
Charming, skill of, 251
Chemistry, between people, 5
Chesterton, G.K., 29
Child-rearing
  communication during, 223
  relationship durability improved by, 221
  religion and, 227
  responsibility for, 220–21
  techniques, 117
Children
  divorce with, 221–22
  education of, 228
  how many, 219–20
  importance of, 215–16
  lifestyle issue of, 193, 215
  money issues with, 228–29
  partner with, 218
  timing for having, 218–19
Children quiz, 216
  scoring, 216
Civil liberties, beliefs about, 231

Class background, shared, 27
Clinton, Bill, 16
Clinton, Hillary, 16
Cohabitation, 45
Collaboration
  decision-making via, 25
  personality amenable to, 129
Collaborative Type, 120
The Colors of Love (Lee), 42
Commitment, 100
  long-term, avoidance of, 19
  outside couple, 233
  total, 50
Communication. *See also* Intimacy
  during child-rearing years, 223
  different styles of, 105, 261
  of emotion, 28
  expectations for, 155
  gender differences in, 155
  high standard for, 266
  key to durability, 260
  lack of, 154–55
  moderation in temperament and, 28–29
  non-hurtful, 262
  pitfalls, 261
  of relationship issues, 155
  ruthless, 261
  subjectivity of, 154
Compatibility
  characteristics of, 13
  insight into, 4–5
  more than personality issue, 193
  most compelling aspects of, 11
Competitiveness, between partners, 24
Complementary differences, 105–6
Complementary factors, 22
Compliments
  criticism v., 265
Compromise, 5, 26
Conditions, behavior under extreme, 27–28
Confidence, 4, 31, 64, 248
Confidentiality
  gender differences regarding, 240
  between partners, 149–50
Conflict
  differences creating, 105
  regarding beliefs, 228